I0569703

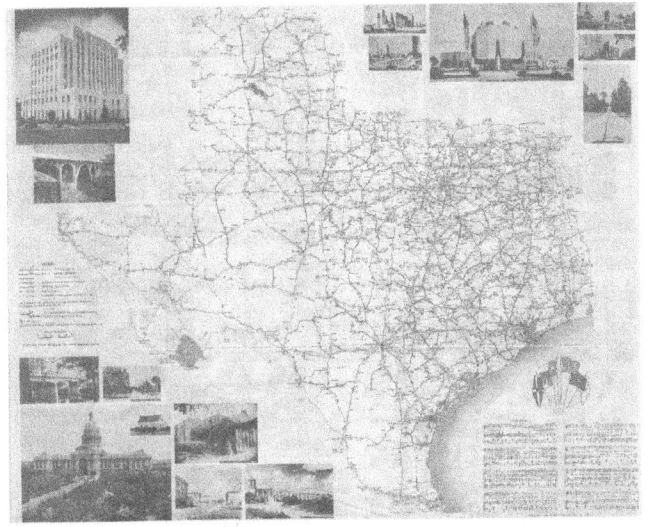

About the Map

The map on the preceding page is a 1936 Texas Centennial road map. It was issued by the State Highway Commission, and the road routes were corrected to March 1, 1936. The opposite side of the large sheet sports dozens of photographs from every part of the state and a few along the Pan-American Highway into Mexico. Several of the scenes will not be found today: abundant tarpon being caught from the beach at South Padre Island, unspoiled pine forests on Highway 105 at Conroe, polo being played on open country at San Angelo, big West Texas sheep ranches, and an empty, winding Fayette County two-lane bordered by pristine limestone fences. Other superb Lone Star vistas shown on the map are thankfully still there to breathe in and remember: Santa Elena Canyon, Dolan Falls on the Devil's River, the Chisos Mountains, and Palo Duro. You can still see the fabulous administration building at Randolph Field and the old church at Independence.

That's the beauty of exploring history in person. Your imagination and some old photos can offer a little glimpse into what was, and sometimes you turn an urban corner and face a quaint time capsule that you assumed was long gone. Here's hoping you find something new in our past.

Also by

Please enjoy these other titles by Mike Vance. They are available where
books are sold and also at www.mikevancewriter.com

Non-Fiction

Getting Away With Bloody Murder

Mud & Money: A Timeline of Houston History

Murder & Mayhem in Houston (with John Nova Lomax)

Houston Baseball: The Early Years, 1861-1961

Houston's Sporting Life

Stand-Up Stories: Tales from Behind the Microphone During Comedy's
Golden Age

Brenham

Fiction

Wingo: The Remarkable Story of an Unremarkable Man

Zeke Gets Glasses. Jungleburgh Children's Reading Community (with
John Swasey)

Undertold Texas
Volume 1

A Curated Journey Through Eclectic History

Mike Vance

Dos Dogs Press

Copyright © 2024 by Mike Vance

All rights reserved.

No portion of this book may be reproduced in any form without written permission from the publisher or author, except as permitted by U.S. copyright law.

Library of Congress Cataloguing-in-Publication Data

Names: Vance, Mike 1959 – author

Title: Undertold Texas Volume 1

Identifiers LCCN pending

ISBN (hardback) 979-8-9879432-8-1

ISBN (paperback) 979-8-9879432-6-7

ISBN (ebook) 979-8-9879432-7-4

Dos Dogs Press

Printed in United States of America

Contents

Foreword

The selection of topics for this first volume of Undertold Texas was entirely subjective. Choices about future volumes will be just as personal. They are not, however, random. I'm hopeful that some of these smaller stories might illuminate a bigger picture. Above everything else, I'm seeking to present a diverse range of stories that reflects the faces of all Texans, both present and past. It is vital that history is preserved in its entirety without kowtowing to politicians who don't understand history in the first place or sanitizing the truth for everyone because a few folks don't want to face it.

Human beings do good things and bad things. All of us do. It is important that we learn from our mistakes and do better as a species. That's why you'll find some people in these pages who you might think are more admirable than others. If we keep in mind that history is the story of that often tenuous humanity taken in context, it becomes very entertaining.

Please note that the stories contained herein are undertold, not un-told. The goal is to present stories from Texas history that will be new to the reader, or at least expand their knowledge on a given subject. I took the two most famous Texans of all time and tried to present a lesser known aspect of their tale or tie them in with much more obscure folks who intersected with their lives. Chances are good that a story in a future volume will again touch one or both of those men. If a name is widely recognized, I hope that I will present new details or add context that might help the reader better understand the story.

In short, some of the chapters may be familiar to some of the readers, but, in Lincolnesque terms, not all of the chapters to all of the people. Much of that will likely be regional. Many Dallasites have certainly heard of Juanita Craft, though many may not know her whole story. The Pease Mansion is known in Austin, and Tom Lea is known in El Paso, but the names might not be as familiar to folks in other parts of Texas. Our state is a big place, just in case no native has reminded of you of that lately. With 48 meaty little stops on the magical history tour, the hope is you'll find plenty that is new to you.

At the suggestion of my friends at Rice University's Glasscock School of Continuing Studies where I am sometimes fortunate enough to teach, I divided the book up into eight regions of Texas. Like the story selection, these regions are subjective. I know people have great and ongoing feuds over what constitutes the Hill Country, for example, and not wanting to wade into that turbulent stream of invective, I will assure everyone that the use of my regions ends with these books.

Neither the individual chapter nor the book overall is meant to be exhaustive. I enjoyed finding the intersection of some tales, though. Those were things that came together in spite of my plans for finding the widest diversity.

I'm approaching this with a long range plan in mind. Honest. I've got this mapped out for a four volume series eventually, so if you don't see your favorite undertold story, it may be coming up. Or drop me a note at mike@mikevancewriter.com to run your idea by me. Please sign up for my monthly newsletter on my website, as well.

Think of this book as an introduction to new history trails to wander. Texas has a past that is more diverse than any other state, and anyone with a healthy curiosity will enjoy a little virtual off-roading through those tales. It may even inspire you to make a real road trip and see where some of this undertold history took place.

Mike Vance. May 2024
www.mikevancewriter.com

West Texas

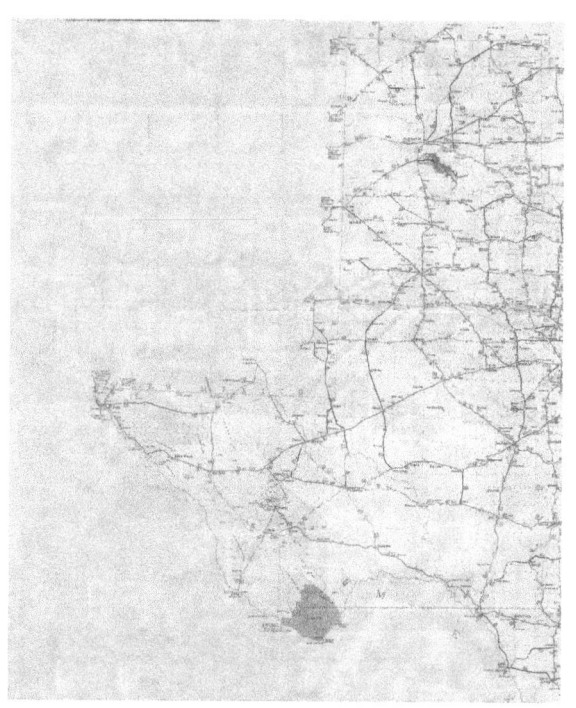

Chapter One

Fray Marcos de Niza

A monument stands near Lochiel, Arizona in the Santa Cruz River Valley where Fray Marcos de Niza crossed what is now the U.S. Mexican border leading an expedition in search of riches. He is credited as the first European to pass west of the Rockies. The date was recorded as April 12, 1539. It signaled the start of a dramatic cultural shift for today's American Southwest, including Texas, since it was the introduction of the Spanish. It led to colonizations, missionization, and the claims of the Spanish crown on the ground as opposed to simply on paper.

The friar may have been most interested in converting the indigenous people to Catholicism, but the Spanish crown, which financed the trip, wanted to repeat their successes in finding riches as they had recently done in modern day Mexico, Central America, and Peru.

The Spanish Empire in the Americas had begun in earnest in 1493 when Christopher Columbus, an Italian Genovese sailing under the Spanish flag, claimed the island of Hispanola for his patrons Isabella of Castille and Ferdinand of Aragon. It was Columbus' second trip to the Americas, and this time he established a colony with livestock, seeds, and agricultural equipment. Isabella in particular, whose land of Castille was richer and more powerful than her husband's, was extremely devoted to the church and spoke of spiritual conquest being of twin importance to military conquest.

Spain's colonies were primarily placed where there was a large indigenous population, and by extension, resources which could be extracted or exploited. Precious metals, stones, and tradable foodstuffs like spices were most desirable. The best estimate is that 250,000 Spaniards relocated to the Americas during the 16th century. At the same time, the indigenous population dropped by as much as 75 to 80%, primarily because of communicable diseases to which the Europeans were resistant, but the native Americans had never been exposed. The decline in the population of the locals, who were both newly converted Catholics and the labor force in their new colonies, alarmed the Spanish greatly. The crown enacted new laws to protect the indigenous Americans as "vassals of the Crown," and that in turn spurred the practice of importing enslaved Africans to labor in their place. This sequence began the creation of the mixed race people that inhabit most of the Americas today.

The first colonies in the Caribbean did not have large populations that required conquest by great Spanish military might. Resistance was nominal compared to what took place in Mexico, and later Peru. Moving forward into the 1520s, the blueprint was that the Spanish military worked in concert with representatives of the church to expand the footprint of Spain.

The Spanish had sighted mainland Florida in 1513, and explorations around the eastern Gulf of Mexico followed. Cabeza de Vaca and several dozen men from the Narvaez Expedition were shipwrecked along the upper and middle Texas coast in November 1528. In spite of all his adventures that filled an epic bestselling book back in Spain, it was really the wanderings of desperate and dying men trying to find safety among their countrymen. The first organized, large scale Spanish exploration intended to cover any part of Texas came from the west and passed through what is today the Panhandle, but it is inextricably connected to the failed quest for the lands between Florida and Mexico for which Panfilo Narvaez had been appointed governor.

Friar Marcos, a native of Nice in France, hence his name, was no stranger to the Americas when he crossed what would become the U.S. border. He had left Spain in 1531 and saw service for his Franciscan order in Peru, and then with Alvarado in Guatemala and Mexico. His journey into modern day Arizona and New Mexico is tied directly to the failed Narvaez Expedition. Roughly 200 Spaniards of that group reached the Texas coast, but only Cabeza de Vaca, Alonso del Castillo Maldonado, Andres Dorantes, and the enslaved African, Esteban, who belonged to Dorantes straggled into Culiacan in Sinaloa seven years later. As their tales spread like wildfire, the biggest take away for the highest placed Spaniards was often that the four men heard rumors of more great cities studded with gold, jewels, and riches such as had been found around what is now Mexico City.

Viceroy Antonio de Mendoza started dreaming about the loot to be found in the Tierra Nueva. Though it did not occur to the Spanish, there were several problems with that tempting gossip. There was an insurmountable language barrier between the Spanish and the American Indian tribes they encountered, especially at first. As early in the Narvaez trip as the area around Tampa Bay, natives had told the Spanish of great wealth to be found near what is today Apalachee Bay, Florida, what the Narvaez group called the Bay of Horses. It repeatedly proved untrue. Whether this was the fault of bad interpretation of hand gestures and pointing, or if the locals just wanted these scary Spaniards to go bother another tribe, we can never know.

None of this deterred Viceroy Mendoza. He tried to enlist at least one of the three Spanish survivors to lead an expedition to the enticing cities of gold, but they all declined. His fallback was to purchase Esteban de Dorantes, the enslaved man who had also survived the failed trip. Esteban had not only been to these distant lands, but he had, in particular, learned enough of the languages that he was serving as interpreter by the time the four survivors reached Culiacan. The viceroy sent Esteban and Fray Marcos de Niza along with some indigenous messengers and guides on a scouting trip to find his riches.

The Franciscan friar and the enslaved interpreter worked out a plan. Esteban and a few indigenous messengers went as the advance party, and if Esteban found something of value, he would send back one of the crosses the expedition brought along as gift trinkets. The messenger would then lead Friar Marcos to that spot. If it was a small discovery, it was to be small cross, and a larger discovery merited a larger cross sent back to the friar. Thus, it was Esteban who was the first non-native to encounter tribes like the Zuni and Apache, and Friar Marcos who was the first European. This was also the first time those tribes had ever seen a horse.

At one point on their journey northward, a breathless messenger arrived with a cross that Friar Marcos later reported was the size of a man, but before the friar could reach him, tragedy struck Esteban. According to the men with him, Esteban found the city of Cibola but was blocked from entering on his first attempt. The following day, Esteban and a few others tried again, but this time they were met with arrows. As Esteban fled, he was killed, or at least the messengers said they never saw him again. The people who reached Friar Marcos said that they were the only survivors. Most likely, the location Esteban had reached was one of the large Zuni pueblos in today's northern New Mexico. When Fray Marcos returned to Mexico, he reported that he had seen the long-sought city of Cibola, albeit from a distant hill, and was ensured of their riches by his Indian informants.

Viceroy Mendoza sent a much larger expedition the following year. This one was led by Francisco de Coronado, the governor of a new province on the Pacific Coast of Mexico, and included 300 Spaniards and up to 1,000 native Mexican Indians. Fray Marcos de Niza was along to lead the way. There were several Spanish officers on the trip, and Coronado dispatched them to lead parties in various directions. Along the way, they subjugated numerous native settlements.

The 1940 commemorative stamp for the Coronado Entrada included a Franciscan such as Fray Marcos. (USPS)

Though multiple participants from the expedition wrote of their experiences, it is difficult to map precise routes and encounters. Evidence shows that members of Coronado's 1540 – 1542 expedition were in the vicinity of Taos, Albuquerque, the Grand Canyon, Dodge City, and Amarillo. Their turnaround point was most likely near present day Salina, Kansas. They were led there in search of the rich city of Quivara that was described by a native of that place whom the Spanish called The Turk. There is little doubt that The Turk was largely trying to keep the Spanish happy by telling them what they wanted to hear. When Coronado found that Quivara contained no riches, he had The Turk put to death.

Overall, Coronado and Viceroy Mendoza were greatly disappointed, though they had seen an enormous swath of what would become northern Mexico and the Southwestern United States. The expedition did nothing to help Friar Marcos' ascendency, though he did remain an esteemed member of the Franciscan order in Mexico. He died there in 1558.

As for Texas, the negative reports largely guaranteed that, though they still claimed the territory, the Spanish sent no further large entrada into the modern state for well over a century. They came to Texas looking for something of value, and did not find it.

Chapter Two

St. Mary's Church - Umbarger

The windswept barrenness of the Panhandle is a far cry from the verdant, rolling Italian countryside, but one large group of Italians were not yet ready to go home. On these flat plains, amongst the tumbleweeds and rattlesnakes near Hereford in the middle 1940s sat a prisoner of war camp. Unlike the dozens of other WWII POW camps in Texas, more than any other state, this one housed Italians instead of Germans.

Just like the German camps which held some hard core Nazis along with men who were conscripted into the service of their country, the Italians in Hereford included several who were solid fascisti backing Benito Mussolini. In late 1943, Italy surrendered, Mussolini was eventually captured by outraged countrymen and executed, and the new government switched to supporting the Allies. Some months later, Italian prisoners held in the United States were offered a chance to return home and perform non-combat service for the Americans and British. The fascists in Hereford, however, declined. They opted to remain as POWs rather than assist the side they still viewed as enemies. That might have been the end of it if not for the fact that several of these men had been artists before the war, and they found a large blank canvas in the nearby town of Umbarger.

Umbarger, Texas is 19 flat miles east of Hereford and 12 miles west of Canyon. In the 1940 census about 150 people were enumerated in what was merely a desolate wide spot on the two lane. Today the number has allegedly doubled, but a casual visitor is hard pressed to square that with visual clues. The grain elevator next to the railroad track is by far the most dominant structure in town.

The people who settled this place were German Catholics who had moved from Schulenberg in south central Texas to the high lonesome of the old John Umbarger Ranch in 1902. Soon there was a general store and a public school, and a Catholic missionary lured more Swiss and German families to the town that he himself laid out.

St. Mary's, the anglicized version of Marienkirch, rose in 1929, but the stock market crashed before the building was completed, and pledges were left wanting. The debt was retired with annual picnics, church suppers, and door to door solicitation. The fall festival, still called Frulingsfest, brought in a few dollars, too. The parish priest, Father John Dolje, declined a salary until the church debt was retired, something that happened only shortly before his death in 1944.

A high altar, side altars, and a tabernacle were donated at the time the Church was built. Alabaster Stations of the Cross were purchased and statues for the side altars were brought from the old Church. There was even a new pump organ. The walls, though, were white. Plain, stark white.

Perhaps something can be read into the relationship that grew between the German residents and the Italian prisoners who had until recently been allied with the nation of the town folk's ancestors, or maybe it was only coincidence, but those imprisoned artists found a project at the little St. Mary's Church on the plains.

The names of the artists are remembered, not lost to time as might have happened. Franco di Bello, Achille Cattanei, Dino Gambetti, Mario de Cristofara, Leonida Gorlato, Carlo Sanvito, Enrico Zorzi, Adriano Angerilli, and Spinello Aretino were the artists. Other Italian POWs came along to help with the scaffolding, clean up, and paint preparation. One of the camp guards, John Coyle, would drive them to Umbarger every day to work at the Church. The prisoners toiled without pay, save for a noon meal prepared by the ladies of the Altar Society and served at a long wooden table Father Krukkert had set up in the church basement.

The artwork they gifted the St. Mary's parish was extensive. The church website describes it as covering the "walls of the Sanctuary, spandrels up to the arch, on the underside of the arch, behind the statues of Jesus and Mary, the chair rail around the Church, across the front of the choir loft, in the choir loft and between the stained glass windows." There are twenty-seven symbolic paintings in the nave of the Church and more are painted above the stained glass windows and along the front of the choir loft. The final piece painted inside the church is a giant oil composition of the Assumption placed above the back altar. It has remained covered by a drape since 1950 and is revealed only on special Marian feast days or for particular visitors.

The Italians incorporated techniques from their homeland, but the paintings include many touches of Umbarger. Inside the sanctuary, mingled with the gold leaf halos of Mary, Elizabeth, and Zacharias in the Visitation and the Angel in the Annunciation, the background of both murals also include local views that the artists saw when they were standing outside of the church on breaks. In the Visitation, a green pasture, trees, stands of ripe grain, and a cluster of farm buildings depict the nearby Meinrad Hollenstein homestead. A little to the side and slightly beneath the radiant dove that hovers over the meeting of Mary and the angel is the Otto Skarke homestead with its sheds and weeping willow trees.

As might be expected, angels abound. Two of them float above an arch at the nave. As the prisoners were creating their images, Achille Cattanei asked some local parents if their daughters, Theresa Westoff and Theresa Evers, could be used as models, and the parents agreed. Franco Di Bello sat on the lunch table in the basement and had the girls sit on a bench with their heads turned towards each other as he sketched their profiles. There is an intricate wood carving of the Last Supper on the front of the altar, as well as the other carved decorations throughout the Sanctuary. These pieces were done by Carlo Sanvito, and the light-colored wood for his artwork was given by Meinrad Hollenstein, the parishioner whose farm is depicted in a painting and who donated one of the stained glass windows. Hollenstein bought the wood from a company in Amarillo that made store counters. Hollenstein also provided oak for other carvings in the form of one-by-six planks that he had gotten to make a cow pen. Like several other Umbarger citizens, Hollenstein came to St. Mary's most every day to watch the artists at work.

The stained glass church windows were also installed by the Italian POWs. The twelve in the sanctuary reference the Eucharist on the west side of the building and Repentance on the east. The windows in the nave are of glorious and joyful mysteries of the church and rosary. John the Baptist graces the confessional. Many of the windows were donated by different Parishioners - people with German names like Friemel, Fischbacher, Batenhorst, or Wieck. Father Krukkert dedicated the newly painted Church on the annual celebration of the Feast of the Immaculate Conception on December 8, 1945.

During the time they were painting the inside of St. Mary's, the POWs would occasionally walk over to the school to talk to the children about Italy. With Christmas approaching in 1944, Franco di Bello drew Santa Claus and his reindeer on the blackboard with colored chalk. The students' thank you note still exists. Scrawled on a piece of tablet paper, it promises that "We shall always remember you and the Prisoners-of-War, Always your friends." It was signed by twenty-three young Umbarger children.

One woman in her seventies still recalled some of the Italian POWs being mesmerized by her fiery red hair when she was in grammar school. Some of the slightly older young women were noticed, too, and decades later they blushingly remembered some of the handsome Italians.

The people of Umbarger did not forget about their imprisoned friends. One man, Franco di Bello, returned many years after the war, and at least one or two of the locals repaid his visit by traveling to his home in Italy. Returning to Umbarger with the artist was his wife, and she found her face, created from wartime longing and memory, reproduced as one of the angels in the oil painting of the Assumption behind the main altar.

Although the rest are all located in Central Texas, in 1983 St. Mary's Catholic Church received designation on the National Register of Historic Places as one of Texas' famous painted churches. There is no resident priest anymore, but with an appointment, one might drive out from the church in Canyon to welcome a curious visitor.

Chapter Three

Ranald Mackenzie

To say that Ranald Slidell Mackenzie came from a connected family of overachievers might be an understatement. His father was a celebrated author and naval officer. His older brother was the United State minister to Mexico, and though the family lived in New York City, he also served as the Confederate minister to France. Mackenzie's Confederate connection was to Louisiana where one uncle was a United States senator and another chief justice of the state supreme court. Ranald Mackenzie's two younger brothers were both senior U.S. Navy officers, and an aunt was married to Commodore Matthew Perry who opened Japan to the West in 1853.

Ranald went from Williams College to the Military Academy at West Point to become the lone Army man in a solid Navy family. He graduated first in his class in 1862. As a newly commissioned second lieutenant, Mackenzie was assigned to the Army of the Potomac just when the cauldron of the Civil War had heated to its hottest. He fought in eight major battles in two years, received seven brevet promotions and six significant wounds, the first coming at Second Bull Run in the form of a .52 caliber ball in the shoulder. He lost two fingers at Petersburg, a wound that led to the Comanches calling him "Bad Hand." The nation's supreme commander Ulysses S. Grant called Mackenzie "the most promising young officer in the Union Army." By the final campaign against Robert E. Lee, Mackenzie had been breveted a major general.

With the post-war rank of colonel in the regular army, Ranald Mackenzie commanded the 41st Infantry, a regiment formed from the wartime U.S. Colored Troops that was reorganized under his command into the 24th Infantry, a unit of the famed Buffalo Soldiers. During his many years in Texas, he was commanding officer at Fort Clark and Fort McKavett. Moving to take over the Fourth Cavalry, he headquartered at Fort Concho and Fort Richardson. Along the way, he spent a great deal of time at military headquarters in San Antonio where he met and grew to fancy a young girl named Florida Tunstall.

In the summer of 1871, Mackenzie led a series of expeditions in the wilds of the Llano Estacado and the Texas Panhandle to drive renegade Indians back onto their reservations near Fort Sill, Indian Territory. He was wounded yet again in a skirmish with Comanches at Blanco Canyon. In 1872, Mackenzie led his troopers on an illegal raid across the Rio Grande and burned a Kickapoo village near Remolino, Coahuila.

Mackenzie's most impactful military year in Texas was that of the Red River War. The federal government had entered the Treaty of Medicine Lodge in 1867 in which several Southern Plains tribes came into reservations around Fort Sill, in southwest Indian Territory, to be cared for and controlled. By the early 1870s, the rations they were promised had become routinely diminished or sometimes absent entirely. White traders in whiskey and guns, supposed to be excluded from the reservations, were thriving. White bandits were coming onto the reservation and stealing the tribes' horses and cattle, then escaping without any pursuit, let alone punishment, from the military and Indian Bureau men who were supposed to be keeping watch. The worst of it was that between 1872 and 1874, White buffalo hide hunters based in Dodge City, Kansas ran unimpeded across the Cheyenne-Arapaho reservation and slaughtered the buffalo herds that supplied everything to those people.

The tribes governed out of Fort Sill were starving, and they decided to take action. A large gathering was called, revolving around a Sun Dance, and Isatia and Quanah Parker, two young war chiefs of the Quahadi band of Comanches, recruited warriors for raids into Texas to avenge the killings of their family members by their mortal enemy, the Texans. Isatia promised that he could bring the dead back to life. Though many Kiowa decided to wait, a combined war party of 700 Comanche, Cheyenne, Arapaho, and some Kiowa headed west from Indian Territory into the Panhandle. At the end of June 1874, they met U.S. Cavalry at the Second Battle of Adobe Walls. It did not go well. Seventy Indians were killed to only three Whites. One warrior was shot from his horse on a ridge three quarters of a mile away, an unheard-of distance at the time, and a very bad omen to the war party.

In July, after several fatal attacks on Whites in Texas, Kansas, and Indian Territory, General Philip Sheridan, with the backing of army head William T. Sherman, sent five commands of cavalry, some 3,000 soldiers, to converge on what they believed to be Indian hideouts up and down the eastern edge of the Llano Estacado. Mackenzie's most decisive battle in the campaign came at the end of September when his men destroyed five Indian villages on the floor of Palo Duro Canyon. His appearance was largely a surprise to the occupants secure in their tipis.

It was his last major battle with the Comanches. Only four people died at the Battle of Palo Duro Canyon, one of the most reliable camp sites of the Comanches, but when the troopers showed up on the canyon rim the Comanches were forced to flee up the steep sides. Mackenzie captured their tipis, winter food supply, and 1,450 wild horses. He allowed his

Tonkawa scouts to select about 300 of the horses, and he ordered his troopers to kill the other 1,100. It was his destruction of the Indians' horses and food, much more than the battle itself, that destroyed the Indians' resistance. Comanche legend says that one can still hear the cries of the horses on the floor of Palo Duro Canyon.

First it was the Kiowa who came into Fort Sill, followed by the Cheyenne and Arapaho. Some Comanches came, but Quanah Parker remained defiant, at least in words. His family tells the story that Quanah went alone into the wilderness, where he covered himself in a blanket to consider his best course. During the night, first a wolf and then an eagle passed, both headed in the direction of Fort Sill. The animals were sent to show Quanah the way. He arrived there on June 2, 1875 with 407 of

Ranald Mackenzie in his brigadier general's uniform. (Library of Congress)

his people and some 1,500 horses. By that time, Ranald Mackenzie had taken over command at Fort Sill and control over the Co-
manche-Kiowa and Cheyenne-Arapaho reservations. Quanah Parker's
arrival marked the end of the Red River War.

After the massacre of George Custer's troops at the Little Bighorn in
1876, Mackenzie was transferred north to the Black Hills to take Custer's
place. He captured Sioux Chief Red Cloud and returned his band to
the reservations. On the upper plains, he led a retaliatory raid against
Northern Cheyenne Chiefs Dull Knife, Yellow Nose, and Little Wolf
in the Powder River Valley. After those successes, Mackenzie moved to
Colorado and then Arizona where his troopers defeated rebellious Utes
and Apache. At age 42, he became the youngest brigadier general in the
Army.

In October 1883, the general was returned to San Antonio as head
of the Military Department of Texas, but those around him had begun
to notice a serious mental decline. He bought land near Boerne and
renewed his acquaintance with Florida Tunstall, by then ten years widowed. A Christmas wedding was planned.

One theory holds that Mackenzie was suffering the final effects of
syphilis. Though he had been temperate for much of his life, he began to
drink heavily. On the eve of his wedding, the general got into a drunken
brawl with San Antonio locals and was found badly beaten and lashed
to a wagon wheel in a sketchy alley. His subordinates had seen enough,
and the wedding was called off. To avoid more trouble, General Sheridan
issued a bogus order for Mackenzie to report to his hometown of New
York City. At the Bloomingdale Asylum, he was diagnosed as insane. At
a fitness hearing, the general was given one option: to be retired from the
Army. He replied, "I would rather die than go to the retired list." It took
five years to get his wish. He alternated his days between the care of his

sister, Harriet, and various mental institutions. Ranald Mackenzie died in January 1889 and was buried in the academy cemetery at West Point.

Chapter Four

Comfort Germans Massacred

T exas has the fourth largest number of people with German ancestry of any state, almost two and a half million, and there was a
time when certain Texas locales were overwhelmingly German. Just like
Spanish and Vietnamese today, the Republic of Texas and later the state
printed some official documents in German. There were many towns
where German language was common on the street. There were German
churches, German newspapers, shooting clubs, singing clubs, sporting
clubs, and festivals. By the late 1840s, several towns in Texas had mostly
German immigrant populations.

Not all the immigrants fit the mold of people who were leaving their
home because they were unemployed or underemployed peasants in
search of a better life. There was a wave of these Germans, along with
some Moravians, Bohemians, Austrians, and a few others from Central
Europe, who were fleeing failed revolutions. These uprisings had a big
element of the educated classes and liberals who valued the enlighten-
ment. Unlike some of the Western nations which had taken on major
democratic reforms by this time, most of Europe, including the German

and Czech states, were still largely underneath a feudal system. There was horrific income disparity, stiff competition for jobs - if you even had a chance to become upwardly mobile - and a building agitation for social justice. Most places had mandatory military service, which was very unpopular, and socialist political theory had begun to emerge.

All of these revolutions and uprisings failed except for one in France which was quickly eaten up by the return of the monarchy anyway. Overall, monarchy still reigned, and suddenly, these intellectuals in Austria and the German states were no longer welcome. There was a crackdown on the press and writings, and many of them soon fled, some to Texas.

This group was called the Freethinkers or 48ers. It included philosophers, writers, scientists, doctors, and engineers. Some of them had money, and they arrived with books, musical instruments, and worldly goods, not just a single trunk of clothes. They established Freethinking communities, each intended to be a utopian, intellectual oasis of true democracy. A few were in Central Texas, Millheim in Austin County and Latium in southwestern Washington County, but the biggest group was in the Hill Country in places like Comfort, Sisterdale, and Luckenbach.

The 48ers held meetings in Latin and were held up as the most cultured people in the South. They were mostly abolitionists, about the only such folk in Texas in the 1850s. Many were atheists or agnostics and either cared nothing about organized religion or were outright opposed to it. Comfort had no church for the first 40 years of its existence.

Germans did not necessarily assimilate well, or want to. The coming Civil War brought that fact to the fore. Many of them were recently arrived and not naturalized citizens and therefore unable to even vote, but despite that, there were enough who were registered to drastically change the vote for secession in some counties. On the southwestern frontier,

Fayette, Bastrop, Travis, Williamson, Uvalde, Blanco, Burnet, Edwards, Mason, and Medina Counties voted against secession, and part of the reason was the heavy immigrant turnout. The other reason was that, like everyone else on the western edge of Texas, the federal government was vital to defending them from raiding Comanches and Kiowas. Breaking the vote down by precinct, it is even more striking to see how strongly German and Czech communities across Texas felt about remaining part of the United States.

The Confederates passed the first ever military conscription in North America in April 1862. All able-bodied men between 18 and 35 were required to join the rebel army. Sixteen year olds must swear an oath to the alleged nation. The great majority of the German immigrants did not believe in secession. They did not believe in slavery. They certainly were not pleased with the potential prospect of getting killed for it. However, faced with little choice, hundreds of German Texans chose the route of least resistance and joined up shortly before the draft would have taken them anyway. A few even became officers, but many others chose a different path, one that did not include compromising their beliefs. They quickly learned that the Confederate government was a very repressive operation.

The C.S.A. did not allow dissent of any kind, and strong supporters of the government sometimes committed murder in its name. That violence happened in every area of Texas where there was a large German population opposed to secession and conscription. As the grumbling and outright defiance festered in those immigrant communities, it brought out the wrath of their secessionist neighbors. Hundreds of German men fled their homes and hid out in the woods to avoid military service, though almost all were eventually found by the Home Guard.

There had been armed resistance and killings up north along the Red River, the other hotbed of anti-secessionist feeling. There was a meeting held at Shelby in Austin County that drew Germans from several communities to discuss what action to take. When the Confederate government found out about the meeting, they put Austin, Fayette, and Colorado Counties under martial law forbidding Germans from holding any assembly that exceeded a handful of people. The state of Texas applied martial law to every space within its borders.

The biggest conflicts and brutalities came where the largest concentration of Germans was located - in the Hill Country frontier out west. Governor Francis Lubbock appointed a San Antonio merchant named Captain James Duff to head the Home Guard, or Partisan Rangers, for that area. Duff had served in the United States Army in the 1850s, reaching the rank of sergeant before he was court martialed and dishonorably discharged. He proved to be a man totally devoid of morality.

Duff's Rangers hanged dozens of German men around Fredericksburg on mere suspicion of holding Union sentiments. The Rangers burned immigrant homes and crops, leaving those men's families homeless and destitute. Hundreds of the immigrants fled to Mexico or Union states. Some managed to return to Europe. The German holdouts who remained in Texas routinely stayed hidden in the woods to avoid *die Haengerbaende*, the hanging band.

On the first of August 1862, roughly 70 German men who had formed a Unionist group met west of Kerrville, ready to head south to Mexico. At least some, if not all, had plans to eventually sail from Veracruz to federally occupied New Orleans, where they would join the U.S. Army and fight for their adopted country. Most were Freethinkers, and others were among the Adelsverein settlers who had come to Fredericksburg. Another immigrant, Charles Bergmann, informed on them, however, and Duff sent almost 100 soldiers led by one of his lieutenants, Colin D. McRae, to attack them. According to an Englishman with McRae's company, Duff had ordered that no prisoners were to be taken.

The rebel infantry and cavalry caught up with the woefully slow-moving Unionist Germans eight days later while they were camped for the night among oaks and cedars on the banks of the Nueces River in Kinney County. A shot fired by an overzealous rebel zinged past one of the few Unionist sentries and awakened the Germans. Twenty-eight of the Unionists managed to slip away from camp and make their way home. Armed mostly with hunting rifles and led by the county treasurer, Fritz Tegener from Comfort, the forty remaining Germans stood for a fight. They repelled the initial pre-dawn charge and killed two Confederates, but they could not hold off the larger force for long. Nineteen of the Germans were killed outright or badly wounded, and another nine were captured. The rest fled into the night hoping for the Rio Grande, still about 50 miles distant.

When the sun rose over the riverside, Lt. McRae's men shot every prisoner through the back of the head. All 28 bodies were left to rot in the August heat of Southwest Texas. By October, McRae and his men had caught up with some of the remnants of the 48ers group and killed eight more as they attempted to cross the Rio Grande. A few of the survivors did manage to reach New Orleans and joined the army.

Three years later, after the war ended, the families from the area around Comfort finally retrieved the bodies of their husbands and fathers and buried them in a mass grave beneath a simple limestone obelisk in Comfort. Some of those hanged by Duff's men rest there, too. The Treue der Union monument is the oldest Civil War memorial in Texas. A 36-star United States flag flies there, permanently at half-staff.

Chapter Five

Nat Love

The story of Nat Love, pronounced Nate, is greatly exaggerated, and parts of it are likely just plain untrue, but in this one instance of history, that might not be the point. Much of the information comes from the 1907 memoir which Love penned himself, and it reads like the best dime novels of the day. The fact is that those western legends are an important part of our history because they spawned real flesh-and-blood pioneers who settled the untamed portion of the U.S., and they built a fascination with the United States in countries around the world. Underlying the legends are many real glimpses of life in the American West.

Nat Love was born into slavery in Davidson County, Tennessee on land that is now suburban Nashville. As the hierarchy of the plantation went, he was relatively better off than most of the enslaved there. His father was a foreman over other field hands, and his mother managed the farm's kitchen. Despite that, Nat wrote that his white overseers were "perfect devils in human form." In his youth, Nat learned to read with the help of his father, Sampson. After Emancipation, Sampson and his family began to farm tobacco as sharecroppers, but he died after planting his second crop. Young Nat worked a variety of jobs and learned that he had a skill for horses, something he described as "break the horse or break my neck." He said of his self-preservation technique: "I held onto his mane and stuck to him like a leech."

In 1869, Love left his family in an uncle's care and headed west with $50 in his pocket, money he said he got by winning a horse in a raffle then selling him. He made the trip from Tennessee by walking or catching rides with friendly farmers, and he eventually landed in Dodge City, Kansas, a 16-year old looking for a job. He walked up on a rough-looking cowboy outfit having their breakfast and sought out someone to talk to. This is how Love wrote his recollection of that morning almost four decades later:

"They proved to be a Texas outfit, who had just come up with a herd of cattle and having delivered them they were preparing to return. There were several colored cow boys among them, and good ones too. After breakfast I asked the camp boss for a job as cow boy. He asked me if I could ride a wild horse. I said "yes sir." He said if you can I will give you a job. So he spoke to one of the colored cow boys called Bronko Jim, and told him to go out and rope old Good Eye, saddle him and put me on his back. Bronko Jim gave me a few pointers and told me to look out for the horse was especially bad on pitching. I told Jim I was a good rider and not afraid of him. I thought I had rode pitching horses before, but from the time I mounted old Good Eye I knew I had not learned what pitching was. This proved the worst horse to ride I had ever mounted in my life, but I stayed with him and the cow boys were the most surprised outfit you ever saw, as they had taken me for a tenderfoot, pure and simple. After the horse got tired and I dismounted the boss said he would give me a job and pay me $30.00 per month and more later on. He asked what my name was and I answered Nat Love, he said to the boys we will call him Red River Dick. I went by this name for a long time.

"The boss took me to the city and got my outfit, which consisted of a new saddle, bridle and spurs, chaps, a pair of blankets and a fine 45 Colt revolver. Now that the business which brought them to Dodge City was concluded, preparations were made to start out for the Pan Handle country in Texas to the home ranch. The outfit of which I was now a member was called the Duval outfit, and their brand was known as the Pig Pen brand. I worked with this outfit for over three years. On this trip there were only about fifteen of us riders, all excepting myself were hardy, experienced men, always ready for anything that might turn up, but they were as jolly a set of fellows as one could find in a long journey. There now being nothing to keep us longer in Dodge City, we prepared for the return journey, and left the next day over the old Dodge and Sun City lonesome trail, on a journey which was to prove the most eventful of my life up to now."

Not that Love set out to illuminate the history of trail rides, but he made some excellent points in that passage. Approximately one in four cowboys in the 19th century West were of African Descent. Most of them were in fact "boys" in their teens. Many accounts exist of pre-teen youths signing on to herd animals up the trail. The fact that the outfit from Duval Ranch numbered but fifteen is not out of the ordinary, either. Barely a dozen seasoned cowboys were all that were required to move a few thousand head of cattle from as far as South Texas to the Kansas railheads.

During his time at the Duval Ranch, Love honed his skills with a .45 Colt and became a good enough all-around cowboy that he was even sent into Mexico as a cattle buyer since he had learned conversational Spanish. He also fought off cattle rustlers, banditos, and hostile American Indians, and he endured hailstorms on the plains that were worse than he had ever imagined. Nat Love stayed on with the outfit in the Panhandle before signing on with the Gallinger Ranch on the Gila River in Arizona Territory. While there, he continued to ride all over the Southwest, including regular jaunts back into West Texas moving longhorn cattle and herds of range horses.

Nat Love photo captioned "In my fighting clothes" in his book. (Library of Congress)

One of the likely tall tales in Nat Love's books involved a trip to Deadwood, South Dakota where he allegedly entered an Independence Day rodeo and won six contests and $200. The trouble with that tale is that the extensive write up in the Deadwood newspaper covered every bit of celebration minutiae, but never mentioned a rodeo. According to Love, that was also the day he earned his second nickname of "Deadwood Dick."

Perhaps the richest tale Love wrote told of his capture by a band of Pima Indians in fall of 1877 while rounding up stray cattle near the Gila River in Arizona. He said he received several of the 14 bullet wounds he amassed on the open range in that fight with the Pimas, but they opted to nurse him back to health since many of them had a mix of African blood themselves, something that does jibe with real history. Though Love wrote that he had the chance to marry a chief's daughter and be adopted into the tribe, he instead stole a pony and escaped into West Texas.

Love's book tells of great adventures and is filled with bold claims. He said he could outdrink any man he met in cattle country, and said that he met Buffalo Bill, Bat Masterson, Pat Garret, and Billy the Kid. It also contains passages that seem to come from the heart:

"Mounted on my horse my ... lariat near my hand, and my trusty guns in my belt ... I felt like I could defy the world."

By the time he was 35, Nat Love married a woman named Alice and gave up the cowboy life in favor of a job with the Denver and Rio Grande Railroad. In 1890, he took on the duties of Pullman car porter for the line and worked routes westward from his Denver home. The family relocated multiple times, living in Wyoming, Utah, and Nevada before settling in southern California.

Love's book contains the boast that everything laid down within actually happened, but without many avenues for verification, the world will never know. No record exists for several of the cattlemen named, but potential doubts about accuracy never slowed America's reading public. The book became a bestseller. The decade and a half following the publication of his autobiography, Love spent as a courier and guard for a securities company in Los Angeles. He died there in 1921 at the age of 66.

Chapter Six

Tom Lea

Not many famous artists could claim of having a police escort to elementary school because Pancho Villa had put a price on his father's head and threatened to kidnap his sons. Tom Lea, Jr., the father of the artist who carried the same name, was a lawyer and the mayor of El Paso when he ordered the arrests of Villa's wife and brother for gun running. The famous bandit revolutionary responded by placing a price of $1,000 in gold on the head of the elder Lea, dead or alive.

Thomas Calloway Lea III grew up in an El Paso that was still filled with frontier elements. Horse-drawn fire engines. A Mexican majority marginalized by the Anglo minority. A years-long typhus epidemic, and a blazing revolution that often spilled across the Rio Grande into the Texas streets. From the El Paso public schools, Lea went to the Art Institute of Chicago to study under acclaimed muralist John Warner Norton. The move to Chicago was suggested by his public school art teacher, and it changed young Lea's life. He stayed there for seven years, working on murals and any commercial job that was offered all the way down to painting window lettering for dime store sales. He also met and married a fellow art student, Nancy Taylor, and the two traveled third class to see the work of famous painters in France and Italy.

In 1933, the Leas packed up and headed south to El Paso for a visit before fulfilling Tom's desire to live in Santa Fe. Lea later described the move and life for the struggling artists.

"I knew exactly where I wanted to go, but we came back to El Paso first and I bought a 1926 Dodge sedan for seventy-five dollars. One of the back windows of this sedan got broken and never was replaced. That was a two-day journey to Santa Fe in that old Dodge, ... and I had enough money to build this one-room adobe house."

The stay was a short one. Nancy had an attack of appendicitis, and the surgery was botched. The couple moved back to El Paso, but she soon died.

Though the rest of the nation was mired in the depths of the Great Depression, the hard times were a lifeline for many painters thanks to the Federal Artists Project. Under the wing of government funding, Tom Lea won competitions to paint murals in the El Paso federal courthouse, the Burlington Railroad Terminal in Lacrosse, Wisconsin, and post offices at Seymour and Odessa, Texas, Pleasant Hill, Missouri, and the Ben Franklin Post Office in Washington, D.C.. He also got commissions for a library in Las Cruces, New Mexico and a mural at the Texas Centennial Exhibition in Dallas.

The subjects of his famous Texas murals varied, but always there was a theme of Texas and the West. In Odessa, cattle stampede under a night sky split by lightning. In Seymour, Comanches gallop across the parched landscape. The mural in his hometown of El Paso was a master work. He spent five months in the studio doing preliminary drawings and then spent ten hours days on site. The artwork follows the timeline of El Paso history from Apaches and conquistadors, for which he had a friend pose in costume, to a determined miner and a wizened and wiry lawman. The face of the miner was also that of a model, but Lea recalled meeting such oldtimers who could "live on coffee, cornmeal and jackrabbits."

A casual Tom Lea posing with his mural work "Pass of the North" in the El Paso Federal Courthouse. (Library of Congress)

The late 1930s were also pivotal in Tom Lea's life for other reasons. In 1938, he married Sarah Dighton, an Illinois woman with a young son. He also made friends with Texas folklorist J. Frank Dobie and book designer Carl Hertzog. Numerous collaborations sprung from those acquaintances, the most famous of which had Lea illustrating two of Dobie's books: *Apache Gold and Yaqui Silver* and *The Longhorns.*

At the outbreak of WWII, Lea took a job as an artist correspondent for *Life Magazine,* one of the most high-profile publications in the United States. For the duration, he traveled the globe, from one war zone to the next. Topping 100,000 miles, Lea visited American forces in the North Atlantic all the way to Greenland, and, sometimes aboard the carrier Hornet, the South Pacific. He visited mainland China and witnessed the landing of the Seventh Marines on Peleliu. At each stop he created unflinching interpretations of what he saw.

Lea remained proud of his wartime work and always stressed that his artwork was that of an eyewitness.

"I want to make it clear that I did not report hearsay; I did not imagine, or fake, or improvise; I did not cuddle up with personal emotion, moral notion, or political opinion about War with a capital-W. I reported in pictures what I saw with my own two eyes, wide open."

One of his most famous studio paintings was a slow adaptation into oils of a snapshot of his wife that he carried throughout his travels for *Life*. It had been taken before the war in their sunlit El Paso backyard on Raynolds Boulevard. In later life, when his painting was confined to the studio, Lea declined portraiture commissions, but the work of his wife, Sarah, was something he called "a painter's votive made in the gladness of being home." It turned out to be a life-sized work in which Sarah stands her full five feet six inches. She is depicted in front of a blue sky with Mount Franklin behind her.

Lea also delved into writing during the post-war years. He wrote novels and illustrated them himself using brush and ink. His first book, *The Brave Bulls*, was turned into a movie, as was *The Wonderful Country*, the volume that followed it. He also wrote and illustrated a non-fiction commissioned history of King Ranch complete with Tom Lea artwork. That two-volume work took four years to complete.

His painting career ended with studio work that had a heavy emphasis on Mexico and the Southwestern United States. He continued to decline commissions saying, "I select my subjects, they don't select me." Many of those later works went to his friends.

Tom Lea's style of artwork was never consistent. He said he used the style his subject demanded. Some paintings are very reminiscent of the

WPA style and Thomas Hart Benton, other work evokes modernism, and some is traditional western art. Lea spoke often about style and subject matter, and his own words about his work include these:

"What I've tried to do as a painter is to express, when it comes down to it, the great privilege of living in such a majestic and mysterious world. We have the privilege of living in this life in this marvelous place."

The Metroplex & North Texas

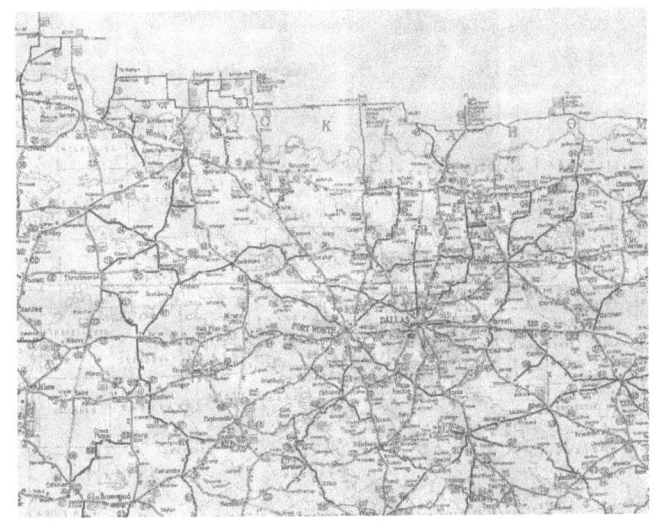

Chapter Seven

1936 Centennial Exposition

T wo other American cities also trumpeted a world's fair in 1936, but that was of little to no consequence to the folks in Dallas. They had outbid their rivals, Houston and San Antonio, when Robert L. Thorton and a committee composed largely of bankers managed to put together an opening cash contribution of $7.7 million in order to land the Texas Centennial Exposition. It certainly helped that the Texas State Fair Grounds were already in place southeast of downtown, and another 26 acres was added to expand the space. While the venue was transformed into a "masterpiece of art and imagination," the annual State Fair was canceled for 1935.

The idea of setting the Lone Star State's centennial as the 100th anniversary of independence from Mexico is Anglocentric, to say the least, but if anyone objected at the time, they were soft voices whispering downwind. The Centennial Commission responded to the occasion with an almost 200-acre, $25 million playground which the newsreels proclaimed had "all Texas playing host." Opening day attendance on

June 6, 1936 topped 117,000. President Franklin Roosevelt addressed crowds six days later.

In true Texas fashion, though backers spoke of a world's fair, only five nations took part. Texas was the only portion of the world that mattered. Three of those visiting nations, Germany, China, and the United Kingdom, were represented largely through restaurant offerings. Mexico offered a small "village." The German restaurant, Old Nuremburg, was also paired with a village that offered ice skating and a rathskeller. All of the foreign attractions were grouped in a quarter-mile long amusement strip.

The United States government was the largest partner nation. That official building was topped by an eagle and relief sculptures of Texas history moments. A highlight was the Department of Labor's Mechanical Man who moved and talked. Uncle Sam was represented in a myriad of other ways, especially given that the mid-1930s were the peak of federal programs aimed to tame to the Great Depression. The Federal Theatre Project staged shows including a short August run of a version of Macbeth with an all-Black cast that was adapted and directed by Orson Welles. It was held in the 5,000-seat amphitheatre with integrated seating, a unique experience for Dallasites up to that time. Audiences were largely positive and enthusiastic about the performances.

The Hall of Negro Life was also sponsored by the federal government. It was the result of pressure from the NAACP and other Black organizations seeking inclusion in the Centennial. The Hall's admission was free and featured six exhibits designed to remind fairgoers that African Americans were contributing members of American society. The hall's exhibits focused on Business and Industry, Art, Mechanic Arts, Agriculture, Health, and Education. Corporations and organizations across the U.S. contributed to the displays inside. One of the most in-your-face visuals in the Hall were several large murals by Harlem Renaissance painter Aaron Douglas. It proved to be a popular feature. Exposition organizers pegged the number of visitors to the Hall of Negro Life at over 400,000. Sixty percent of those visitors were White.

Federal Exhibits Building 1936. (Library of Congress)

One of the most popular attractions at the Exposition was a spectacular called The Cavalcade of Texas, a historical pageant covering Texas history, though the organizers' notion of history started in 1519 with the Spanish. Indigenous Texans before that time were evidently on their own. Sweaty visitors in cotton dresses, straw hats, and shirtsleeves ate it up.

Other exhibits abounded and astounded. There was an aquarium where people could press their noses next to fish. The House of Magic where, among other wonders, visitors saw popcorn cooked by radio waves, was a favorite stop. Kilgore Rangerettes escorted celebrity fairgoers to a replica Jersey Lily where "Judge Roy Bean" pronounced a sentence. There was a Texas Rangers exhibit, and square dancing on the ground and on horseback. Scantily clad women were on display, plus a show boat and an exhibit called Midget City. Visitors saw model railroads, boxing dinosaurs, shiny new cars, and a plethora of Texas product promotions including fruit-bearing citrus trees transplanted 600 miles north of the Rio Grande Valley. Hamburgers were a dime and sodas a nickel.

No fair is complete without a Midway, and the Centennial Exposition had that, as well. The Rocket Speedway, an English carnival ride that raced in a circle and climbed up the walls as it gained speed, was billed as making its first American appearance. The roller coaster remained in operation for later State Fairs, but the other rides moved on. Adding to the excitement that summer, a Gene Autry movie called *The Big Show* was filmed on site.

Buildings around the central lagoon were painted in a tawny off white to lessen the blinding bounce of the Texas summer sunshine. The group design took place under the direction of George Dahl, a mid-century Dallas architect. Though Dahl had over 3,000 buildings to his credit when he died, those at Fair Park were the highlight of his portfolio.

The sleek modern architecture with notes of the Spanish frontier was only the beginning. Texas was presented as the most modern of states, trumpeting television as a medium of the future and commercial air travel celebrated by the state's carriers such as Braniff. Several of the fair buildings offered air conditioning that mesmerized visitors on 100-degree summer days.

The *New York Times* wrote that the Centennial Exposition was still about cattle, cotton and oil, and there was indeed a robust presence for commercial concerns with business in Texas. AT&T was the first major exhibitor to sign on. They were soon joined by General Motors, Chrysler, Ford, Westinghouse, Kraft, Standard Brands, Beech-Nut, Texaco, and Gulf Oil. Being Texas, visitors also saw plenty of Dr. Pepper. Industries were grouped together in Food & Agriculture, Travel

& Transportation, Home Planning, or Electrical & Communications buildings.

At its core, the Texas Centennial was one giant advertising campaign to encourage more investment in the state in the midst of the Great Depression. The planners depicted Texas as "a land of opportunity and second chances," and part of that was a very conscious decision to lead the state away from its Southern identity and make it over as part of the West. Sculpture, paintings, and photographs embraced cowboys and cowgirls. Visitors saw every colorful myth laid out by Tom Mix and Zane Grey, and though the state may have started the year 1936 picking cotton, it left Dallas wearing a ten-gallon hat.

After a five-month run and well over six million tickets sold, the Texas Centennial Exposition closed on November 29. The bonds that had been issued lost money, leaving some of the backers in the red, but public reaction was so positive, and the attention brought to the City of Dallas so great, that no one seemed to mind too much. Ten thousand temporary jobs were created. Driven by those who motored to Dallas, state fuel tax revenue in Texas rose $9.3 million over the two years of the Exposition. Hotels and railroads saw a 35% increase in traffic, and general retail sales in the area rose as much as 40%. It was estimated as a $50 million windfall for Dallas, and it went a long way toward softening the pain of the Depression there.

The exhibits changed and reopened the following year as the Texas & Pan-American Exposition. Though the second time around offered a much more international experience, with 20 nations from across the Americas taking part, a disappointing 2.3 million people strolled the grounds during an even longer fair run.

There is still a tangible legacy from the Texas Centennial Exposition. The event lives on in the 30 buildings which remain at Fair Park. Those were collectively designated as a National Historic Landmark in 1986, fifty years after the fair. The Dallas Historical Society now occupies the Texas Hall of State. The General Motors Building is now the Music Hall. Other highlights among the lasting buildings are the Old Mill Inn, Magnolia Lounge, Hall of Religion, Museum of Nature and Science, and Museum of Natural History. Architectural historian Karen Shopoff says, "Fair Park in Dallas is the largest collection of TRUE art deco architecture anywhere."

One structure that modern visitors would search for in vain is the Hall of Negro Life. It was demolished for the 1937 Pan American Exposition season, under the guise of needing more space for building new exhibits. It was the only building demolished. Despite protests, the State Fair of Texas remained segregated for three more decades.

Chapter Eight

Fannin's Pocket Watch

T hough most nineteenth century Texans would disagree, it is difficult to cast James Walker Fannin as a hero. Even disregarding his earlier activities as a slave trader, Fannin is unlikable on his Texas Revolution record alone. He alternated between vacillating and whining as the Texas revolutionary commander at Goliad. He failed to go to the aid of the besieged Alamo when he was asked to do so. Ultimately, his choice to stop his troops in the center of an open prairie without water or natural defenses led to the loss of the Battle of Coleto Creek and set in motion the massacre of more than 400 brave men under direct orders from Mexican General Antonio Lopez de Santa Anna.

On paper, the Georgia-born Fannin was one of the most likely officers the Texas revolutionaries possessed. He had entered the United States Military Academy at West Point at the age of 14 and a half. Going at the time by the name of James Walker, and only adding his estranged father's surname later, his record at the Point was poor. It was filled with unexcused absences and disciplinary infractions. He failed courses and was held back one class. He resigned two years in, writing two separate letters of resignation giving slightly different reasons in each one. It may easily be interpreted as an indicator of his later dithering as a revolutionary colonel.

That formal military training was the primary reason that Fannin lobbied to be named commander in chief of the revolutionary Texas army instead of Sam Houston. He forever after bore a hatred of Houston that was lined out in letters to officials of the interim government, and he ignored several of Houston's common sense orders. His letters from the presidio at Goliad oscillated between excoriating General Houston and declaring that he himself was wholly unfit for command.

It was not a matter of cowardice. More than once during his short service in the Revolution, Fannin showed great personal bravery. At the Battle of Concepcion in the early stages of the Texian victory at Bexar in late 1835, Fannin was one of the co-leaders, along with James Bowie, who routed a superior number of Mexican Centralists deployed by General Martin Perfecto de Cos.

A few months later, on the ground that would become known as the Coleto Creek battlefield, though it was not immediately near the creek, Colonel Fannin halted his column of men to have lunch and let the oxen pulling wagons and guns graze. Inexplicably, he had not thought to have the oxen fed before they departed the presidio to flee the oncoming army of General Jose Urrea, a force known to be hot on his heels. They had gone but a few miles before the stop, and some of Fannin's junior officers urged him to at least move along to the cover of the tree line two miles distant. He declined to do so, and soon Urrea's troops had the Texians surrounded.

Fannin ordered his men to form a battlefield square with his artillery pieces at the corners. It was a textbook move from the military manuals of the times. The brave Texians held off an assault until nightfall. By that time, Mexican sharpshooters had picked off many of the gun crews, and the cannon themselves were too overheated to keep firing back at the Centralists. Both the guns and the dozens of wounded badly needed water that they could not reach. In the morning of March 20, Urrea's own artillery arrived, and he fired a loud and ominous warning shot directly over the head of the besieged Texians. Fannin signaled to surrender. Though many modern Texans claim that the colonel was duped by dishonest Mexican Centralists, the signed surrender document clearly states that the capitulation was without conditions.

Fannin left the field with a severe wound in the right thigh and bruises from another shot that was miraculously deflected by his coin purse clasp. Dozens of other Texians carried injuries from balls and artillery fire. Along with the rest of the captives, they were taken back to the presidio at Goliad which they had just fled. Most men were crowded into the Lady of Loreto Chapel to the point that there was not sufficient room to lie down. They were thrown pieces of beef for food. Water was scarce since the Mexicans feared that the fort's wells had been poisoned in anticipation of their arrival. Fannin and other wounded stayed in a makeshift hospital, tended to by Texian doctors who also saw to the Centralist casualties.

The fate of the captured rebels is well known. Those who could march were divided into three groups and told they were being taken to ships where they would be sent back to the United States. That tale was a lie. Instead, the groups were halted about a mile from the fort where they were summarily executed under ironclad orders from Santa Anna himself. Some 28 men escaped amid the fog of musket smoke and disappeared into the nearby San Antonio River. The rest of the bodies, over 340 of them in three separate fields, were left to rot in the Texas sun where they provided food for the wolves, coyotes, and turkey vultures.

A few of the captives, many of them Irishmen who shared a religion with the Mexicans, were spirited out of line and survived. The men suffering from wounds, however, were not spared from execution. Many had to be carried outside in order to be shot. By that time, the volleys of musket fire made clear to them what would happen next.

James Fannin was a colonel in the regular Texas army according to the rebellious Texas government, but to the Mexican army, he, like all the Texians under arms, were rank pirates. After he was led to a place for his execution, a Centralist captain of the Tres Villas Battalion pronounced "That for having come with an armed band to commit depredations and revolutionize Texas, the Mexican government was about to chastise him." The chastisement meant death.

Fannin asked to see the post commander, Lt. Colonel Jose Nicholas Portilla, but the request was refused, so he laid out a series of requests with Joseph Spohn of the Alabama Red Rovers providing the translation. Perhaps because of his bilingual abilities, Spohn was later spared. Once again, Fannin seemed to misunderstand his bargaining power. He asked that he be shot in the chest instead of the face, that the rifles be placed a decent distance away so his face was not scorched, and he requested to be properly buried. Some eyewitness accounts say that the Mexican captain nodded and bowed. Fannin gave the officer money from his coat to sweeten the request. The captain placed Fannin on a chair, blindfolded him, and the musketeers stepped to within two feet, shot James Fannin dead and rolled his body into a dry ditch with other bodies. His belongings that were not deemed worthy of looting lay scattered beside him. The rest were taken.

The most noteworthy item taken from him was a "valuable gold watch." Fannin had told the captain that it belonged to his wife. An eyewitness named Coy understood Fannin to mean that he wanted it returned to her. The Mexican captain nodded and pocketed the watch.

Today, at the Dallas Historical Society, resides a gold watch of the time period. They display it, along with Fannin's epaulettes and an original painting of the man, as that very timepiece that the doomed colonel pulled from his pocket one last time on that late March day in 1836. But believing it is the genuine article might require more than a little bit of squinting at the historical facts.

A generous Dallas collector gifted it to the Society, but it certainly did not arrive with any sort of indisputable chain of provenance. In the watch's inscriptions, Fannin is misspelled. Twice. Of course, with no public school system in the early 19th century, misspelling is not out of the realm of possibility.

The bigger problem is the story to be inferred by the two inscriptions, one on the timepiece and one on the case. The later one bears the name of William Houston Jack who fought as a private at San Jacinto and later went on to some fame in early Texas. He and his brother Patrick even have a county named after them. It is true that throughout the Texas Revolution, Mexicans looted from dead Texians, and Texians returned the favor by rummaging through the pockets of dead soldados. Trouble is that the Mexican forces who defeated and then massacred Fannin's men were those under General Jose Urrea, a separate army of Centralist forces who largely followed the coast. General Santa Anna's group who lost at San Jacinto had moved out ahead of the army who came through San Antonio and then chased Sam Houston's ragtag bunch across Central Texas. Two entirely different armies in two entirely different places.

There were a literal handful of the escapees of the Goliad Massacre who made it to San Jacinto. Could one have somehow gotten the watch from the Tres Villas capitan? No, because they had already been led away from the presidio and the soldados had already fired into the captive groups by the time Fannin was shot. Did the captain in Goliad ship the watch to Santa Anna himself to curry favor, and William Jack found it in the generalissimo's luggage? That feels like a major stretch.

The Fannin pocket watch is not alone as far as artifacts with highly questionable authenticity. The amazing collection of Alamo artifacts compiled by renowned rocker Phil Collins has drawn more scrutiny than anything in the last several decades. After the singer donated his artifact collection to the Alamo for a future museum, one that has now come to magnificent realization, *Texas Monthly* published a lengthy and scorching article. Though the bulk of the collection is undoubtedly represented correctly, certain items are called into question with detail that is tough to dispute. A William B. Travis knife is perhaps top of the list. The seller who sold the knife to the man who passed it along to Collins says flatly "It's a fake! I saw it a hundred times." The initials W.B.T. were most assuredly carved into it before it was sold to Collins, but according to that previous owner, it was a matter of months, not two centuries. The same may well go for a Bowie knife which experts say they can trace to being made by a famous counterfeiter of Bowie knives in London in the 1970s.

Fake documents related to early Texas have sold by the hundreds over the years. In fact, James Bowie himself and his brother Rezin, ran a land grant forgery operation in the 1820s that famous historian William C. Davis called "of industrial proportions." The Bowie Brothers were trying to cheat longtime landowners out of their property and make top dollar off newcomers to Texas. Modern day con men and well-intentioned amateur historians and archaeologists continue to muddy the historical waters.

A very private archaeological dig at the History Shop near the Alamo attributed horseshoes to Mexican Colonel Andrade's camp outside the surrounded Alamo when in fact, San Antonio records show indisputably that there was a blacksmith's forge on the site where they were digging. It is infinitely more likely that the shoes were removed from the steeds of everyday San Antonio horses at the start of the 20th century.

The Texas Revolution is one of those subjects that fire the passions of enthusiasts to the white heat of an iron furnace. There is still intense debate over the minutiae of cannon sizes and the flags that graced certain battlefields. It is natural that high profile artifacts will draw close attention.

The descriptions and sales pitches for these highly enticing artifacts often contain carefully hedged language, huge missing pieces in the chain of provenance, Grand Canyon sized leaps in logic, and sometimes deliberate disregard of known historical record. But there is money to be made. Illustrious Texas Revolution historian Stephen L. Hardin calls these big money collectors a "bird's nest on the ground" for those who want to exaggerate an artifact's history or just flatly fake and lie.

Like UFO believers or Kennedy Assassination conspiracists, if a person desperately wants something to be true, they convince themselves despite every evidence to the contrary. No one can say with certainty whether the pocket watch that sits proudly at the top of the Dallas Historical Society collection is genuine or not.

Chapter Nine

Doak Walker

It is not uncommon for the entire populace of a small town to get caught up in a local high school sports hero. It feels much rarer when the town is as big as Dallas. When that icon has and takes the opportunity to then star for a major college, still without leaving home, only a handful of people come to mind. Houston's homegrown basketball legend Clyde Drexler is one, but in Texas football annals, only Doak Walker truly fills the bill.

After several crushing years of brutal warfare in the early 1940s, Dallasites, like millions of people around the world, were looking for distractions. Many found that release in the gridiron exploits of Highland Park High School. Teammates Bobby Layne and Doak Walker provided the show. By 1944, Layne had graduated, and the Scotties were Walker's show. He led the team deep into the high school playoffs, and the week before Christmas, the sports eyes of Texas were on the state semifinals.

Port Arthur beat Lufkin in the southern bracket, and the Scotties stopped San Angelo to make it to the finals. Both teams had gone into the semi-final game as the underdog, but almost 20,000 cheering fans willed the local Dallas boys to the next round. The game stories landed on the same page of the newspaper as word of Joe Routt, the first All-American in A&M history, being killed in Belgium at the Battle of the Bulge.

Just as the state's sportswriters whiffed on predicting the winners of both semi-finals, they missed again in the title game. The Port Arthur Yellow Jackets put up 20 points to Highland Park's 7. The Port Arthur line was too big and strong, and though Walker passed for 191 yards, it was not enough to prevail.

Immediately after graduating from high school, Doak Walker and Bobby Layne joined the Merchant Marines together and remained in that service through war's end. They got off their boat with a discharge at New Orleans at the end of October 1945 and stayed over to watch the SMU – Tulane game before heading back to Texas. Layne was signed to play football for the Longhorns in Austin, and Walker was expected to follow. As luck would have it, their coach at Highland Park, Rusty Russell, was by then an assistant for the SMU team, and Coach Russell offered Walker a lift back to Dallas. By the time Doak got out of the car, he was a player for the Mustangs. Both boys were enrolled at their respective schools quickly enough to face each other on the SMU campus barely a week later. It was a touchdown pass by Layne that beat the Mustangs 12-7. Despite playing only five games in 1945, both Walker and Layne were named to the All-Southwest Conference team. Walker also earned a trip to the East-West Shrine Game in San Francisco where he threw a touchdown pass of his own.

Ewell Doak Walker, Jr. was called by his middle name since birth to distinguish him from his father, a teacher and coach in the Dallas schools. Doak's mother, Emma, was also a teacher, and though their son was definitely undersized at 5'11" and 170 pounds, they both encouraged him to play sports. He lettered in five different ones at Highland Park and, along the way, set the city of Dallas on fire.

Like his high school, Southern Methodist University was just a stone's throw from the Walker family home on Stanford Avenue. Doak Walker had another detour to make before he could settle in on campus, however. Despite his Merchant Marine service, he was drafted by the U.S. Army in 1946 and did not begin to play full time for the Mustangs until the 1947 season, when he was a sophomore.

Doak Walker as an SMU Mustang
back (SMU Libraries)

That season was a whirlwind for the halfback who also punted, kicked, and returned punts and kickoffs from his opponents. Walker earned the first of three All-America honors and the Maxwell Trophy. He led the Mustangs to the Southwest Conference title and a Cotton Bowl berth that year. In 1948, he did it all again and topped it by becoming the first junior to ever win the Heisman Trophy. In an homage to Babe Ruth, witty scribes referred to the Cotton Bowl as "The House that Doak Built" since SMU was forced to move its home games there to accommodate crowds too big for its on-campus home. The Cotton Bowl was hastily expanded to add another 30,000 seats.

Walker's position was listed as halfback, but he did everything on offense. The numbers tell the tale. In 35 games at SMU, he put up these figures: 288 points scored, 2,076 yards rushing, 1,786 yards passing (on 128 of 222 attempts), 454 yards receptions, 750 yards on 50 punt returns, 764 yards on kickoff returns. He averaged 39.6 yards on punts.

An SMU teammate, Francis Pulattie, said, "Having Doak on our team was like having loaded dice or marked cards. We just felt like we had to do our part and Doak would do the rest. The most amazing thing is that he did it all so effortlessly. He made it look so simple."

Walker received his degree and entered the NFL draft where he was taken by the Boston Yanks. The Cleveland Browns of the AAFL took him for that league, but when the dust of arbitration and two trades settled, Doak Walker was reunited with his high school friend Bobby Layne in the backfield of the Detroit Lions. He also married his high school sweetheart that year. Though Walker himself had already graced the cover of *Life*, he and his fiancée wound up on the cover of *Collier's*. He was America's football hero before he ever played a professional game.

In Detroit, he did not disappoint. As a rookie, he led the NFL in scoring with 128 points. It was the smashmouth era of the T-formation which put four players in the backfield. The numbers do not compare to the gaudy figures of modern football, but that was the third highest single season point total in league history at the time. Statistically, it is impossible to translate eras, but Walker ran, caught passes, kicked extra points, and occasionally punted and returned kicks. He added a second league scoring title and was named an All-Pro four times. With his buddy Layne, the Lions won the NFL championships in 1952 and '53. Then, after six years, already sitting in third place for all-time points scored in the National Football League, Doak Walker was done. He retired to have a private life. As he told an interviewer many years later, "What else was there to do?"

His number 37 was retired at SMU and in Detroit, the first such honor afforded by each institution. He made the College Football Hall of Fame in 1959 and the professional Hall of Fame 17 years later, joining his Highland Park High teammate Bobby Layne. In 1990, an award was created in his honor to be given to the nation's top college running back.

After Doak Walker remarried to ski racer Skeeter Werner in 1969, the couple relocated to Steamboat Springs, Colorado where he concentrated on his several business interests. It was on those slopes that Doak Walker, then aged 71, hit a change in terrain that launched him more than 20 feet in the air and sent him flying 75 feet down the mountain. One of the greatest football athletes the country had ever known was left paralyzed from the neck down. He died of complications from the accident about nine months later.

The weekend after his death, Ricky Williams of the Texas Longhorns, the college home of Walker's old friend, was facing the Iowa State Cyclones in Austin. Williams had won the Doak Walker Award as a junior the previous season, and along the way he had become friends with the man who was said to epitomize leadership, sportsmanship, and athletic achievement. Williams viewed the much older Walker as a role model. On the field that day, Ricky Williams was allowed to wear number 37 instead of his regular burnt orange 34 jersey. Though the game meant little in the scheme of things, Williams ran for 350 yards and five touchdowns, the most in a single game by anyone who won the Heisman Trophy, something Williams accomplished that year with a 37 decal on his helmet.

In writing up the story of the unlikely connection between the two men, *Sports Illustrated*'s talented Rick Reilly said of the departed legend, "He's Doak Walker, and he was as golden as golden gets. He had perfectly even, white teeth and a jaw as square as a deck of cards and a mop of brown hair that made girls bite their necklaces. He was so shifty you couldn't have tackled him in a phone booth, yet so humble that he wrote the Associated Press a thank-you note for naming him an All-American."

Chapter Ten

Juanita Craft

A little way southeast of downtown Dallas sits the home of a former hotel maid that welcomed both Lyndon B. Johnson and Martin Luther King into her living room. By that time, Juanita Craft was recognized as an important civil rights leader in that North Texas city. She was influential enough that her 1,300 square foot, one-story house, where she lived for 50 years, is now a museum that continues her vision for inclusivity and education.

Craft was the granddaughter of emancipated slaves, and like many who shared her experience, those family stories impacted her greatly. The pain of relentless discrimination could not help but shape her outlook, and the hurt and humiliation came in many forms. Craft's mother, a teacher, as was her father, died from tuberculosis after being refused hospital treatment at the state sanitarium in San Angelo because of her skin color. There were no state hospitals for Black Texans. Despite having a college degree earned at Prairie View and Huston-Tillotson universities, the best work Craft could find was as a drug store clerk in Galveston during a brief marriage. She then got work as a maid at Dallas' Adolphus Hotel. Later, she worked as a seamstress. Saving her money, she bought the house and supplemented her income by taking in boarders. It was not until 1937, when she remarried to a salesman and gambler named Johnny Craft, that Juanita gained some measure of financial stability.

Rather than focus on her resentment of oppression, Juanita Craft fought back. Joining the NAACP in 1935 was a pivotal choice in those battles. The organization was tailor made for her, and in turn, she made it stronger. By 1942, Craft was the Association's Dallas membership chair elevating the chapter to the third biggest in the nation. In 1946, Craft was hired as Texas field organizer. Working with Lulu B. White of Houston, the two women organized 182 rural NAACP chapters in Texas, Louisiana, and Oklahoma. In the same decade, she started a local NAACP Youth Council, which became a nationwide model.

The 1940s saw several small steps toward racial fairness in Texas, and these were gained through court victories. After *Smith v Allwright* ended the state's Whites Only Democratic primaries in 1944, Juanita Craft became the first African-descended woman to vote in such an election in Dallas County. She later served two decades as a party precinct chair. Craft got into the habit of sitting in Whites Only sections during her frequent train travel around the state, refusing to move when challenged.

Like everywhere else in Texas, racial segregation was a constant issue in Dallas. Some cities saw more difficulties than others. One flashpoint had come in 1938 when educator and local NAACP officer George Porter arrived for jury duty. When dismissed due to his race, Porter refused to leave the courtroom. Two men threw him down a flight of courthouse stairs causing a head injury that left Porter blinded. No arrests were ever made. Thurgood Marshall, the national lead counsel for the NAACP, came to Dallas to investigate. Leaving a meeting with a judge, Marshall was chased by the city's police chief. He was likely saved bodily harm by a Texas Ranger. While in the city, Marshall met Juanita Craft, and the two remained friends.

Following the 1950 death of her husband in a basement maintenance room of segregated Parkland Hospital, Craft doubled down on her civil rights work. She encouraged the NAACP youth council members to lead voter registration drives beginning with their parents. Craft raised money to take the young people to the National NAACP Conventions, something she continued to do for over 25 years.

One of those youth council members, Joe Atkins, became the admissions test case at North Texas State College in Denton, Texas (now University of North Texas) in 1955. Craft urged him to file suit over his denial of acceptance on the grounds of race. Dallas attorney U. Simpson Tate was joined on the legal team by Robert L. Carter and Thurgood Marshall. They won the case a year later, but by then Atkins had begun studies at Texas Western in El Paso. He never attended North Texas State. Juanita Craft was also involved in efforts to integrate the University of Texas Law School and the Dallas Independent School District.

One annual thorn of segregation was the Texas State Fair held in Dallas. Beginning in 1955, Craft encouraged the youth throughout the state to boycott "Negro Achievement Day," which was the only day Blacks could attend the Fair. With her leadership, marchers picketed the Fair on that day for decades in protest against the longstanding racial segregation.

Along with the successes were plenty of roadblocks. In 1956, Texas Attorney General John Ben Shepperd tried to shut down the Texas NAACP. A trial was set in town of Tyler, a place with no hotels for the NAACP attorneys. It was Craft who drove them to and from Dallas every day for the duration of the six-week trial.

By the start of the 1960s, African Americans worked to integrate public facilities through sit-ins and picketing. Craft and her NAACP Youth Council were active at many Dallas businesses including restaurants, theaters, public transportation, and other venues. In 1967, thanks in part to her years of protest, the State Fair of Texas finally desegregated without conditions.

At age 73, Juanita Craft ran for elective office for the first time ever. The campaign against her Republican opponent was "raucous," but Craft prevailed for the vacated seat. She won reelection to a full two-year term in 1976. Among her council concerns were a drug and alcohol reduction program, subsidized housing, animal control, historic preservation, and strengthening environmental ordinances.

Though civil rights work was thankless and dangerous in the 1940s and 50s, recognition came to Juanita Craft over the later decades of her life. She was invited to the White House by President John F. Kennedy in 1963, and again in 1966 for a civil rights conference sponsored by President Lyndon Johnson. In 1970, under Richard Nixon, she participated in a White House Conference on Children.

Craft's funeral was attended by a myriad of state officials, including Governor Mark White. Former President Jimmy Carter and Thurgood Marshall, by then a Supreme Court Justice, sent glowing messages about her life's work. Juanita Craft's remains are buried in Evergreen Cemetery in Austin, next to her family in the city where she attended a segregated high school over 60 years before. She is honored in Dallas by a city park and a recreation center. There is also recognition on the Texas State Fair Grounds that she once picketed. She received the NAACP Golden Heritage Life Membership Award in 1978 and the Eleanor Roosevelt Humanitarian Award in 1984, one year before her death. Her living legacy, however, resides in her old house.

The Juanita Craft Civil Rights House and Museum in Dallas.

The Juanita J. Craft Civil Rights House and Museum is one of the newest such facilities in the Metroplex. It opened in May 2023 in Craft's longtime residence at 2618 Warren Avenue. It builds on the spirit from which Craft dedicated her life to fighting for human rights before that specific term was even in vogue. The mission is hers and seeks to improve the quality of individual lives through community engagement, discussion series, music programs, and clubs that center around books, crafts, and healthy food.

Chapter Eleven

Martin Irons & the Great Southwest Strike

The Knights of Labor had been on a roll, and the country's top railroad magnate, Jay Gould, was tired of being on the losing end. Then a spark ignited in Texas set another multi-state railroad strike aflame. It turned out to be a defining moment not only in Texas, but for labor organizing across the nation.

The founder of the Noble and Holy Order of the Knights of Labor was a Philadelphia garment cutter named Uriah Stephens. When he was a child, his family had lost everything in one of the nation's frequent economic panics, and he was forced to work as an unpaid apprentice learning to be a mechanic. With that chip already on his shoulder, Stephens found difficulty with ownership as an adult when his garment cutters trade union was forced to disband because they failed to get a wage increase. Stephens came to believe that all laborers needed to be joined together. At first, his Knights of Labor was a secret society, but soon, they went public. A decade later, and under new management, a

Pennsylvania machinist named Terrence Powderly, the Knights decided women needed to be a part of the labor movement, too. It was a radical notion.

The Knights of Labor were also leading the fight against other injustices. They wanted to end the use of child and convict labor because the competition was cutting the wages of working adults. They fought for equal pay for women. They wanted binding arbitration for worker – management disputes. The Knights favored the nationalization of the railroads and the brand new telephone industry because both were vital to the health of the nation and should not be a source of private profit. The Knights also pushed for a graduated federal income tax, something that eventually happened in 1913. And here's one more thing – the Knights of Labor opened their membership to Blacks. That was not as radical as it seemed because, as brutal and discriminatory as things were in the 1880s, the brunt of Jim Crow did not gain its legal stranglehold until the 1890s. One issue on which the Knights were anything but progressive was foreign workers. The Knights supported the Chinese Exclusion Act because they saw those immigrants as nothing more than unneeded competition.

By the middle of 1885, the Knights of Labor claimed over 700,000 members including 30,000 in Texas. The bulk of the membership had come on board recently thanks to a pair of stunning successes. The first came just a year prior, when the Union Pacific railroad cut workers' wages by 10%, the Knights immediately organized a strike and shut that railroad down. It took only four days before the U.P. gave in. Three months later, the railroad put forward the same wage cut again, and the Knights organized another strike. This time it took five days before the Union Pacific surrendered for real. The governors of Missouri and Kansas, pushed by public opinion, had backed the Knights. Contemporary newspapers and journals specifically noted positive changes for union workers at railroad shops in Palestine and De Soto, Texas.

There was a second major success against the Wabash Railroad system in the Midwest and Southwest, a line controlled by Jay Gould. Under his orders, the Wabash terminated all shop men who were members of the Knights of Labor. Immediately, union members on other lines refused to operate any trains that included Wabash cars. The union solidarity wrested a promise from Gould to stop discrimination against members of the Knights. The peace with workers lasted less than a year.

In late February 1886, a foreman named Hall with Jay Gould's Texas & Pacific Railway was fired for attending a union meeting in Marshall. The excuse given was that Mr. Hall had exceeded his leave of absence granted for the meeting. In response, machinist Martin Irons, a Scots immigrant who had formed District Assembly 101 to organize the workers on Gould's railroads in the southwest, ordered his union men to leave work. He took this action because the firing was in clear violation of the agreement reached over the Wabash. The strike, with the silver-tongued Irons acknowledged as leader, spread quickly. In St. Louis, strikers boarded a train and intentionally killed the engine.

Gould sent in hired Pinkerton strike breakers to escort scab workers and initiate violence against the strikers. This eventually cost at least ten union lives. The union retaliated with sabotage. On March 20, strikers began burning railroad bridges in Texas. Railyard fires were set. Moving trains were assaulted, and locomotives were disabled. Threats of violent retaliation were issued against train engineers still reporting to work.

In the days before aviation and long-distance trucking, it is difficult to overstate the nation's reliance on railroads. Most manufactured goods shipped by rail. Long distance travel was exclusively by train. With American freight operations at a near standstill, the crisis was soon dire.

Before the end of March, the governors of Kansas, Missouri, Arkansas, and Texas issued demands that railroads in their jurisdictions resume business. After discussions between Gould and the Knights of Labor executive board, the strike was thought to be over. It was not.

Industrialist and robber baron, Jay Gould. (Library of Congress)

In April, during hiring discussions, Jay Gould specifically ordered that any railroad worker who had taken part in the strike had forfeited his job permanently. A few days later, more violence erupted at Fort Worth between strikers and police. Three deputies were killed. Six days after that, police and militia fired into a crowd of strikers, killing six. More lines joined the strike, and eventually 200,000 United States railroad workers walked off their jobs.

Reaction from authorities was harsh. Texas Governor John Ireland sent state militia and Texas Rangers to corral the strikers at Buttermilk Switch in Fort Worth. Irons and other Knights of Labor leaders called for their members to continue the strike, but unlike 1885, the railroad showed no signs of giving in.

Congress formed a committee to bring about an end to the Great Southwest Strike, and on May 4, they strongly advised the Knights to go back to work. Unlike the previous Knights strikes which were supported by sentiment in favor of the working man, the public grew weary of the violence and of disruptions in commerce and transportation. Finally, Knights president Powderly decided that continuing the strike was a hopeless proposition.

The failure was more than the organization could bear. Amid infighting over the loss against Gould, the Knights dissolved. Less than a year after its peak, the most powerful American labor organization developed to that point in history had largely ceased to exist. They were replaced by the American Federation of Labor under Samuel Gompers, who promoted a back-to-basics organization that supported self-organizing along trade lines for job-related goals. American unions eventually got back to the bigger picture, but the Great Southwest Strike caused a decades-long setback.

What Jay Gould had attempted after the Wabash Strike in 1885 became the rule on his railroads. Strikers were blacklisted. That included the Texas labor leader Martin Irons. He found jobs in St. Louis, Little Rock, and Fort Worth under assumed names, but each time, he was discovered and sacked. He finally settled in Bruceville near Waco where he lived out the rest of his days promoting the causes of labor and workers when his health allowed.

Gould had less than a decade to live, but he spent those years in great luxury. By 1890, he had investments in several railroads and owned controlling interest in four: Missouri Pacific, Texas & Pacific, St. Louis & Southwestern and the International & Great Northern. They represented one half of all track mileage in the southwestern quarter of the United States.

Chapter Twelve

Blind Lemon Jefferson

H is name was parodied by Redd Foxx in *Sanford and Son* and adapted for a rock band, but beyond the memorable moniker, Blind Lemon Jefferson's contribution to American music is relatively forgotten these days. Though his songs were covered by Bob Dylan, Elvis, B.B. King, and the Beatles, only the most diehard of modern fans can identify Jefferson's authorship. There was a time, however, when the ground broken by Blind Lemon was understood and celebrated by the top musicians in blues, jazz, and country.

Like several other blues music pioneers, there are lots of holes in Jefferson's biography. His given name was recorded in three censuses as Lemon, sometimes Lemon Henry Jefferson, but the date of his birth is inexact. The 1900 census puts it as September 24, 1893. When Jefferson himself filled out a draft registration for the first world war, he gave his birthdate as October 24, 1894. Other speculation has put his birth as much as a full decade earlier.

It is accepted that he was born to sharecroppers Alec and Clarissy Banks Jefferson on a farm in the Couchman community near Wortham in Freestone County. It is generally thought that he was blind since birth, but the condition may have come on within the first few years of his life. The cause of the blindness or whether it was profoundly complete or if he had some partial sight is also debated. Even what he looked like is a tad sketchy since only two photographs of Blind Lemon Jefferson have ever been identified, and one of those is very probably bogus.

He could not attend school or do farm work because of his blindness, so at some point in his youth he turned to the guitar. Where he got his training as a "blues songster" is another unknown, but blues historian Alan Govenar speculates that Jefferson may have been exposed to "Texas" Alexander or "Ragtime Texas" Thomas who are known to have traveled and played around Freestone and Navarro Counties.

By his latter teenaged years, Lemon was playing around the east end of Elm Street, called Deep Ellum or Central Track, in Dallas. He was apt to show up anywhere from bordellos to church services to country barbeques. For a time, he played almost every day at the corner of Elm and Central in East Dallas. Other recollections have him playing aboard the interurban train that ran all the way from Waco to Denison. There are even stories about Jefferson earning extra money as a wrestler.

Blind Lemon was a big man, weighing some 250 pounds. Some specific accounts note that he always looked sharp with an ever present Stetson and a box-back black suit from Model Tailors in Dallas. Another report called him "fat, and a slovenly dresser." For a large person, his voice was high pitched, covering a full two octaves.

One of his closest friends in North and East Texas was Huddie Ledbetter, known to later generations as Leadbelly. The two played together beginning in 1912 according to Ledbetter's most reliable later stories. Musicologists credit Jefferson with being a prime influence on Leadbelly's work, and in turn, Leadbelly wrote of his friend several times in lyrics and song titles.

Though Jefferson clearly spent a great deal of time playing around Dallas, no known records indicate that he made his home there. In the 1920 census, he is enumerated with his half-brother back in Freestone County. His occupation is listed as "musician" and his employer as "general public." Sometime over the following few years he married Roberta Ransom, a woman ten years his senior.

Toward the end of 1925, Jefferson was noticed by a talent scout for Wisconsin-based Paramount Records. Soon he was brought to Marsh Laboratories in Chicago to make records, the first of which hit wax possibly around the New Year. The date was not noted. The following March, he laid down two classics: "Long Lonesome Blues" and "Got the Blues." Other blues musicians, mostly women, had passed along this route before him, but none hit, as the industry might say. Blind Lemon's records were soon selling nationwide.

Most early musicians were regional phenomena. Travel was often difficult and expensive, especially for someone who was the child of sharecroppers. Thanks to the nascent record industry, however, Blind Lemon Jefferson visited a good chunk of the eastern United States. Along the way, he interacted with a wide variety of other musicians, Black and White, and he both came away with new ideas and left much of himself behind.

In Johnson City, Tennessee, Jefferson met a White guitar picker named Clarence Greene who used some of Lemon's licks in his "Johnson City Blues." In Virginia, he hung around ragtime guitarists Stephen Tarter and Harry Gay. They in turn, introduced Jefferson to a young man named Lesley Riddle. Not long afterwards, Riddle passed on his blues knowledge to fellow Virginian A.P. Carter who was developing a touring act with his family. In that manner, the plucked notes of Blind Lemon Jefferson's guitar first made it into American country music.

The longer he recorded, the more varied his innovative playing became. His guitar style likely comes from ragtime piano with a left and right-hand approach. Some notes he picked with his thumb. He used various tunings, and some songs are rhythmic with a traditional blues repetition while other melodies show more complexity. His frequent guitar turnarounds were readily imitated. Country music virtuoso Chet Atkins credited Blind Lemon as being "one of his first fingerstyle influences."

While the Father of Texas Blues was acknowledged as a guidepost for artists including Eric Clapton, Bessie Smith, Louis Armstrong, Carl Perkins, Mance Lipscomb, and Charley Patton, at least two of the all-time greats knew him firsthand. Sam "Lightnin'" Hopkins, who grew up in Crockett, and Oak Cliff's Aaron "T-Bone" Walker both served as guides for the famous artist when he was in their hometowns. Hopkins was only eight years old when he met Jefferson but was still allowed to play music with him.

Blind Lemon recorded nearly 100 sides for Paramount, mostly in Chicago. Two were spirituals done under the pseudonym of Deacon L.J. Bates. In March 1927, Okeh records in Atlanta lured Jefferson into the studio, but Paramount threatened legal action after just one record was released. Six other songs from that session were lost, never issued. Many of the songs that survive have been covered by later artists. The Rock and Roll Hall of Fame named Jefferson's "Match Box Blues" as one of the 500 songs that shaped rock and roll.

Just like his early life, Blind Lemon's death at a young age is also clouded in mystery. He died on December 22, 1929, a cold day in Chicago. A contemporary resident of Wortham said later that Jefferson had "got in with the wrong bunch." One story had him poisoned by a lover, a tale that was also used for the early death of Robert Johnson. His death certificate says, "probably acute myocarditis," a heart attack, but there are even variations on that. One version is that he was to have been picked up from the train station by a person who never showed, and that Jefferson became lost trying to make his own way in a snowstorm and died. His two record producers claimed that Lemon suffered his heart attack in the car and was abandoned in a snowbank by his terrified chauffeur.

No matter how it went down, Paramount Records paid to have the bluesman's body shipped back to Wortham, Texas by rail. He was buried in an unmarked grave at the local Negro Cemetery. In 1967, his resting place was given a Texas Historical Marker in a ceremony that included musicologist Alan Lomax and guitar player Mance Lipscomb in attendance. Some thirty years later, a granite marker was added. It contains a lyric from one of Blind Lemon Jefferson's most famous tunes: "Lord, it's one kind favor I'll ask of you. See that my grave is kept clean."

Central Texas

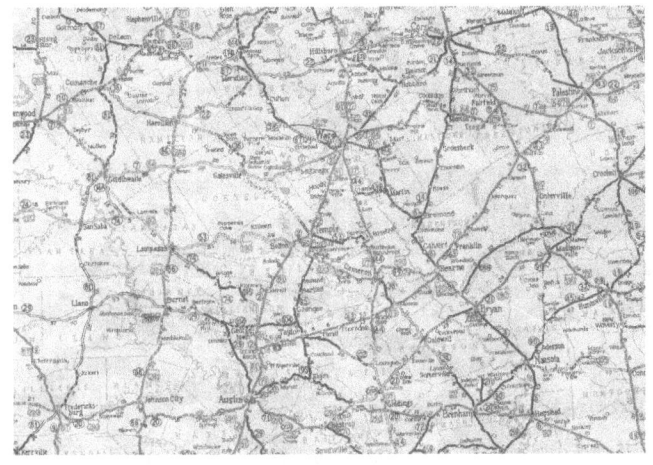

Chapter Thirteen

The Birthplace of Texas

M ultiple locales make the assertion that they are the birthplace of Texas, and all of them are bogus. Some, such as the lost Brazos River town of Washington, might be more correct with slight tweaking and the addition of a word or two. On the other hand, the places that truly could come closer to making the claim choose not to do so because they are located in other nations.

Washington, which for the last century has gone by Washington-on-the-Brazos, makes a case that it is the birthplace of Texas because that was where the Texas Declaration of Independence was signed. It is certainly true that on March 2, 1836, sixty men signed such a document declaring that they were independent from Mexico. The declaration itself had been written earlier, largely cribbed from the United States declaration that was penned mostly by Thomas Jefferson, and brought to the convention at Washington by Tennessean George Childress. It is notable that of the 60 signers, 57 of them were not from Texas, or even the nation they were claiming freedom from. Three signers were Mexican born, but only two of those, Jose Francisco Ruiz and his nephew,

Jose Antonio Navarro, were natives of Texas. But if Texas already existed, then how could Washington be its birthplace?

The town's statement might be altered to call itself the Birthplace of the Republic of Texas, but that might be viewed by many as wrong, too. There were at least two previous declarations of Texas independence. Three months before the convention at Washington, Old 300 colonist Ira Ingram read a document to citizens and militia assembled inside the presidio at Goliad. Ingram's text announced that Texas should be a "free, sovereign and independent State," and that those undersigned pledged their mutual determination plus their "lives, fortunes and honor" to make that happen. The response was enthusiastic, and 91 men stepped forward to place their John Hancocks on the paper. Included among them were Tejanos Jose Miguel Aldrete and Jose Maria Jesus Carbajal. Philip Dimmit, the commander of the garrison then at the presidio, and his men, signed gleefully.

Ten days later, on December 30, 1835, the original of the Goliad Declaration of Independence arrived at the de facto capital of American Texas, San Felipe de Austin. The ayuntamiento, or council, there was suddenly put in a bad situation. They were awaiting negotiations with Federalists from Northern Mexico to determine if, in fact, the sentiments of Texas leaned toward total independence or an adjusted position within the Mexican Republic to which it already belonged. The Goliad Declaration was filed away with no further action save a stern warning to its deliverers to keep their mouths shut.

Yet there was another declaration of Texas independence, and it had come a full 20 years before Goliad or Washington. It was so early that the signers were declaring independence from Spain since Mexico did not yet exist as a nation. It was part of the Guterriez-Magee rebellion which in turn was a portion of Mexico's revolution against the Spanish Crown.

On April 6, 1813, the rebels proclaimed from the captured city of San Antonio de Bexar that Texas was now an independent republic attached to the as yet fictional Republic of Mexico. For good measure, the men behind the Declaration of Independence also wrote a Constitution for Texas. Spanish troops soon met the rebels at the Battle of Medina, and through that victory and the subsequent murderous purges in Bexar, they disabused Tejano revolutionaries of such notions for another two decades.

The name Texas, and where it comes from, however, is much older, else there would be no such entity to assert its freedom. Under the Mexican Constitution of 1824, the abandonment of which sparked the Texas Revolution, Coahuila y Texas was the northeastern most state in the Mexican Republic. Its capital was at Saltillo, and for a short time, Monclova. Since the laws governing the region were administered there, could Saltillo be the birthplace? Some of the legislation, including the exemptions and obfuscations of slavery, was unique to Texas. Those laws, though, required oversight from the federal government at Mexico City, so perhaps the answer lies there.

Texas as a government region within New Spain, later Mexico, was well known under the Spanish Crown. There was a governor and a governor's palace in San Antonio. Its planning dates to 1722, and it was completed in 1749 with the coat of arms of Spain's then King Ferdinand VI. It officially became the capital of Texas in 1772, and it was there that Moses Austin first got permission to bring a limited number of Americans to settle along the lower Colorado and Brazos Rivers. If any place in or near present day Texas has the right to call itself a birthplace, even of American Texas, it is San Antonio.

The very name of Texas reaches back even further, however. Since 1907, Texas schoolchildren have learned that Texas was the Caddo Indian word for friend, and that a Spanish friar, Damian Massanet, first recorded it in his diary at an East Texas mission in 1689. It is a story engrained in our very being. Even the state's motto, "Friendship," is based on Fray Massanet.

However, that tale, too, is likely wrong. An historian named Jorge Luis Garcia Ruiz now lives in San Antonio, but he was born in Madrid, a city that as home to the royal Alcazar Palace, also has a legitimate reason to call itself the Birthplace of Texas. Garcia Ruiz caused a bit of a stir in 2019 when he rightfully pointed out that the Spanish were using the word Texas many decades before Fray Massanet's diary entry.

Maps are an amazing source of history, and one used by Juan de Onate around the start of the 17th century clearly has an area marked "Tejas" that sits right where Texas should be. Maps and documents that predate the "original" of anything are tough to refute. Onate, by the way, might also plant his flag as a founder of Thanksgiving since he brought together his expedition and native Texas Indians at San Elizario near El Paso and gave thanks for having been delivered across the Chihuahuan Desert by divine providence and saved from starvation by the friendly natives.

Part of Garcia Ruiz's common sense theory is that it was not in the nature of the Spanish explorers to use native Indian words. They almost unfailingly used Spanish. Case in point can be found in the names they gave the Texas rivers such as Brazos, Trinidad, Colorado, Guadalupe, Nueces, and so on. Why on Earth would the name for Texas be different? If the word Tejas did not come from the Caddo, then, where did it originate?

Garcia Ruiz suggested an answer to that question, as well. He simply looked through a Spanish dictionary from 1495, and he found an entry for "teja" or "texa." It was a word for a yew tree, a plant held in high regard in 16th century Spain. When the Spaniards first landed in East Texas and explored a bit of the modern state's Gulf Coast, they did not find the yew trees that lived at home, but Garcia Ruiz theorizes that a bald cypress tree would have been both very notable and similar to the yew. So, he believes that someone, prior to 1606, named this land for the interesting tree they found on it – Texa, or in plural, Texas.

Chapter Fourteen

Calvert & the Chinese

The land underneath Calvert had been settled as early as 1827 as part of Robertson's Colony, but official platting came via the Houston & Texas Central Railroad in 1868. It was all part of the changing 19th century equation for how best to move agricultural products from where they were produced to the ports where they could be shipped to lucrative markets. Cotton was widely grown in the area from the 1830s, but because the nearby Brazos River proved unreliable for steamboats, it was problematic for shipping bales to Houston and beyond. Consequently, overland wagon travel became the slow and only option.

All the way back in the days of the Texas Republic, entrepreneurs had been talking railroads in Texas. Charters were granted, but little capital was raised. In the 1850s, Houston businessmen Paul Bremond, William Marsh Rice, William Robinson Baker, and Abraham Groesbeck decided to build the Houston & Texas Central line. Once early progress was underway, a plantation owner named Robert Calvert, who had over 3,800 acres in cultivation, convinced Groesbeck to buy 1,000 acres where the Calvert townsite is now located. He promised that it would be a wonderful investment for both men.

Before Emancipation, railroad backers in Texas loaned or leased slave labor to do the work of track laying. It was a cost-effective way for men of property to get richer. The Civil War brought that heinous practice to an end. In fact, the war was a years-long interruption for railroad construction in general, and the tracks did not reach Robert Calvert's lands until 1868, a year after his death. Groesbeck fared much better. The townsite he had bought at $3 an acre grew to be worth as much as $2,000 an acre.

There were acute labor shortages in the South after the Civil War. Though roughly the same number of African Americans remained as in the years immediately before the war, some planters sought alternatives to hiring their former slaves to work out of either distrust or spite. In 1869, there was a convention of planters and railroad financiers held at Memphis, and among the topics discussed and publicized was the importation of Chinese labor.

Newspaper editorials took both sides. *The Galveston News*, with the largest circulation in Texas, saw Chinese as "the best, cheapest and most reliable labor ever known." Their opinion was that bringing in the Chinese would force the freedmen to lower the asking price for their toil. At the other end of the spectrum, the *Dallas Herald*'s racist rhetoric went beyond the pale, calling the Chinese "miserable yellow imbecile dwarves." Public opinion seemed to side with the *News*.

The first Chinese laborers brought to Texas, in fact the first group to arrive anywhere in the South, were those who came to work construction for the Houston & Texas Central. The railroad's agent had contracted with businessman Chew Ah Heang of San Francisco for 300 men. Many had just completed work on the transcontinental railroad, and they traveled via that line to Council Bluffs, Iowa. There, according to *Harper's Magazine*, they crossed the frozen Missouri River on planks to reach the railroad on the opposite bank so they could continue to St. Louis, New Orleans, and on to Texas. The group arrived in Houston on January 10, 1870 and were quickly transferred to the H&TC tracks where they were sent to Calvert.

The first section of track the Chinese worked on ran eighteen miles from Bremond to Thornton. Between 247 and 267 workers had arrived in Central Texas. All but one were male, and most were in their late twenties. The agreement between Chew and Walker called for the workers to be on the job 26 days a month in return for $20 in silver per man. Their primary job was grading the track bed.

The railroad was also contractually required to provide shelter and food. The housing, specified as tents or huts, was established as camps along the line, and the food on offer was what the Chinese men were thought to prefer: rice, pork, dried fish, vegetables, and tea. They wore light cotton shirts and pants along with wide straw hats described by the *Galveston News* as looking like "inverted washbowls" that sat atop queued hair. Aside from one or two of the foremen, none of the immigrant workers spoke English. They kept almost entirely to themselves, celebrated Chinese holidays, and largely stayed free of the nearby towns. When they did venture in, they did not patronize the merchants. To all observers, they were "sojourners" who had no desire to stay in Texas or even the United States.

That lack of commerce may have been one reason that the *Calvert Enterprise* switched its tune from praising the lack of drunkenness on the part of the Chinese workers by saying they would provide better labor than their Irish and Black fellows to lamenting one month later that the Asians were a failure and the railroad wanted rid of them. There were underlying factors. The immigrant Irish workers disliked the Chinese to the point that 150 of them left. Perhaps looming largest was that the railroad encountered a bit of a financial bump, and likely wanted shed of the contract. By September of 1870, the workers had been released and had filed a lawsuit at Dallas suing for fulfillment of their contracts.

Though a good portion found their own way back west, many of the workers initially stayed in the area and switched to farming. James Hanna and John Drennan are two of the Calvert area planters who hired Chinese men as either sharecroppers or wage laborers. Some of Hanna's contracts still exist including an 1872 agreement with John See and Sin Yong to farm 30 acres, with 20 in cotton and 10 in corn. The crops were to be evenly split.

Over the next few years, the majority of the original Chinese railroad workers moved away from Texas, but James Hanna liked their work ethic so much that he brought in 59 more Chinese laborers through the Port of Galveston in September 1874. They had most likely sailed from Cuba.

By the 1880 census, only 136 Chinese-born Texans remained, and 72 of those lived in Robertson County. Only two other counties, Galveston and Travis, were in double digits. All the Robertson County Chinese residents lived on farms except for one "huckster" in town. They were still exclusively male, and only four of them were married even a decade after they arrived. Of those married men, three had taken an African American bride and one a White. Though the official census records indicate that all traces of the Chinese immigrants of the 19th century were gone from Robertson County by the early 20th century, that is not the case. It is simply that the listings had changed to Black, White or Mulatto.

Locally, their descendants were known as "Black Chinese," and some still remain in the area around Calvert. Families still found in Robertson

County include descendants of Lee Chopp and Tom Yepp. Bar Low, one of the immigrants to James Hanna's farm in 1874, also has descendants in Calvert. Chopp was born in Hong Kong, Guangdong Province in 1848 and came to the U.S. via San Francisco at age 18. He was among the initial group from the transcontinental railroad who took work in Calvert after that job was finished.

Today well more than five million people identify as Chinese-American. None in Texas, however, can boast a longer claim than those descended from a handful of families near Calvert.

Chapter Fifteen

Round Top Rifle Hall

A handful of Germans mercenaries snuck illegally into Texas with the filibustering expeditions that sought to wrest potions of the land from the Spanish, but there were not many. By the time the Republic was established in 1836, barely 200 Germans lived here. A decade later there were thousands, mostly living in the fertile land between the Brazos and Colorado Rivers. They came from many of the 41 member duchies and states that made up the German Confederation that lasted between 1815 and 1866.

Much of the immigration was spurred by glowing reports of Texas that were published in German newspapers, and travel books by the likes of Detlef Jordt, Hermann Ehrenberg, Ferdinand von Roemer, and Gustav Dresel. The writers told of a beautiful country, cheap land, and high wages. The first settlers wrote home with warm reviews. These personal reports and letters from family filled the boats to the Gulf Coast.

Though some of the Freethinkers who came after the failed revolutions of 1848 arrived in Texas with money and substantial belongings, hundreds of these immigrants, the ones without cash to hire or buy wagons, walked from the coast to their new homes. When they found someplace that looked good, especially if it resembled the German countryside, they dropped stakes.

The first permanent German settlements in Texas came in the early 1830s at the Austin County towns of Industry and Cat Spring. By the time Texas joined the United States, burgeoning communities of Germans stretched from the northwest reaches of Harris County all the way to the Hill Country. Most came through Galveston or Indianola; others entered at New Orleans before coming to Texas.

The Germans died disproportionately from yellow fever because they carried no immunity, unlike a major percentage of Americans who had spent long summers near the Gulf Coast. Despite the hardships, neighbors shared farming techniques, and the immigrants in the Hill Country even got help from a few friendly Comanches.

They brought with them the traditions of Prussia, Hannover, Mecklenburg, or Holstein. Those traditions were well established across Texas by the Civil War. Turnvereins, or athletic clubs, thrived in the larger cities, offering everything from group calisthenics to competitive bowling. Sangerbunds were singing societies, and ofttimes a band was associated with them. Agricultural societies dotted rural areas. The one in Cat Spring is the oldest in Texas, founded in 1856.

German newspapers abounded. Every medium sized town where they settled had a German language paper including a handful like the *Zeitung* in San Antonio that were distributed statewide. The larger cities like Houston had more than one. There were meat markets serving smoked pork and beef in butcher paper and sausage ground to German tastes. Those are one of the three underpinnings of modern Texas barbeque. There was also beer. Lots of beer. Though other cultures brewed beer, none held it as closely as the Germans, and that love accompanied them to Texas. Many of the republic's and state's earliest breweries were

German owned and operated, and German saloons were on seemingly every other street corner.

But another institution was almost as ubiquitous. The schutzenverein, or shooting club, was a mainstay in every Texas community that had more than a dozen Germans. The first one in Texas came at New Braunfels in 1849, just three years after the first one in the United States was opened near Philadelphia. Soon after New Braunfels, others followed until there were more than 200 German-immigrant schutzenverein in the Lone Star State. Kentuckians and Tennesseans loved rifle shooting contests, but it was the Germans who mixed that with their unquenchable thirst for codified organization.

The clubs were strictly German. The one in Brenham, like several others, did not even allow first generation Americans. Members, men only, were required to have been born in a German state. Both target shooting, with rifles or pistols, and trap shooting were offered. The Round Top Schutzenverein, founded in 1873, also listed bicycle riding, games, and dancing in its purpose.

Like other German clubs, and they were a people who insisted on their clubs, the schutzenverien became social gathering places where immigrants could congregate with their countrymen. Though some shooting clubs were smaller than others, they all had two constants – a place to shoot guns and a place to drink beer. The Bluff Schutzenverein just south of La Grange was conveniently located on the grounds of the Kreische Brewery. Balls and band concerts were frequent occurrences at the clubs.

The camaraderie also brought friendly competitions. Annually, usually in late May or early June, a Koenig, or king, was chosen for the club. Members and visitors fired at wooden targets with a dozen or so concentric rings, and the man accumulating the most points was declared king for the year. It was both an honor and a tax since the Koenig was expected to use some of his small winnings to pay for a keg and quench the thirst of all those he had defeated.

Toward the turn of the 20th century, large regional, or even national, shooting competitions were big doings in Texas, and many of the top shooters were German immigrants and their offspring. The contests began at the grounds of schutzenverein. The Sunny South Handicap started in Brenham, but had outgrown the space by 1909 and moved to Houston. It was a six-day long tournament replete with sponsors galore and teeming crowds.

Ad and Plinky Topperwein pose in front of a sign for Plinky's sponsor Dead Shot Powder. (Robert P. Cochran)

The most famous target and trick shooters in America were the Toepperweins, a husband and wife team who lived in San Antonio. His name was Adolf, a German-Texan known to the world as Ad, and he and wife Plinky kept setting world records for tossed or launched targets. Ad was a native of Leon Springs, the son of a German immigrant gunsmith. A product of the schutzenverein tradition, Ad Toepperwein was an accomplished shooter by age 10. He met his future spouse, Elizabeth, known to the world as Plinky, when he visited the Connecticut headquarters of his sponsor Winchester Arms. Plinky was working there as an inspector. They performed together for 40 years, shooting targets while standing on their heads, riding in cars, or lying on their backs. Plinky set numerous trap shooting records. In 1907, Ad shot for 68 ½ hours firing Winchester .22 rifles at 72,500 targets and missing only 9. The demonstration only ended after Ad had allegedly used all the .22 cartridges in San Antonio.

Changes came to the shooting clubs eventually. When virulent anti-German furor bubbled up with WWI, most clubs adopted English as their language of choice. Insistence from the Ku Klux Klan gave them a nudge in some cases. One change, however, brought the end of dozens of the schutzenverein. Prohibition, in places where the sheriff chose to rigorously enforce it. In other locales, the beer-swilling German-descended populace rode out that absurd experiment with much less hardship. At those clubs that survived, women were allowed to shoot by the post WWII years.

Only about 20 Texas clubs remain. The original in New Braunfels, San Antonio's Alamo Schutzenverein, which dates to 1857, Boerne, Vogel's Valley, Fredericksburg, and Round Top are among them. Round Top is typical, sitting on just over 10 acres, the dance hall dates to 1882.

That same year, the town's Fourth of July celebration moved to the grounds, a demonstration to their Anglo neighbors that, though the immigrants clung tightly to their language, they embraced their new Americanism.

The Round Top Schutzenverein, called a Rifle Club since incorporation in 1921, still offers the general public a taste of the 19th century tradition. On the first three Mondays of every month, the club sells cheeseburgers to the public. The sense of community is raucous and palpable, and the food and beer, prepared and/or served by club members, is delicious.

Chapter Sixteen

Rube Foster

Ask the name of the greatest Black baseball player of all time and the answers will likely include Jackie Robinson, Henry Aaron, Barry Bonds, and Willie Mays. Phrase the question differently and seek the name of the single person who had the biggest impact on Black baseball, and the answer is undeniably Andrew "Rube" Foster of Calvert, Texas. He was the best African American pitcher of his day, a groundbreaking manager in terms of strategy, and he started the most successful segregated baseball league of all time.

Andrew Foster was born in 1879, one of six children of former slaves. Only he and two sisters escaped death from tuberculosis. In addition to a life as sharecroppers, work shared by the entire family, Foster's father, also named Andrew, was a Methodist Episcopal preacher. Baseball proved to be young Andrew's way out of the Central Texas cotton fields. Though specifics were not found, Andrew reportedly started with the Austin Reds, a Black team in the state capital. A year later, in 1898, he joined the Waco Yellow Jackets, one of the top Black ball teams in the state. Andrew Foster pitched well, and for the first, but not the last, time in his playing career, legends of his prowess spread. One dubious story said that the young man had pitched a scoreless game every day for 11 days straight.

The next big chance for Foster came in 1902 when Frank Leland, a top Black baseball entrepreneur, brought him north to play for the Chicago Unions. Foster, away from Central Texas for the first time, struggled. He journeyed even further north to play for an interracial club in Otsego, Michigan. When that season ended, he moved on to the Cuban X-Giants, a top team that played out of Trenton, New Jersey, across the river from Philadelphia. He led them to a championship and began getting national recognition in the bargain. The club's manager declared Foster, with a good fastball, a devastating curve, and a baffling fadeaway, to be the greatest moundsman he had ever seen. In 1904, the Philadelphia Giants, crosstown rival of the X-Giants, lured Andrew Foster away with a higher salary. Though Foster understood that the constant team-jumping of star players was holding back Black baseball as a product, he readily took advantage of it.

Playing for his new team, Foster led them to the city title over his former squad. Hits were hard to come by against him, and his strikeouts were plentiful, as many as 18 in a game. A false legend arose during this time period claiming that the New York Giants manager John McGraw quietly hired Foster to teach his fadeaway pitch to star Christy Mathewson, who was the same age as Foster, but the White Giants star already held that tool in his repertoire. Somewhere in these years, Andrew picked up the nickname Rube after the white Philadelphia Athletics star twirler, Rube Waddell. White sportswriters began to write compliments such as "If Andrew Foster had not been born with a dark skin, the great pitcher would wear an American or National League uniform. ... Foster has never been equaled in a pitcher's box."

Still seeking the biggest payday, Rube Foster returned to the Leland Giants in Chicago and his first chance to lead a ball club as player-manager. He carried the childhood lessons of strict religion with him. Though he personally avoided alcohol, he allowed his players to drink, but if they arrived hungover to the ballpark, they were summarily sent back to their hotel.

He developed an aggressive but disciplined style of play for his teams. His ball clubs loved to steal bases. Negro Leagues historian Larry Lester credits Foster with introducing the hit and run, drag bunt and squeeze play to baseball. In 1907, his Leland Giants went 110 and 10. After the season, they took two out of three from a White big league all-star team with Foster the winning pitcher in the victories.

Such inter-racial games were not uncommon in the depths of Jim Crow America. Despite ingrained prejudice, many ballplayers respected both their counterparts' talent and the big box office that such contests earned.

Rube Foster poses with manager of the White Joliet ballclub prior to a 1916 exhibition game.

After a season shortened by a broken leg, Rube Foster planned a careful barnstorming tour in the South for 1910. His club, boasting some future Hall of Famers, won 123 out of 129 games that season. More importantly, back home in Chicago, Foster entered a partnership with a White businessman named John Schorling. When the American League's Chicago White Sox opened their new Comiskey Park, Schorling bought their old field, South Side Park, at 39th and Wentworth, built new bleachers to accommodate 9,000 fans, and installed Rube Foster's team, which was rebranded as the Chicago American Giants.

The ball club flourished, winning roughly 75% of their games over the next several seasons. Again, favorable comparisons to the White big leagues were commonplace. When a new White baseball enterprise called the Federal League started in 1914, Rube Foster publicly offered optimism that the White owners would be forced to integrate in order to fill roster slots with quality players. It did not happen.

Though star Black baseball players were making good money, there were many problems. The jumping between teams remained a constant. Umpiring was suspect. Press coverage was uneven. There were even violent episodes between ball clubs such as when Foster's American Giants squared off against the rival Indianapolis ABCs with bats, and an umpire pulled a gun and hit Giants star Pete Hill across the nose with it. Organizing the barnstorming tours to the West Coast and Havana to maximize gate receipts was an exhausting and expensive proposition. Foster began to coalesce thoughts of something better.

The final straw may have been a deadly race riot in the summer of 1919 that forced Foster's team to play for weeks on the road. The following February, he convened a meeting of other Midwestern Black team owners at the Paseo YMCA in Kansas City. The goal was to organize a league that had business discipline like the White-only majors. After several days of working out details, the Negro National League was born with the Chicago American Giants, Dayton Marcos, Detroit Stars, Cuban

Stars, Indianapolis ABCs, Kansas City Monarchs, St. Louis Giants, and a crosstown team called the Chicago Giants as charter members.

Foster was installed as both league president and treasurer. Though he would come under continuing criticism for his iron rule, no one could doubt his work ethic. His son recalled that Foster left the house at 8:30 every morning and returned home at midnight. Player salaries rose to new heights, and teams traveled in Pullman train cars like their White counterparts.

Rube Foster preached competitive balance as a vital ingredient to a strong league, but his American Giants won the first three titles. Though he personally was no longer playing, stars such as the Cuban outfielder Cristobal Torriente sustained them.

There were personal setbacks. In 1921, Foster's five-year old daughter died. The same season, he was arrested in Atlanta for stealing from his players, though he professed his innocence and was released. In his defense, he reminded people that he had raised the players' salaries tenfold in just three seasons.

Though his great successes were tied to Chicago, Rube Foster did not forget Texas. His American Giants held spring training in Houston in March of 1924, and the local African American sporting world feted Foster with a banquet. Though his team did not win the league that year, Foster helped plan the first Colored World Series against a Philadelphia area team named Hilldale. Supposedly, Foster surreptitiously signaled pitches to Jose Mendez, the NNL Champion Kansas City Monarchs pitcher, throughout the decisive game.

At the start of the following season, a younger half-brother, Bill Foster, was brought up to pitch for the American Giants, and he would go on to his own Hall of Fame career. Things were looking bright.

In June of 1925, some of the American Giants players discovered their owner-manager unconscious on the floor in front of a gas heater at the boarding house in Indianapolis where the team was staying. He had accidentally inhaled gas fumes from a leaky pipe. He was revived, but the episode damaged his brain. His wife Sarah later talked of Rube hearing voices and hallucinating. He was found wandering the street in front of his house, and at one point he locked himself in his office and refused to leave. In early September 1926, Rube Foster was declared mentally irresponsible and confined to the Illinois state mental hospital at Kankakee. He spent his next four years there, dying at the institution on December 9, 1930. He was buried at Lincoln Cemetery about 90 blocks south of the American Giants ballpark on Chicago's south side.

Almost on cue, the Negro National League fell into disrepair after Foster's death, even though he personally had not been involved for four seasons. The Great Depression proved too big an obstacle to overcome, and the league folded in 1931. Joe Green, a Leland Giants teammate, said: "When Rube Foster died, Negro baseball died with him."

There was a revival in the middle 1930s, and in the decade that followed the second Negro National League, along with a Negro American League on the East Coast, thrived using the model that Rube Foster created. Dozens of future major league greats got their start in those leagues, and in 1946, Jackie Robinson was plucked from their ranks to finally re-integrate professional baseball. Ironically, it was the development that brought a quick end to the Negro Leagues, but it did finally fulfill Rube Foster's prophecy from 1914.

Foster was enshrined into the National Baseball Hall of Fame in 1981.

Chapter Seventeen

Texas Guinan

H er catchphrase was "Hello, sucker!" and it was often followed by "Come on in and leave your wallet on the bar." This daughter of Waco turned a vaudeville career into movie stardom as one of the first silver screen cowgirls, but she was perhaps best known as simply a bawdy character who embodied a large portion of America in flaunting Prohibition.

She was christened Mary Louise Cecilia Guinan, the daughter of grocery store owners most commonly put down as Irish immigrants, but her Waco pals knew her as Mamie. Her reputation at Sacred Heart Academy during the last decade of the 19th century was not sterling, but among the lessons she learned in Central Texas were how to ride a horse and throw a lasso. Her father's co-owned grocery store went bankrupt in the 1890s, and the Guinans moved to Colorado, but the family found money to send their daughter to a music conservatory in Chicago for two years. Some reports claim that she got a scholarship, but in any event, she did not emerge as the mainstream singer her parents had in mind.

Instead, Mamie Guinan took to vaudeville stages with a Wild West Act. There was a brief marriage to a Denver cartoonist, but ultimately the young lady sought stardom as a chorus girl, alone in New York City

Through the illegal bootlegging operations, Guinan also met her fair share of gangsters including Arnold Rothstein and "Legs" Diamond. Another mobster named Larry Fay enticed her into a partnership at the El Fey Club and gave her half the profits. Texas Guinan, often perched atop a grand piano, was at the center of every show, and lines stretched around the block to pay a $25 cover charge and hear her sassy wisecracks and reminders to "Give the little ladies a great big hand!" The bottle prices were steep, too. Twenty-five dollars for a fifth of Scotch or $30 for a bottle of champagne. By her own account, she and Fay made a profit of $700,000 in ten months.

Prohibition in New York City, like many other American locales, was spotty and subjective. Still, crusading politicians frequently sought raids to burnish their law-and-order credentials. Guinan was caught up in their nets several times. In the summer of 1928, she was among 104 people hauled in and charged with federal crimes. She and Helen Morgan, another nightclub owner, faced up to two years in prison and fines of $10,000 each. Both were acquitted.

Texas Guinan always claimed she did not sell alcohol, and the arresting authorities never found the paperwork to prove that she even owned the clubs. Guinan said it was all an act she was paid to put on and offered $100,000 to anyone who had seen her personally take a drink. She never served meaningful time for any of her arrests, but she also never failed to get the most colorful publicity out of every charge. Getting a good laugh was job one. She once said of the NYPD vice squad that "Some people are so narrow-minded that their ears touch in back."

When the bother and payoffs of Manhattan authorities proved too burdensome, Fay and Guinan opened a club in Miami Beach, but the two had a falling out, and she returned to New York. She opened her own club called Texas Guinan's on West 48th St.. When the police shut down one club, she opened another. She was also staging other shows, and she starred in two talking pictures that were unsuccessful, including one in 1929 called *Queen of the Night Clubs* in which she played a fast-talking club owner with a heart of gold.

Her fame was national. Writer and literary critic Edmund Wilson wrote that she was "a formidable woman, with her pearls, her prodigious gleaming bosom, her abundant yellow coiffure, her bear trap of shining white teeth." Even New York effetes who did not like her admitted that everyone should go to her nightclub "once in a lifetime."

When the Depression hit the country with full force, Texas Guinan looked to move to Europe, but ran into difficulties on that front. Scotland Yard had her on a list of "barred aliens." She signed a contract with a Paris nightclub, but French employment law made things very difficult for non-citizens to work there. Instead, Guinan made the most of the trouble, putting together a touring show called *Too Hot for Paris*.

The show featured a full cast and was booked for several North American cities. In Chicago, coinciding with the World's Fair of 1933, she had the misfortune of staying at the Congress Hotel. It coincided with an outbreak of amoebic dysentery that was later traced to tainted water. Not realizing that she was ill, the tour continued. In Vancouver, she was hospitalized with debilitating abdominal pain and underwent surgery, but there were complications. After several days, Guinan asked to see "all her girls," forty of them from the show cast. She told them that she was not likely to make it through the night, but asked them to not be sad, since death would be a relief from the pain she was in. She died on November 5, one month before the repeal of Prohibition.

Her funeral was held on Broadway back in New York, and estimates of the attendees ranged from 7,500 to 12,000. Her pallbearers included journalist Heywood Broun, bandleader Paul Whiteman, and two of her lawyers. At her request, there was an open casket "so the suckers can get a good look at me without a cover charge."

Chapter Eighteen

The Lomax Family

W hen John Avery Lomax started at the University of Texas, he was a 28-year old farmer from Bosque County who had an undying love for old cowboy music. Much of his excitement about starting an academic career was crushed when his English professor told him the traditional cowboy song lyrics he had studiously collected since childhood were worthless and simple. Lomax took his hard-earned bundle of notes behind Brackenridge Hall, the dorm where he lived, and burned them.

Lomax settled down to mainstream English literature, got his UT diploma, then a job as school registrar and personal secretary to the university president. From there he started teaching English at Texas A&M and got married. His interest in cowboy songs continued to nag at him, though. In 1907, he heard that two Harvard scholars were researching folklore, and he moved to Massachusetts for a chance to work with them. Their encouragement not only changed the life of John Avery Lomax and got the young man his master's degree, it bettered the entire landscape of American music.

With the backing of those men, John Lomax was awarded a grant to research and collect his precious cowboy songs. His work was racially inclusive. Several tunes were credited to Black cowboys including "Get

Along Little Doggies" and "Home on the Range." Other songs, including "The Buffalo Skinners" were praised for their "Homeric quality" by the likes of Carl Sandburg. When Lomax's anthology was published in 1910, Theodore Roosevelt penned the introduction. John A. Lomax had become famous.

Back home, Lomax and UT Professor Leonidas Payne co-founded the Texas Folklore Society. Among other things that came out of the fast-growing group was Lomax's suggestion that folklorists mine the oral traditions of "the large Negro and Mexican populations of the state." He continued his own research and went on lecture tours all while again working as part of the UT administration. Then in 1917, John Avery Lomax was one of seven Longhorn faculty members fired as a result of petty crusading on the part of the state's colorfully corrupt governor James E. Ferguson. Though others were hired back after Ferguson's removal from office, Lomax chose to maintain a career in banking.

That might have been the end of the Lomax contributions to American music and folklore if not for a string of misfortune. In 1931, John's wife Bess died. Around the same time, his Dallas bank failed, forcing Lomax to telephone a string of depositors and explain to each that their investments were gone. He fell into a personal depression.

John Lomax, Jr., the oldest of four children, coaxed his father to revive his lecture touring, and the two took to the road, camping along the way to save cash. They eventually made a stop at the New York headquarters of MacMillan Publishing where the senior Lomax, now 65 years old, pitched an anthology of American folksongs with an emphasis on the nation's African Americans. The publisher accepted. From there, father and son headed to the Library of Congress to peruse the recorded holdings. They found it woefully inadequate. By the time the Lomaxes left Washington, D.C., they had an agreement to tour the country gathering field recordings for the national collection. It turned into an archive of its own, and all four of the Lomax children became involved in amassing this great treasure.

John, Jr. served as a sort of family manager while he carried on his day job, and the next youngest son, Alan, joined his father on the road in June 1933. The two mounted a 315-pound acetate phonograph disk recorder into the trunk of their Ford and drove south. They concentrated their efforts on Texas, Louisiana, and Mississippi. They recorded sharecroppers and small-town balladeers, Spanish vaquero songs on the Rio Grande, and French Acadians in the Louisiana swamps. The biggest gold mine was found following the recommendation of their Library of Congress predecessors that "nearly every type of song is to be found in our prisons." Just as today, an outsized percentage of Black males were incarcerated.

In Texas penitentiaries and prison farms, John, Sr. and Alan recorded work songs and blues from men such as James "Iron Head" Baker, Mose "Clear Rock" Platt, and "Lightnin'" Washington. At Angola in Louisiana, they found a 12-string guitar player named Huddie Ledbetter who went by Leadbelly. Two decades earlier, Leadbelly had been a running buddy of the famed Blind Lemon Jefferson.

Though it is popular to accuse John Lomax, Sr. of paternalism in "tailoring Leadbelly's repertoire and clothing," he and his sons were nonetheless the ones who made Ledbetter a commercial success. Within months of his release from Angola, something helped by appeals from Lomax, Leadbelly was playing for elite audiences in New York and Philadelphia. Though he had an irreparable break with the Lomaxes shortly thereafter, he enjoyed another fifteen years of well-paid performances and influenced generations of guitarists.

*"Aunt Harriet" McClention being
recorded by John A. Lomax, Sr. at
Sumterville, Alabama. Not the record-
ing rig in the trunk of the car. (Library
of Congress)*

John Lomax, Sr. served as an advisor for the Federal Writer's Project in
the 1930s and was the first to direct the gathering of the Slave Narratives
that have become an invaluable resource for modern historians and the
public. He died of a stroke in 1948. A few months later, Leadbelly gave
a concert at the University of Texas where he sang songs that had been
recorded into a car trunk at the Angola Prison.

The family story did not end there. John, Jr., settled by then in Houston, founded the Houston Folklore & Music Society in 1951. Members,
including himself, sang and shared old music. No amplified instruments were allowed at the sessions which were often held at the Lomax
home. Lightnin' Hopkins was a family friend and group member, as
were Mance Lipscomb, Towns Van Zandt, Guy Clark, K.T. Oslin, and
Lucinda Williams. John, Jr. also managed Hopkins and helped arrange

films about Lightnin', Lipscomb, and Clifton Chenier, who recorded his early zydeco records in Houston. A grandson of the original musicologist, John Lomax III, later managed Van Zandt and several other artists including Steve Earle.

Alan Lomax made as much of a mark on folk music as his father had on genres such a cowboy songs and the blues. After wrapping up their field recordings, Alan became the first paid employee for the Folk Song Archive at the Library of Congress, a collection that now has tens of thousands of recordings. He also recorded oral histories with legendary musicians including Jelly Roll Morton, Muddy Waters, Woody Guthrie, and a wealth of famous British and Irish performers. Along the way, he produced a series of folk albums for Decca Records.

In the 1950s, Alan resided mostly in London where he edited world music for release on the new LP records. When he returned to New York in 1959, he produced a groundbreaking concert at Carnegie Hall. He included Muddy Waters and Memphis Slim, Jimmy Driftwood, two top gospel groups, Pete and Mike Seegar, the Stony Mountain Boys, and a rock group called the Cadillacs. He chose the lineup to carefully make a point. As he told the audience: "The time has come for Americans not to be ashamed of what we go for, musically, from primitive ballads to rock 'n' roll songs."

John Avery Lomax, his sons John, Jr. and Alan, his grandson, John III, and his great-grandson (and this author's long-time late friend) John Nova Lomax all wrote extensively about music and its history. Their books and recordings brought previously obscure sounds to a broader audience and no doubt saved thousands of traditional American songs and musicians from the historical landfill. Without John, Sr. and his son Alan, the shape of American music today would be infinitely poorer.

Edwards Aquifer

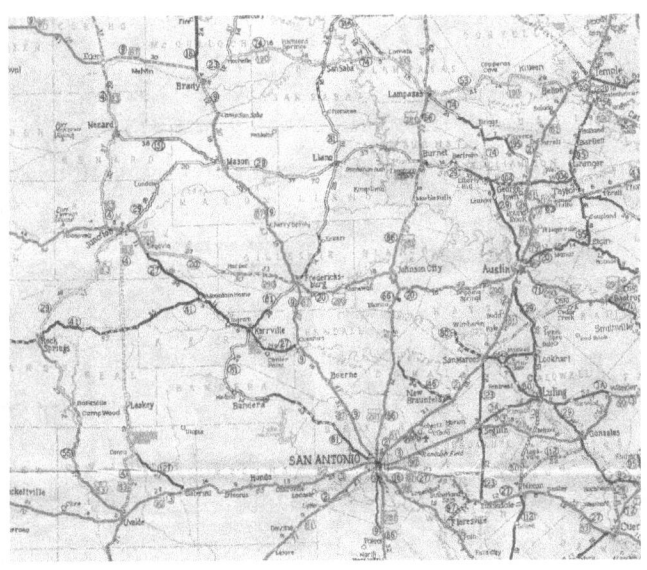

Chapter Nineteen

San Pedro Springs

I t is the tenth oldest public park in the United States and by far the oldest in Texas, but it could be argued that San Pedro Springs is simply one of the most culturally important sites in the entire American Southwest. The several springs and a small natural lake emerged from a fault at the base of a limestone bluff a few miles northwest of downtown San Antonio. The springs were declared an ejido, or public land, by King Philip V of Spain in 1729, and two years later the local military authorities designated it as temporary farming land for the first group of 56 Canary Islanders who settled the community.

The history of the springs goes back much further, however. In fact, the stories predate history. For thousands of years, indigenous Indians of Texas used the location as a place to camp and meet, and before them it was a gathering spot for animals. Among the bones and fossils found there were tigers, wolves, extinct horses, and mastodons, along with projectile points and stone tools crafted and used by some of the earliest inhabitants of Texas. The first name given to it was Yanaguana by a band of Coahuiltecans known as the Payayas.

The name of San Pedro was bestowed upon the springs by Father Isidro Felix de Espinosa who was part of an early entrada by the Spanish who had become greatly alarmed by 17th century French claims to Texas. Father Espinosa wrote of a place "bordered by many trees and with water enough to supply a town. It was full of taps and sluices of water, the earth being terraced. We named it Agua de San Pedro."

A second missionary who came to the area in that same year of 1709 was taken with the friendly Payaya people and sought to build a mission for them. It took nine years before he got his chance, but Antonio de San Buenaventura y Olivares eventually constructed a small building out of brush and grapevines just west of the springs and offered mass. Martin de Alarcon, the Spanish governor who was so instrumental to the settling of Texas, sited his presidio on San Pedro Creek just below the springs. These buildings from 1718 were the start of first permanent European settlement in San Antonio.

Olivares called his mission San Antonio de Valero, and it gave the new town its name. A year later, the missionary moved the mission to the east side of the springs to take advantage of better farmland. It was resituated one more time before it was finally relocated to the banks of the San Antonio River. It was at that location, while housing Spanish troops from the town of Alamo de Parras, that the name Alamo became forever attached to the mission complex.

Though the villa of San Antonio grew along the river to the south, the area around San Pedro Springs, and nearby San Antonio Springs, continued to be vital to its existence, primarily by supplying important water via an acequia built under orders from Alarcon. Seven of the canals eventually irrigated the area's farmland, and the seemingly mindless meandering of several streets in the modern Alamo City is due to the fact that they were constructed to follow the turns of those canals. Limestone from the northwest side of San Pedro Springs was used to build the earliest structures in San Antonio, as well.

The biggest connection of the springs to early San Antonio, though, was as the growing city's space for entertainment. Not long after the Texan victory at San Jacinto, Ranger Captain Jack Hays oversaw a company stationed in San Antonio. Texas memoirist John Duval wrote in detail of contests of horsemanship that the buckskin-clad Rangers held at San Pedro Springs against Mexican vaqueros in tall sombreros and Comanche warriors in a "finery of paints, feathers and beads." There were multiple events of horseback acrobatics, firing arrows or bullets at a target while at full gallop, and snatching a spear from the ground. Duval described a Comanche "rushing at full speed, and as he passed the spot where the spear had been placed, without checking his horse for an instant, he swerved from his saddle, seized the spear, and rising gracefully in his seat, ... he wheeled again and galloped back, dropping the spear as he returned at the same spot from which he had taken it... The same feat was then performed by a dozen or so each of the Rangers, rancheros, and Indians."

In the mid-19th century, the springs served as a stable for the camels that the U.S. Army were trying to mobilize in South Texas. The springs were also a temporary camp for the African American cavalry known as Buffalo Soldiers. During the Civil War, there was a small prisoner of war camp there. But in 1864, Jacob Duerler, who had been given a city deferment for the house which he built on public land, received a 20-year lease to create park improvements. He installed fish ponds, flower gardens, and added an exhibition building with a ballroom and bar. There were boat rentals, a horse-race track, a small museum, and a zoo complete with a "bear garden." The local German Turnverein exercised at the park, and after a mule-drawn cart started running continuously between the springs and Alamo Plaza, families and beer drinkers filled the park every weekend.

Most of San Antonio's sporting firsts happened at San Pedro Springs. Occupying Union troops possibly played the first baseball games in the city. It was the site of the first polo match and cricket game. The Alamo Gun Club held clay shooting there, and in the late 1800s, there was a board-covered and banked racetrack for bicyclists.

For years there were several legends that clung to the springs. One had a cache of buried gold and silver hidden in a cave, and another told of a secret tunnel between the Alamo and the bear pit. An oldtimer's reminiscence that made the local newspaper in 1911 involved a man named Pedro Lara who lived in the block house at the springs. He would lure travelers to spend the night in a small hut where he would rob them, kill them, and dump their bodies in a hidden pit. The gory plan was allegedly ended by a suspicious man named Vincent Boone who awoke to find Lara hovering over him with a knife and shot him dead about 1851. In the process, Boone also saved a young girl named Lolita who Lara kidnapped and used as a lure to his unwary victims. The entire tale might be easily dismissed, except that in 1900, city workers extending San Pedro Avenue unearthed a shallow cave with three skeletons.

The centerpiece of the park is, of course, the springs themselves. In 1891, the very year that the city took back management of the park, the first wells were drilled into the Edwards Aquifer. Though the city soon made park improvements, adding new plantings, pathways and bridges, building decorative walls around some of the springs, demolishing Duerler's buildings, and filling in his fish ponds, the continued drilling of wells in the area took a heavy toll. Each new well sunk into the aquifer sucked up water that would have flowed from the springs.

1930s-era postcard of the swimming pool at
San Pedro Springs

When the City of San Antonio opened Brackenridge Park in 1912, many of the San Pedro visitors began going there. That same year, the zoo animals were sold and shipped to Kansas City. Some new amenities were added: a library, tennis courts and a theatre. The saddest irony among the new additions was that the city made the old lake bed into a "naturalistic" swimming pool, the first municipal pool in town. Within 20 years, the continuous pumping of water, coupled with the drought years of the 1930s, had rendered the native water supply insufficient to fill it. The San Pedro pool sat empty for a decade. In the mid-1950s, grocery store magnate Howard E. Butt paid to build a rectangular pool filled with chlorinated water just like everywhere else.

New generations of San Antonians grew up with no recollection of water ever flowing from the San Pedro Springs. That changed with abnormally heavy rains in 1991 and 92. As the official Edwards Aquifer keeper put it: "long-forgotten tiny springs bubbled up all over the Park." Though it was officially forbidden, for a few years at least, hundreds of locals once again took a dip in the San Pedro Springs.

Chapter Twenty

The Pig War

T he British have the War of Jenkin's Ear. The Ashanti Kingdom of Ghana has the War of the Golden Stool. Mexico has the Pastry War, the starting point of the splendidly bizarre saga of Santa Anna's leg. And in Texas we can claim the Pig War. Never mind that no one actually died, except a few unfortunate pigs, or that the name was blatantly stolen by later historians and applied to a conflict over a different martyred pig in the San Juan Islands between Vancouver Island, British Columbia and Bellingham, Washington. Texas had the name first. Fair and square.

Our Pig War, the real one obviously, was a not-so-diplomatic conflict between the Republic of Texas and France that played out at the start of the 1840s. It was a setback in what promised for a brief moment to be a lucrative relationship between an ancient country and an infant one.

Sam Houston, first president of the Republic, knew the score. He and more than 90% of Texas voters wanted to become an American state. The trouble was that the United States did not want Texas. A majority of politicians in Washington, D.C. believed that adding the Lone Star State would upset the delicate and contentious balance between slave and free interests. Many Americans could feel the creep toward greater sectional strife or even violence, and they wanted to avoid it at all costs.

It was Houston's belief, when confronted with that unwanted reality, that if the new Republic of Texas cozied up to European powers, the United States would fear the loss of a huge opportunity and would correct the errors of her ways regarding annexation. In fall of 1838, President Houston dispatched James Pinckney Henderson to Europe. Andrew Jackson had given official U.S. recognition to the Republic of Texas as a legitimate foreign country, but after more than two years, there the list still stood. Mexico was distracted by their beef with France, but most international observers knew that someday soon the Mexican Army would cross the Rio Grande looking to reclaim its temporarily lost territory. Recognition by the nations of Europe might forestall the Mexicans.

Henderson's targets for diplomatic relations were Britain and France. The issue with the former was that they had recently outlawed slavery behind a decades-long citizens crusade, and national pride in their parliamentary action was running extremely high. Never mind that the British later supported the Confederacy and wholly justified the subjugation of darker-skinned people across their Empire, the British government of the moment was not about to recognize a new nation formed largely around the protection of slavery. Furthermore, the Brits had extensive commercial interests in Mexico, and Mexico unequivocally claimed that Texas was still theirs. The best Henderson could muster in London was a commercial agreement to potentially do business.

In Paris, however, things were quite different. France and Mexico were then engaged in the aforementioned Pastry War, and French ships were blockading Mexican ports until their demands for repayment of 600,000 pesos in debts were repaid. Still, the French had already studied the matter of Texas and determined that the possibilities were extremely high that the region would either revert to Mexico or join the United

States. The French initially saw little upside for their potential efforts and expense of establishing foreign relations. News of the commercial agreement with Britain changed things a bit. The French did not want to fall behind their centuries-old rival when it came to expanding business and influence. They agreed to send a discreet envoy to analyze the situation in Texas and report back.

Their choice was a 29-year old bachelor secretary attached to the French Embassy in Washington, D.C.. His name was Jean Pierre Isidore Alphonse Dubois de Saligny. The de Saligny part was something Dubois appended to his moniker when he began referring to himself as a Count. He was not. It took him three months to arrive in the Republic's capital at Houston in February 1839. In addition to the town of Houston, he also saw Galveston and traveled down the coast as far as Matagorda. He also met with former President Houston and the new President Mirabeau Lamar. When he sent his final report up the French diplomatic ladder, Dubois inflated the numbers of Texas population and agricultural output then concluded that France must not miss out on this "opportunity to establish ourselves on this continent." The French government saw a chance to beat the British to a growing new market for its goods and a strategic navigational stop in the Gulf of Mexico. A formal treaty of recognition was ratified in October 1839 making France the first European nation to fully acknowledge the legitimacy of the Texas Republic. On its part, Texas very much wanted an extremely large loan from the French government, so they were overjoyed.

The next step was to establish a legation, and Alphonse Dubois was sent as charge d'affaires since Texas did not warrant a full ambassador. It is possible Dubois had written so glowingly of Texas with this exact posting and promotion in mind. While the French were building a beautiful legation complex on the east side of the new capital of Austin,

Dubois moved out of Richard Bullock's hotel, a place that drew his frequent complaints, and settled into temporary quarters in a "wretched wood shanty" on Pecan, later to become Sixth Street. Though he wrote disparaging letters about the frontier village of Austin on the edge of Comancheria, Dubois did entertain local dignitaries with his stash of fine French wine.

Dubois began promoting a Franco-Texian Bill in the Republic's Congress that would give three million acres of Texas land to a private French company to settle 8,000 families from France. The company would build 20 forts housing 10,000 French soldiers, establish mining operations and have exclusive rights to trade with New Mexican merchants. Unfortunately for the French, David G. Burnet's powerful opposition doomed the bill's passage. It did not leave a good taste in Dubois' mouth.

Then came the pigs. The rough edge hotel owner Bullock was in the habit of letting his pigs, of which there were many, run loose on the dirt streets of the capital. At the interim French legation three blocks away, several of the porkers had gotten into the stables, broken down the wood fence around the garden, and eaten the sovereign French corn. Unsatisfied with that fare, some of Bullock's imperious pigs busted into the charge d'affaires' bedroom and made a meal of his imported linens and some official papers. Dubois ordered his butler, Eugene Pluyette, to shoot the pigs on sight. It was a directive Pluyette took to heart, killing at least five of the hungry swine. Bullock, who already disliked Dubois over an unpaid hotel bill accrued when he first arrived in town, demanded reparations for his slain livestock. Dubois invoked diplomatic immunity and "the law of nations," so Richard Bullock gained his satisfaction by beating the stuffing out of the French butler on an Austin street corner, pelting him with rocks as he fled, then threatening the diplomat himself.

The French government demanded a summary punishment of the hotel owner, but instead, the Republic's Secretary of the Treasury paid Bullock's bail and opined that Bullock should have shot Dubois instead. Alphonse Dubois de Saligny was so incensed that he personally broke off diplomatic relations with the Republic of Texas and decamped for New Orleans. The French government had not approved his course of action, but they mostly backed their man. Dubois remained in Louisiana for a year before his bosses finally negotiated a "compromise" deal with Sam Houston who had by then returned to the Texas presidency. Dubois returned to Texas in April 1842, albeit Galveston since the Texas government had fled Austin out of fear of Mexican invasion. His last meager efforts to keep Texas independent failed.

If Dubois' highhandedness was at all a stain on his career, retribution was a long time coming. After annexation, Dubois was posted to the Netherlands, Russia, and finally Mexico under Emperor Maximillian. He was eventually recalled to Paris after being accused of fraud in 1864. He brought with him a Mexican wife and their son. Bullock's remaining pigs resumed their ramblings around Austin, and the Texas government lost the opportunity to mortgage itself and become a de facto French colony. It continued to wallow in crushing debt until the United States changed its tune and admitted Texas in 1845.

Chapter Twenty-One

Henry B. Gonzalez

T he Civil Rights movement is often associated solely with African Americans, but the nation's Mexican Americans, especially in South Texas, had long faced similar discrimination, subjugation, exclusion, and violence. Just as Barbara Jordan was the first Black member of the Texas Senate since Reconstruction, Henry B. Gonzalez was a similar pioneer for Latinos. In fact, the wait for Hispanics was even longer. The one and only person of Mexican descent to grace a State Senate desk prior to 1957 was fellow San Antonio native Jose Antonio Navarro a full century earlier. Another Bexareno, Navarro's uncle, Jose Francisco Ruiz, had served in the Senate of the Texas Republic.

Henry Gonzalez's parents had fled the State of Durango during the Mexican Revolution. His father, Leonides, was mayor of the small mountain town of Mapimi, and in the family's new home of San Antonio, Leonides went to work for a Spanish language newspaper called *La Prensa*. It was a household that supplied Henry with a solid political education. To lose the heavy accent that brought ridicule from other children, he read aloud with a mouth full of rocks, copying Demosthenes. For his more formal and advanced schooling, Henry went to San Antonio Junior College, the University of Texas, and then St. Mary's

Law School in his hometown. By the time he graduated, he had married Bertha Cuellar. After law school, Gonzalez served the remainder of WWII as a censor in military intelligence.

Following the war, Henry Gonzalez worked in public service. First came three years in the juvenile probation department, but just when he earned the position as chief officer of the department, he resigned after being told that he could not hire a Black assistant. He next worked in the city housing department, and after losing his first political campaign, an attempt to go to the State House, Gonzalez was elected to San Antonio City Council in 1953. His top priority there was to desegregate city facilities which had been denied him personally since his birth there almost 40 years prior. He experienced what he called "many lonely votes" on the matter.

When he made it to the Texas Senate, Gonzalez became known for a pugnacious style of legislating. It fit with the boxing that he had done as a younger man. He needed that bluster in a building where he was often referred to as simply "that Mexican."

It was a contentious and interesting time in the South. *Brown v. Board of Education* had just ordered integration of the nation's public schools, and President Eisenhower had sent federally-sworn troops to oversee the integration of Central High School in Little Rock, Arkansas. Southern state governments were doing everything in their power to resist the changes. In Mansfield, outside Fort Worth, Black students won a lawsuit that would allow them to attend the local high school. Loud threats were made, and Black effigies were hanged and burned. The school principal refused to let one hanging mannequin be removed. With the opposite goal of Eisenhower, Governor Allen Shivers sent in the Texas Rangers to prevent any African American students from registering.

Doubling down on that sentiment, Texas House members passed 13 bills aimed to further enshrine segregation in the state. Among them was even one that would prevent any members of the NAACP from holding a state or local government job. The bills next worked their way to the Senate where a small group of six men from South Texas tried to stop them. Perhaps most odious of the group were five bills that would give local school officials 17 criteria to deny entry to any given student and another that would provide state tuition vouchers to any Texas parents who did not want their child in an integrated school. It would take public taxpayer money and send it to private schools to maintain segregated privilege. Another bill, allowing the governor to immediately shutter any school where federal troops were sent to enforce integration, had already passed.

The leading voice against the five bills was Henry B. Gonzalez, a man in his first legislative session. Dressed in a light blue suit with a yellow tie and pocket handkerchief, Gonzalez, alongside fellow Senator Abraham "Chick" Kazen, a son of Lebanese immigrants from Laredo, held the Senate floor for three straight days and nights. Yielding to anyone else, sitting down, or even stepping out to go to the bathroom would have ended their filibuster. It was Gonzalez's show, and he personally spoke for 22 and a half hours. When Kazan or one of the other allies spelled him, Gonzalez asked his fellow Senators interminable questions to fill time. He spoke with great eloquence about the specific injustice of a "tuition grant" of taxpayer money to attend a private school and the much larger tragedy of the bills sent before the Senate with but a single goal: to keep Texas schools segregated by race. Such actions would destroy the state's public schools.

Gonzalez and Kazen spoke to each other in Spanish, perhaps a first for the Texas Senate floor. "The lion judges everybody by his own condition" and "Everybody looks yellow to the jaundiced eye" were among those passages. They reminded people that among the many good Americans were "thousands of Negroes and Mexicans who had recently fought and died on world battlefields from Anzio to Iwo Jima." Gonzalez decried the short memories of his fellow Texans on that matter. He read from books. He even read telegrams as Jimmy Stewart had in "Mr. Smith Goes to Washington." In the 21st hour of his erudite stand on the floor, exhausted and sometimes having to lean against desks, Henry B. took off his shoes and paced in his yellow socks. He had refused to yield to various calls to allow the tuition vouchers in return for the pulling of other bills. "Compromise on one, and you're sunk on all," he answered. He also reminded his fellow senators and the growing eyes of Texas of something else: "What a noble opportunity to enlist in a cause that's eternal – the maintenance of the dignity of a human!"

With minimal help, Gonzalez and Kazan defeated eight of the 13 bills. Another was later found unconstitutional.

Henry Gonzalez had an unsuccessful campaign for governor in 1958, but he succeeded in getting elected as the Congressman from San Antonio's 20th District in 1961 with the endorsement of President John Kennedy, Vice President Lyndon Johnson and Governor Price Daniel, a man who had opposed his efforts in the state legislature. LBJ actively campaigned for Gonzalez. Henry B. served 18 straight terms, never gaining less than 60% of the re-election vote, and he retired as the longest serving Hispanic in U.S. Congressional history.

When Gonzalez took his seat as the first Mexican American ever in Congress, his initial assignment was to the House Banking Committee, and he learned his role flawlessly. He sought to increase transparency at the Federal Reserve. In 1979, Gonzalez began warning his House colleagues that the "excessive deregulation" of the savings and loan industry would soon have massive and dire consequences for taxpayers. His fellow House members ignored him. Nine years later, with seniority earned, Gonzalez ascended to the chair of that committee and launched hearings into an S&L crisis that was already hurting the nation. With Gonzalez pushing hard, a bill with major reforms passed in 1989 - a decade after he sounded the alarm. Included in the mess were hearings into the illegal activities of California S&L chairman Charles Keating. Not only did Keating go to prison, but five U.S. Senators were publicly embarrassed when they tried to lean on investigators on his behalf.

Henry B. Gonzalez (St. Mary's University)

One of the final windmills of corruption at which Henry B. tilted was the so-called Iraqgate. In the course of House investigations, Gonzalez learned that several officials of the Reagan and Bush Administrations had used an Atlanta, Georgia branch of an Italian bank to open an illegal multi-billion-dollar line of credit with the aim to funnel arms to Iraq prior to the Persian Gulf War. As the truth unfolded, Bush officials tried to silence Gonzalez on grounds of national security. Members of his own party tried unsuccessfully to replace him as Banking Committee chair. Despite the intense opposition, Gonzalez showed that administration officials had used seemingly innocuous U.S. agriculture loans to illegally boost the conventional and chemical weaponry of Saddam Hussein's Iraq prior to their invasion of Kuwait. Those same weapons were used against American service people just months later. Henry B.'s attempts to start impeachment proceedings against George H.W. Bush went nowhere.

Many called Gonzalez a "maverick," a term that came from a San Antonian of a previous century. His more bitter opponents called him everything from "eccentric" to "crackpot." Twice Gonzalez called for the impeachment of Ronald Reagan, once over the invasion of Grenada and once over the shameful Iran/Contra affair. Neither gained any traction. The fact remains, though, that Henry B. Gonzalez's unpopular opinions were often proved both honest and right.

The Kennedy Center honored Gonzalez with the Profiles in Courage award in 1994. Among the phrases in the writeup was a "voice for the voiceless." It was something Henry Gonzalez himself had long ago said that he sought to be, and he said it in the wee hours of the morning in May 1957 speaking to a Texas Senate Chamber that was completely empty save for two reporters and a janitor.

Chapter Twenty-Two

Elisha Pease

Outside of the City of Austin, where his 8,000 square foot mansion anchors the Old West Austin neighborhood near Shoal Creek, Elisha Pease is just another forgotten Texas governor whose name graces a street sign here and there. He was, however, one of the state's more successful leaders in the 19th century, and part of that success may be attributed to his schooling and upbringing in Connecticut and Massachusetts which gave him a different view of what government might accomplish.

Like most who came to Texas in the 1830s, Pease came seeking opportunity and adventure. Arriving in 1835 at the age of 23, he quickly built up his Texian credentials. He fought at the Battle of Gonzales, took part in the convention at Washington that drafted a Texas Constitution, and became the Republic's first comptroller of public accounts. As a legislator, Pease authored the Republic's first criminal code of law, then he won the governorship on his second try.

The Pease Administration's greatest accomplishment was finally settling the negotiations with the United States over money owed to Texas from sale of the Republic's land claims to parts of Oklahoma, Colorado, and New Mexico. In 1854, Pease ushered ten million dollars into the state coffers. With the funds, he retired a great debt and saw to it that the state built a hospital for the mentally ill, schools for the deaf and blind, a state orphan's home, a new General Land Office building, and the Texas Governor's Mansion. A new state capitol opened the year he took office. When he left office after two terms, Texas was on good financial footing for the first time in her history.

The 1853 Texas Capitol sat on the same grounds as the current building.

Two other Pease policy areas are best assessed as being noble ideas which were executed with very poor planning. The first was public education. It was something Elisha Pease had seen succeed firsthand in New England, but that was virtually unknown in most areas of the South. An 1851 northern visitor to Houston wrote a letter to the editor of the *Telegraph and Texas Register* complimenting the town's business community and churches, then remarked "I was astonished to find that in a city some sixteen years of age, containing a population of between three and four thousand souls, and much wealth and intelligence as there is, there was not to be found one single edifice built for Educational purposes – not even the most common school house!!"

Pease vowed to remedy the situation, but he chose a decentralized path that provided stipends to pay private tuition at existing schools. The 1854 "Act to Establish a System of Schools" handed the duties of establishing said schools to the counties, and it did so without much funding. Pease stated a hope that the next session would provide "li berally." That term would never become applicable to Texas education funding, and more than 170 years later, Texas schools are still waiting. The sole legacy of Pease's bill was the creation of the Permanent School Fund. That grand notion remains in existence, having been resurrected in the state's 1876 constitution. Pease placed two million dollars of the money from the United States in his 1854 fund to get it started.

Texas counties each performed a scholastic census as required by the law, and the surviving lists are goldmines for genealogists and historians. They also show the woeful local response to educational opportunity. In Houston, for example, only 83 of some 700 school age children were attending classes. Reports from elsewhere told the same sorry tale.

Overall, only 89 counties made an effort to take part in the new school system in 1854 and just 74 were still there the following year when the first disbursement of funds was made. Much of the trouble was due to a lack of organization. In Bastrop County, for example, there were 29 common school districts formed, but only three of them went so far as to elect trustees. Brazoria County had only one district follow through, and in Fort Bend, not a single district organized to claim money available under the new law. Dallas County seems to have had one of the best results in Texas, reporting in 1857 that the state funds were paying almost "two-thirds of the tuition for those who attend school." The most frank and dismal assessment came from the Chief Justice in Nacogdoches who reported that "There is but little interest taken in the school law."

Even during the Civil War, a semblance of school districts was maintained in some places, though by then the government only supported students who were proven to be indigent, in which cases their teachers were directly compensated by the county.

Unfortunately for the future of Texas education, the Pease administration placed an equally high value on seeing Texas gain new railroads. Soon after the start of the schools program, the bulk of the "set aside" fund was loaned to start up railroads in the state to bolster track construction. The interest the railroads would owe was to further augment the public schools. The state got a very different result.

As with many other corporate ventures, most of the railroads went bankrupt, undermined by poor and greedy management and then the upheaval of the Civil War. Wartime governor Pendleton Murrah said in December 1863 that the distribution "to the schools for the last two years is insignificant." Specifically, he noted that the railroad companies owed the school fund about a quarter of a million dollars with another $166,000 in interest due on top of that. Much of the school fund had vanished with the would-be train entrepreneurs' dreams.

Famous Texas historian Eugene Barker summed up the mid-1850s attempt at schools thusly: "It proved a miserable failure. Doubtless it contained some element of merit but the enormous loss that accrued to the School Fund is eloquent testimony to the fact that not all finely conceived theories work out in practice."

The Civil War and Confederate budget realities of the early 1860s brought an end to the school program entirely. One and a quarter million dollars was taken out of the two-million-dollar school fund principal and transferred to the Texas military board, and investment income in general withered like rye grass in summer. A law setting aside all revenue from the sale of public lands for education was repealed. On top of it all, the few railroad companies which were keeping up with at least a portion of their interest payments began doing so in Confederate currency, an instrument that depreciated until it was used as wallpaper.

After serving his two terms as Texas governor, Elisha Pease remained in Austin, vocally opposing secession. He quietly held his Unionist view throughout the Civil War, even when his biggest Unionist ally, Sam Houston, grudgingly came to accept the Confederacy. When the war ended and Union forces occupied the state, General Phillip Sheridan appointed Pease as provisional governor replacing the unapologetic Confederate James Throckmorton. This second turn as governor brought conflict with both the former rebels and many among the Texas Republicans, a party he helped form. Pease resigned less than two years into the job.

For a time, it seemed as if Elisha Pease wanted to play both sides of the aisle. The Republican was chosen as chair of the Taxpayer's Convention of 1871, a mostly Democratic gathering that opposed most everything that Reconstruction-era Governor Edmund Davis suggested including legislative redistricting, prohibition of carrying firearms on the street, and using state police to enforce election integrity. The biggest complaint of the Taxpayer's Convention was over Governor Davis's school law and school tax that established the first true public education system in Texas. Though he stayed active in politics, Pease mostly practiced law in Austin until his death in 1883.

Chapter Twenty-Three

Sam Ealy Johnson, Sr.

W e are all a sum of our parts. Those who are remembered as great and influential people may bring important change, but the forces that shaped their ideas are rarely noted. In the case of Lyndon Baines Johnson, the stunningly complex man whose presidency did more to improve the lot of modern Americans than any other, no one shaped his ideals and convictions more than his father and his paternal grandfather. Both men, Sam Ealy Johnson, Sr. and Jr., were embodiments of the agrarian populism that provided the roots of American liberalism.

Sam, Jr., like his father before him, was a risk taker. His business life was boom and bust. He reached such highs in Hill Country real estate that he hired a teenaged boy as his chauffeur and paid cleaning ladies to help his wife. At one time he owned multiple ranches, a small movie theatre, a weekly newspaper, and the only hotel in Johnson City. The cotton futures market ate it all and chased the Johnson family back into poverty. As his son, the president, put it, "My daddy went busted waiting for cotton to go up to twenty-one cents a pound, and the market fell apart when it hit twenty."

In Texas, a state where the 1901 adoption of the poll tax rendered elections a realm brutally dominated by White Democrats, the choice was between the party conservatives who were unflinchingly pro-business and the populist-leaning Democrats who worked for the interests of common citizens. Money almost always spoke loudest.

Lyndon's daddy served five terms in the Texas Legislature. He got there when he was 27, and supported causes like an eight hour day for railroad workers, drought relief, and a franchise tax for corporations. Mostly, though, Sam Jr. lost. The rich guys with the business interests generally carried the day. After two terms, Sam Johnson, Jr. declined to run again because he was personally broke. Though patronage from railroads and other big business supplemented the incomes of a majority of state legislators, it was never offered to Sam, Jr.. In the eyes of those with the deepest pockets, he was not a team player.

Sam, Jr. went back to the Hill Country and worked to rebuild a living. One thing he never lost was a reputation for honesty and friendliness. When a Texas House seat came up in a special election in 1917, a full decade after he left the capitol, so many of his neighbors asked Sam, Jr. to fill it that he ran unopposed. Two full terms followed before Johnson left state office for good in 1923.

Sam, Jr. had learned his lessons at the foot of his father, referred to inside the family as Big Sam, and Junior even used the record Sam, Sr. amassed as a populist to burnish his own reputation as a legislator of the people. The family commitment to helping the common man and solving the American plague of poverty came from Sam Ealy Johnson, Sr. and from deep in the Hill Country soil.

Sam, Sr. and his brother Tom came back from the Civil War and hit it big in Blanco County in the Hill Country. The town of Johnson City bears their name because of their cattle driving success after the war. But as writers have pointed out for many years, West Texas is fickle. Drought, unseasonable cold, and a heaping helping of slack business dealings and unfortunate ranching choices against a volatile commodities market sent Sam Johnson and his family to Buda for almost two decades. Lyndon's father, Sam, Jr., was born there. They managed to salvage a life in Hays County thanks to assistance from the family of Big Sam's wife, Eliza Bunton. Several Lyndon Johnson scholars have remarked about his shrewd practicality being inherited from his grandmother Bunton.

Before populism became a word coopted by right wing authoritarians, it meant exactly what the word's Latin roots suggest – a movement for the people. Two groups that came to power in Texas during the 1880s proved a high point for that notion. The first was the Farmer's Alliance, which started in Lampasas. The goals of the Alliance centered around cooperative power. They established warehouses and took in individual farmer's cotton as a deposit. The large stock of collective cotton could then be used to stabilize prices and gain better interest rates than the exorbitant ones offered by banks. Above all, the Alliance wanted farmers paid with a federal paper currency divorced from the gold standard that kept the playing field permanently tilted in favor of banks and big buyers.

The day after the Farmer's Alliance state meeting of 1891, an organizing convention was held for the Populists, called the People's Party of Texas. Big Sam Johnson was a prominent speaker at both. Though there was debate over how best to accomplish it without alienating too many White ex-Confederate Democrats, the Populists added Blacks to their state executive committee. In Blanco County, there was also a "Mexican" representative. It was an imperfect start, but in the hot racism of a time only 25 years removed from slavery, it was also a bold statement. In addition to the Farmer's Alliance platform, the Populist coalition advocated a federal income tax, a regulation of monopolies, an eight hour work day, collective bargaining, and much greater support for public schools.

The Johnson family had moved back to the Hill Country in 1889 and settled on 950 acres along the Pedernales River in Gillespie County. They bought land that had been decimated by another record drought and years of grazing that had robbed the soil of its protective native grasses. The hard road faced by American farmers and strong memories of his own bankrupted troubles made Sam Johnson go all in for the Farmer's Alliance and then the Populists. The Alliance chose him as lecturer for the area, and he gave innumerable speeches for the people's cause.

A Johnson Family gathering about 1912. The future president leans against the car grille. Sam Johnson, Jr. is the tall man behind the car, third from left, in the white hat, and his wife, Rebekah Baines Johnson, is in front of him. (LBJ Library)

His daughter-in-law described Big Sam as "highly gregarious" and said that "he met his friends with a handshake, friendly greetings, and a hearty resounding laugh" – attributes tailor made for a politician. In 1892, Sam, Sr., still a struggling farmer, was a nominee for the Populist Party for the Texas House seat representing Blanco, Hays, Comal and Gillespie Counties.

To call that election cycle a volatile one would be gross understatement. At the top level, Governor James Hogg, a mild progressive, faced railroad lawyer George Clark, a staunch conservative. The Republicans, whose relevance was by then on the verge of extinction in Texas, declined to field a candidate in order to back Clark. The Populists hoped that the anti-Clark vote would help them in the Hill Country house district.

That House race was a four-person affray from which two at-large winners would be selected. Sam Johnson's Populist running mate was his wife's first cousin, and one of his Democratic opponents was his son-in-law, Clarence Martin. In some cases, the political foes Johnson and Martin made joint campaign appearances. Presidential grandson Lyndon later told of the two riding together in the same buggy, but there is no confirmation of that. It is certain that the campaign was bitter. At a heavily Populist stop in Blanco County, Martin was shouted from the stage by hecklers then stabbed in the abdomen. He lived, but the sails were gone from Big Sam Johnson's campaigning. Though the somewhat progressive Hogg was reelected governor, the conservative Democrats carried the two Hill Country House seats by two to one. It was the only political race of Big Sam Johnson's life.

After one and a half terms in the legislature, Clarence Martin and his wife, Frank, moved to a place just up the river from Sam and Eliza Johnson. When they reached their sixties, the elder Johnsons moved into the old farmhouse with their daughter. Eliza and Big Sam died there.

Senator Lyndon Johnson later purchased the old place from his Aunt Frank and added on much more space. It became his Texas White House.

One trait that Johnson family biographers note about the two Sam Johnsons is an endless thirst for education. Sam, Jr. taught at one-room schools in the Hill Country, and Sam, Sr. had an every-other-day ritual of fording the Pedernales River to pick up his many newspaper subscriptions at the Stonewall Post Office. Sam, Sr.'s grandson had his famous array of White House televisions so he could watch news on each channel, and the President's first job out of college at San Marcos was as a teacher.

When Lyndon Baines Johnson gave his inauguration speech in 1965, following one of the biggest presidential election landslides in history, he laid out the blueprint for his Great Society. Noting America's "great wealth," he called for an unprecedented government investment in fighting poverty, providing health care to the elderly, improving education across the nation, and ending discrimination against minorities. Each of those ideas were deeply rooted in the beliefs of Big Sam, the populist grandfather that President Johnson spoke of with great pride.

Chapter Twenty-Four

Jacob DeGress

I n 1870, the federal government called Texas "the darkest field educationally in the United States." The state had a 17% illiteracy rate among Whites and 90% among Blacks. Crime was high. The homicide rate was double any of the other 37 states. Edmund J. Davis, elected governor in 1869, decided to improve the situation and signed a schools act into law in April 1871. Provisions included common statewide curriculum, a system of teacher certification, establishment of grade levels, continuing education for teachers, and central administration of schools.

Davis appointed Jacob Carl DeGress to be the first Supervisor of Public Instruction. The Prussian-born DeGress was only 23 when he came to Texas in 1865 as a brevet colonel with the Freedmen's Bureau, but he was battle tested. DeGress was a twice-wounded commander of Union cavalry who had fought at Vicksburg and in Louisiana before traveling as a staff officer on Sherman's march through Georgia. With the Freedmen's Bureau, DeGress served at Houston and Galveston in multiple civil affairs capacities, including some related to schools. While in Houston, he met and married Betty Buckner Young, a Confederate war widow. From the Bureau, he was sent to West Texas as a regular

Army captain commanding the Ninth U.S. Cavalry, a troop of African American veterans being dispatched against Indians.

DeGress' new schools job came with great authority. The governor, attorney general, and supervisor of public instruction were in charge of the system all the way down to selecting county school boards and teachers and setting their salaries. A subsequent head of the state schools said that the 1871 statute was "only a few sections and less than three printed pages... but it gave to the Board of Education powers that might well excite the envy of the autocrat of all the Russias."

The ex-Confederates, a minority in political power, railed against the centralized oversight. True to the new federal laws, DeGress appointed both Whites and Blacks to school board positions, further angering the unreconstructed rebels. The taxes required to fund the schools were the biggest sticking point. The state's well-to-do objected to the mixed social conditions public schools created. They were able to educate their own children via tuition and thought it unfair that they should be taxed to educate the children of others. Many flatly refused to pay up.

Jacob DeGress

Initially, Governor Davis was having none of the protests and non-compliance. He ordered Attorney General William Alexander "to threaten seizure of their properties if payments were not made." Local tax collectors and sheriffs, however, did not often comply with those orders from Austin.

The opposition was not all economic. A good part of the squawking was rooted in simple bigotry against both the newly freed African Americans and any Yankee interlopers who dared to bring public education to Texas. The idea of educating Blacks, though never illegal in Texas as it had been in a handful of other Confederate states, was repugnant to some Whites. Many in the press were outraged. The *Houston Telegraph* opined: "We may let our children work in the fields or shop with the children of our former servants. They may hunt or fish or play together, but to attend the same school never!" The *Galveston Daily News* was more virulent: "Colored children are not sufficiently advanced in civilization to be fit companions for white children."

Despite rampant rumors to the contrary, Supervisor DeGress pledged to keep the schools segregated, and he honored his word, likely afraid of potential consequences both violent and political. His decision angered the most prominent of the freed people. On the other hand, DeGress was well known for protecting and standing up for freed people during his time with the Freedmen's Bureau, and that alone made him hated by many ex-Confederates.

Other protest groups had their own blatant self-interests at heart. Germans, prevalent across Texas, were afraid the public schools would be used to "de-Germanize" them, a goal that was openly stated by some who favored assimilation of foreign minorities. The Baptists believed that examining teachers for competency was humiliating. Catholic leaders opposed the public schools as an infringement upon their rights. They refused to allow teachers in the church schools to take the state oath, even though the new law mandated that all teachers in any school pass a competency test. In San Antonio, the bishop even went so far as to refuse the sacraments for parents who sent their children to public school. It is unknown if the Catholic DeGress was ever denied communion. Eventually the church gave in, and Catholic teachers were certified.

In the end, many Texans couldn't afford both public school taxes and private school tuition, so they brought their children into the state system. In the neighborhood of 1,100 private schools either closed or joined the state system in 1872.

On the positive side for most people, a popular provision in the law stated that all religious instruction was prohibited in the public schools, and violations resulted in teacher termination.

Despite a rash of problems, including extreme difficulty in finding places for the white teachers of African American students to board, there was success. Salaries for teachers, who faced entrance exams for the first time, were generous, ranging from $75 to $110 a month, with principals even higher. Black schools flourished, enrolling 1,500 children in Harris County alone. A statewide curriculum was adopted, and textbooks were furnished at state expense. Schools were open for 10 months of the year and at least six hours a day. At one fleeting juncture in the first year of the new school law, DeGress felt reassured that common sense and a desire for education would prevail. He was wrong.

Texas Democrats, seeking a wedge against the Northern-led Republicans, made the Republican schools their top issue. Democratic campaign rhetoric railed against educating Blacks, and charged that Texas children would be learning manners and morals at odds with those of their parents.

It did not take long for the ex-Confederates' efforts to turn personal. The Texas Senate convened hearings aimed at DeGress and his alleged party favoritism. DeGress did indeed sometimes bow to party pressure, appointing certain freedmen to posts in order to turn out the vote, and forcing one Galveston board member out of his job for being "a spy in the camp." That man quickly complained to the Democrats in the Senate that DeGress was asking for kickbacks from building contractors and sellers of the schoolbooks and slate boards that students used. The investigating committee called dozens of witnesses and found no wrongdoing on the part of DeGress. Still, some Democrats stated that even though they'd found nothing, he was probably guilty.

Democrats managed an injunction to stop tax collection, though that was overturned on appeal and the property taxes declared constitutional, but meanwhile the school finances fell further into arrears. After serious election losses, Republicans at the state level preemptively cut school costs, eliminating 23 of the 35 district supervisor jobs, increasing class size and cutting teacher pay. They even added a new fourth class level that applied to most rural schools and paid teachers only $25 a month.

As 1872 continued, Democrats filed more and more injunctions to declare the school law unconstitutional, all of which were shot down by the Texas Supreme Court. Nonetheless, Governor Davis and Superintendent DeGress continued the cost cutting to reflect continuing unpaid taxes. In some places such as Houston, teachers went without any pay whatsoever for a full year. Various county sheriffs skimmed some school tax money off the top, further adding to the woes.

When new governor Richard Coke took charge in 1874, Supervisor of Education Jacob DeGress found himself out of a job. Though he had been branded a Yankee carpetbagger, he remained in Austin and was elected alderman and then mayor in the late 1870s. The summer of 1880 was devastating to DeGress: a lawsuit successfully challenged his eligibility to serve as mayor, and his wife and two of his three daughters died. Two years later, he remarried to a cousin of famed Confederate General Joseph E. Johnston and re-emerged in Republican politics. Presidents Garfield and Harrison each appointed him to terms as postmaster of Austin, and another lawsuit reinstated his service as alderman in the interim. From 1885 to 1888, he even served on several committees concerned with construction and dedication of the new Texas Capitol. Jacob C. DeGress died of complications from his war wounds on St. Joseph's Day in 1894.

The good schools that he tried to create were not entirely dead, but they were greatly weakened. In 1875, and ratified in 1876, came a new school law that was less centralized and greatly limited taxes. It was even weaker than what a committee of Democrats, recently gaining the majority of elected offices, had recommended. There were no supervisory positions at all. The entire system was run by the State Comptroller. Compulsory attendance was eliminated and would not return for over a generation. School taxes were only allowed in incorporated cities and towns. Statistics for the 1878-79 school year told the tale. Using the same criteria as the Reconstruction Republican law had laid out, only 39% of Texas children were in school. Monthly teacher pay, equal for the sexes under the Reconstruction law, now averaged $48.13 for men and $28.31 for women, and in some locales, the school year was allowed to drop to only 72 days.

South Texas

Chapter Twenty-Five

Americo Paredes

"**I**'m working and I'm gonna study nights. Sometimes I get to thinking and I say to myself, 'Who the hell am I? Just a poor Damn Mexican that's worth less than a dog in this cursed country.'"

Those words from *George Washington Gomez*, the first novel Americo Paredes ever wrote, were not autobiographical, but they hint at one theme of his life's work – to get Mexican Texans a rightful place in history. He authored the book during his second year of junior college in his hometown of Brownsville, but the book was not published until 1990, more than a half century later. *George Washington Gomez* became his widest read work.

Though he gained acclaim as a champion for Tejano history and letters, he was given his first name to honor an Italian explorer, "the result of a promise to an aunt and her Italian sailor husband." His father's family were Sefardic Jews who came to the Americas in 1580 and converted to Christianity. In 1749, the family settled in the Lower Rio Grande Valley with Jose de Escandon. Americo Paredes spent his career exploring and documenting those border traditions including the double American and Mexican culture of South Texas.

His father composed ten line poems called decimas, and that love of poetry and rhythm in speech and song was passed on to Americo. He followed his father's lead, and his first recognition for writing was winning a poetry contest in his teens, an award that led to his acceptance at junior college in 1934. *George Washington Gomez* tells the tale of a young man of that time, struggling through life and an educational system that was complex for a Tejano in a dual culture society. The parallels are inescapable.

Paredes worked his way through school with a job at a grocery store and as a cub reporter for the *Brownsville Herald,* starting at $11.40 a week. With his associates degree in hand, he continued working at the newspaper and started publishing his poetry in *La Prensa*. He was getting paid to write in two languages. He also bought his first guitar from a co-worker at the grocery and taught himself to play. There was a brief marriage to Brownsville singer Chelo Silva, and the two performed together on occasion.

With the war effort ramping up, Paredes left the Valley to work for Pan American Airways installing .50 caliber machine guns into their aircraft under a very quiet contract with the War Department. Because Pan Am had a much more extensive cross-ocean fleet of planes that the military, the airline was readying to take part in the American war effort. When Americo Paredes enlisted in the U.S. Army, he was sent to the Pacific as a journalist for *Stars and Stripes*. Among his assignments was an interview with Hideki Tojo, the imprisoned former head of the Japanese Army. At the end of his service, he remained in Asia working as a journalist and writing for himself when time allowed. While in postwar Japan, Parades met and married Amelia Nagamine, who was half-Japanese and half-Uruguayan. The couple was forced to overcome visa problems before they moved back to the United States in 1949.

At age 35, Americo Paredes became attached to the institution with which he would be most closely identified. In the first half of the 1950s he earned a bachelors, masters, and Ph.D. from the University of Texas at Austin. He was reportedly the first Tejano to get a doctorate from UT. He served as a graduate teaching assistant, and within a year of gaining his Ph.D., he was offered a tenure-track professorship in the English Department. Two decades later, he was given faculty status in Anthropology, as well. All along the journey, Paredes continued to write short stories and poems.

In 1958, University of Texas Press published Parades' doctoral dissertation as a book. *With a Pistol in His Hand* examined a story that had passed into border folklore as a corrido, a traditional Mexican border ballad that often told of a hero's exploits or a bandit's escapades. Along the Rio Grande, the subjects were sometimes the same. Paredes had been in love with the corrido as an art form since childhood, and at UT Austin, he made it a field of study.

A cabinet card of Gregorio Cortez with a handwritten account of his capture (Texas State Library and Archives)

The book revolved around the tale of Gregorio Cortez, and it told of his life and the various interpretations of his legacy. Cortez, who lived a few miles from the town of Kenedy in Karnes County was questioned about a crime by the sheriff and two deputies at his family's residence in 1901. One Cortez brother had served a penitentiary sentence for horse theft, another had been charged for that offense but released, and the broad brush of local opinion had tarred Gregorio. Thanks to a series of bad interpretations on the part of a somewhat bilingual deputy, gunfire erupted from the lawmen. Sheriff Morris seriously wounded Romaldo Cortez and narrowly missed Gregorio who responded by shooting the sheriff dead. The ten day manhunt ranged across several Texas Counties. Rangers were brought to South Texas by train. In Gonzales County, a shootout left that sheriff and a ranch owner dead. With each passing day, the Tejano community grew more sympathetic to the slippery outlaw, and Whites, livid about the sheriff-killer, retaliated with violence. At least nine people of Mexican descent were killed in the resulting tensions. Legal defense groups were formed, Cortez escaped a huge lynch mob, and was he pardoned in 1913. A corrido about the affair surfaced immediately after the killing of Sheriff Morris, and the Cortez mythology grew from there.

Americo Paredes challenged the Anglo narrative about Cortez and told some uncomfortable truths about such state icons as the Texas Rangers and some of the more racist narratives of Walter Prescott Webb. One Ranger threatened to kill Paredes for tarnishing the agency's name.

The book sold fewer than 1000 copies over the first seven years of its existence, but things changed with the emergence of the Chicano movement in the later 1960s and early 1970s. Ultimately because of that awakening, Americo Paredes expanded the teaching narrative at the University of Texas, just as Tatcho Mindiola was doing at almost the same time at the University of Houston. Paredes was instrumental in founding the university's Center for Intercultural Folklore and later the Center for Mexican American Studies. His earlier work was rediscovered, and Paredes became a bit of an underground hero. *With a Pistol in His Hand* became required reading for several college courses in Texas and beyond. In 1982, the book was made into a movie starring Edward James Olmos.

During his academic work, Paredes proved that the simple corrido was not a Mexican invention, but rather a product of the border culture of the Rio Grande. He frequently brought a guitar to class and taught via music. He trained generations of folklorists and continues to influence Mexican American writers and historians. Many have said that Americo Paredes provided a model for their work to stand on its own rather than strive for assimilation into more Anglo-centric corners of academia.

There were honors that came to him for his work. He was awarded a Guggenheim Fellowship in 1962 and the Charles Frankel Prize from the National Endowment for the Humanities in 1989. A year later, he received the highest honor offered by the Republic of Mexico to a foreign citizen, the Orden de Aguila Azteca, the Order of the Aztec Eagle.

Two less conventional pieces of recognition and appreciation were also given. In 1995, Austin singer Tish Hinojosa, wrote a song for him called "Con Su Pluma en Su Mano," "With His Pen in His Hand." Just three years later, the Austin Independent School District handed him a shovel to break ground for the Americo Paredes Middle School. It is one of at least three public schools that bear his name. Paredes died in Austin on Cinco de Mayo 1999.

Chapter Twenty-Six

The Gonzales Cannon

R evisionist history is a wonderful thing. When done correctly, it brings new sources into the conversation or debunks mythology steeped in bygone notions of morality and race. Just because history is long past does not guarantee that it was recorded correctly. Often the closer one gets to an event's time period, the more axes there were to grind, so the addition of both new information and time can offer a clearer picture.

The famous Come and Take It cannon at Gonzales is a wonderful example of the positivity of revisionist history. Though the flag with those words can be annoyingly ubiquitous in the Lone Star State, far fewer Texans than desired have a grasp on the events surrounding it. Even fewer know the story of the artifact itself.

A large majority of leaders and citizens in Texas at the start of 1835 were against the idea of declaring independence from Mexico. Most wanted to see a restoration of the Mexican Constitution of 1824 and the recognition of Texas as a state separate from Coahuila, but as things unfolded that year, thoughts began to change. Still, even many of those who longed to see Texas as an American state, did not believe the time was right. They did not think it was a fight Texians could win.

There had been plenty of agitation by the discontented or naturally recalcitrant. Texians had attacked Mexican troops. They were not paying taxes or import tariffs, and they were smuggling all the time. The Mexican government finally said enough is enough.

Stephen F. Austin had always been the voice of reason in the foreign colonies of Northeast Mexico, but he had been imprisoned in Mexico City for suspected treason. Antonio Lopez de Santa Anna, once a hero to the liberal Federalists in Texas and elsewhere in the Mexican Republic, had switched sides to lead the conservative Centralist faction that served the church, the army, and the wealthy. By the time Austin was released from confinement and made his way back to Texas in August 1835, his taste for compromise had evaporated, left behind with barred windows and prison rats. Both sides knew that Texas was a powder keg whose fuse had been lit.

Around the same time, General Martin Perfecto de Cos led a Centralist army into San Antonio de Bexar with orders to make the unruly Coahuilans and Texians behave and to arrest all those opposing Presidente Santa Anna on both sides of the Rio Grande. He joined Colonel Domingo Ugartechea, the military commandant for Coahuila y Texas. Ugartechea, like Santa Anna himself, had been part of the Spanish Army that brutally put down the rebellion at San Antonio in 1813. Perhaps his biggest role in the unfolding drama was to dispatch Lieutenant Francisco Castaneda to Gonzales.

It had come to Ugartechea's attention that four years prior, the garrison at San Antonio had loaned a six-pounder cannon to empresario Green DeWitt so that the colonists at Gonzales would have better defense against Indian raids. Given the delicate political situation, the colonel believed it better to retrieve the artillery piece lest it be used against his own forces. Castaneda, the son of a Spanish turned Mexican soldier, had lived in the Alamo mission complex as part of the military company there. He understood the Texians well. When he left with 100 mounted dragoons, he was given orders not to provoke a major conflict.

When Castaneda and his men reached the west bank of the Guadalupe, they found the river in flood. To make matters worse, the small band of Texians had pulled all of the possible ferry boats to their side. Communicating by shouts or messages swum across the swollen river, Castaneda made his demand for the cannon, and the Texians stalled for time. Soon, the frantic messengers returned with reinforcements from towns like Columbus and Mina, now Bastrop. When the Texian force had grown to about 140, Lt. Castaneda decided to return to San Antonio empty handed.

The Texians who had ridden to Gonzales were there for a fight, and they resolved not to go home without one. It was the Texians who crossed the river hauling the very cannon, now mounted on wheels, that Castaneda had come to retrieve. Following the Mexican army unit about nine miles through pitch darkness, the Texians rode into Castaneda's camp just east of the present community of Cost. When a Mexican sentry fired his musket, a Texian horse reared up and threw his rider, who hit the ground and broke his nose. That might be considered the first casualty of the Texas Revolution.

As the sun rose on the foggy morning of October 2, 1835, Castaneda rode out under a flag of truce. The Texian representative, John Henry Moore, briefly tried to entice Castaneda, a Federalist himself, to switch sides, but the soldier stuck to his orders and duty. Upon reaching their respective lines, Moore ordered the cannon fired at the Centralist troops on top of the rise, and the Texians unfolded a painted banner that read

"Come and Take It." As historian Stephen Hardin said, "If they were serious about it, they would have painted it in Spanish."

The cannon boomed and rifles cracked. Two Mexican soldados fell dead before Castaneda and his mounted men bugged out for the safety of San Antonio. The Battle of Gonzales was really a small skirmish. Though blood had been spilled between the two sides on several occasions before, it is considered the start of the Texas Revolution because there is a direct through line to the Alamo, Goliad and San Jacinto.

The same Texians who gathered at Gonzales at the start of October 1835 left almost at once to take the fight to Bexar. There they laid siege to Perfecto de Cos's troops who were headquartered at the Alamo mission complex. Texians tightened the noose around him with a series of fights, and Cos finally capitulated in December. Both sheer logic and a voluminous historical record shows that those Texians, spoiling for a fight and headed to battle, took the contested cannon with them to San Antonio. It joined other artillery pieces the Texians had gathered from Harrisburg and Matagorda.

After the victory in December, all of those cannons, along with one captured from the Mexicans at the Battle of Concepcion and several others, were incorporated into the artillery defenses at the Alamo, by then left under the command of J.C. Neill. In turn, they were recaptured by Santa Anna's army, along with the entire mission complex, in the predawn hours of March 6.

In 1936, a 100-year flood unearthed a small cannon on the banks of Sandy Creek. The location fit a reminiscence of early Texas memoirist Noah Smithwick to a tee. Smithwick said the Texians had abandoned a cannon there on their march to San Antonio after its carriage failed. Research was compiled about 1980, and the good folks of Gonzales dearly held that the small cannon thereafter displayed in the Gonzales Memorial Museum, the one dug out at Sandy Creek, was the Come and Take it cannon. It is not.

Gregg Dimmick, a medical doctor in Wharton, is a passionate historian of the Texas Revolution. His work on the Mexican retreat after San Jacinto was groundbreaking. Along the way, Dr. Dimmick taught himself to read 19th century Spanish handwriting and poured through Mexican Army archives for 1835 and 1836, documents largely unavailable to American researchers for decades. Among those papers and volumes, Dimmick found plenty about the borrowed cannon at Gonzales.

For starters, it was big. Made to shoot a six-pound ball, it weighed about 600 or 700 pounds. Dimmick unearthed a receipt and letter showing when a wagon driver named Tumlinson had brought the cannon from San Antonio in March 1832. That information joined a dozen other Texian accounts of the action at Gonzales and the subsequent military events during the Siege of Bexar. All of the documentation showed that it was a big, bronze cannon that the Mexicans wanted back if the Texas trouble turned to war.

Around this time, an archaic Spanish word found its way into the mouths of Texas military historians. Long vanished, the term is esmeril. It denoted a small artillery piece that did not require wheels and a gun carriage. It should be carried on the back of a mule or horse. The piece might be a signal cannon to summon men in an emergency, or it could be quickly carried out to chase marauding Indians. Subsequent research showed that the Spanish and Mexicans had at least seven of these small brass pieces in Texas, and that the one in Gonzales, handling a ball of just a quarter pound, was perhaps the smallest of them all.

The Gonzales esmeril displayed at the
Gonzales memorial Museum (Library of
Congress)

The expanded story and the research of Gregg Dimmick were first
included in a documentary called *Washington on the Brazos and the
Politics of Revolution* that was produced and directed by the author of
this book. Not long after, in 2014, historian Jim Woodrick released a
wonderfully detailed volume about the two cannons. The proof that
the famous Come and Take It cannon was not the small piece in the
Gonzales Museum was undeniable. That did not make it well received.

Woodrick and Dimmick saw a silver lining. Documentation had also
been found showing that the Texians had both a medium piece and the
esmeril, so both artillery pieces were present at the skirmish in Gonzales.
It was cold comfort to many of the old timers there. At the documentary premiere in Gonzales, a handful of locals stormed out during the
post-screening discussion. Gradually, led by a man named Chris Kapp-
meyer who was passionate about Gonzales history, some people came
around.

Learning that a long held belief is not true can be jarring, but it is
necessary to maintain an accurate understanding of our past. We should
always seek the truth in history whether it is what someone wants to hear
or not.

Chapter Twenty-Seven

Benjamin Franklin Yoakum

M any southern Texas communities that started around the start of the 20th century were first populated by Midwesterners who bought their new land sight unseen. One of the biggest lures for those Iowans and Nebraskans was the chance to plant fruit orchards. The Houston suburbs of Pasadena, La Porte, Deer Park, and the aptly named Pearland are cases in point. When it comes to the complete transformation of a region, those places pale in comparison to what was started by the transportation and land dreams of Benjamin Franklin Yoakum.

Yoakum was a railroad man. Born in Tehuacana in Limestone County, he started carrying chain for a survey crew at age 20. He used his smarts and savvy to amass control of multiple lines by the start of the 20th century and came relatively close to challenging the great behemoth Southern Pacific for control of the business between New Orleans and Houston then down to Brownsville. Though Yoakum gathered a tidy fortune for himself, his lasting contribution relates to the potential he saw along the lower Rio Grande Valley.

The Valley, as Texans know it, consists of four counties: Cameron, Hidalgo, Willacy, and Starr. The first two are the most populous, and they were settled earliest. Jose de Escandon colonized the area starting in 1749 when he subdivided and sold land. Today's Cameron and Willacy counties were sold by Escandon as large land grants, intended for ranching, of many leagues apiece. Today's Hidalgo County was mostly long porciones roughly ¾ mile in width that ran 11 to 16 miles north from the Rio Grande River. There things stayed for a century.

In the Treaty of Guadalupe Hidalgo at the end of the Mexican War, all doubt was removed over ownership of the land between the Nueces River and Rio Grande. Mexicans who owned land now firmly in Texas were allowed to keep it. Though Brownsville became the United States' most crucial entrée to Mexico, the land of the Lower Rio Grande Valley remained mostly large ranches. Cows and sheep vastly outnumbered humans.

Two glaring problems with the Valley served as impediments to growth. The first was water. The area averages about 25 inches of rain per year, but it can be sporadic. Growing crops was dicey. The other was transportation. There was one single 150-mile-long dirt road that led from Matamoros and Brownsville north to the rest of the United States. Zachary Taylor's men had constructed a military road connecting the forts along the north bank of the river, but it was a track even worse than the other road. To move up the Valley, most people crossed at Brownsville and took the Mexican National Railway as far along as needed before ferrying back across to Texas. Port Isabel offered the only way out by boat. An 1889 hurricane had changed the course of the river and created so many sandbars that navigation upriver was all but impossible. When a railroad reached Laredo in 1885, Brownsville and the Valley began to lose its shine.

Ben Yoakum, already successful as a railroad executive, felt that there was money to be made. Yoakum had gained experience from a variety of lines. As general manager of the San Antonio & Aransas Pass, working for Uriah Lott, he had the town of Yoakum named in his honor in the 1880s. He followed that with three years as general manager of the Gulf, Colorado & Santa Fe. It was during the decade of the 1880s that B.F. Yoakum first saw the Rio Grande Valley and became enchanted with the rich possibilities. Then in 1897, he became vice president and GM of the Frisco Line. By 1904, Yoakum was chairman of the board. A year later, still in charge of the Frisco, he was named chairman of another major Midwest line, the Chicago, Rock Island & Pacific. Throughout those years, Yoakum was working with a capital investment firm in St. Louis to expand and acquire enough track and stock to challenge the venerable Southern Pacific with Houston as a hub.

Benjamin Franklin Yoakum about
1900

He saw the key as expanding freight and passenger service to Brownsville, but since no railroad existed past the Corpus Christi area, Yoakum would have to build it. He chartered the St. Louis, Brownsville & Mexico Railway to run from Houston all the way to the Rio Grande River including a railroad bridge to Matamoros in partnership with the Mexican government. Along with dozens of other stops, it provided a viable land route between Corpus and the Valley for the first time ever. Several South Texas towns were created as the track building worked its way south. Those included Kingsville, Robstown, Bishop, Sarita, Raymondville, Lyford, Sebastian, and Harlingen. The first through passenger service to Houston from the border city began in April 1908.

By that time, Yoakum and his main partner, Uriah Lott, had created a system called the Gulf Coast Lines. By buying several small and troubled regional railroads, they planned to cover South Texas and create a network that ran from Mexico City to Chicago. In an oddity, since the GCL holdings ran east to New Orleans all trains leaving from Houston toward Brownsville were labeled as westbound as opposed to southbound.

In addition to his grand railroad dreams, B.F. Yoakum recognized great agricultural potential at the southern end of his new railroad, commonly called the Brownie. He collected a group of St. Louis investors to form the American Rio Grande Land and Irrigation Company with a capital stock of $1.25 million. The company purchased 250,000 acres plus the townsite of Mercedes. Historically, the site was part of the 18th century Spanish grant to Juan Jose Ynojosa de Balli. It was operated as a ranch by the Cavazos Family until it was purchased by a developer named Lon Hill, Jr.. Hill turned a tidy profit by quickly selling it to American Rio Grande for their Valley headquarters.

The company operated at first out of a boxcar that sat on a siding of its Sam Fordyce rail spur. They soon constructed a two-story building and an electrical plant. The plant was critical since their entire plan hinged on irrigation. The idea of irrigating Valley land was not original. A Frenchman named George Brulay had done it for growing sugar nine miles below Brownsville. A handful of individual farmers had built ditches, mostly for sugar or rice, but larger scale plans never got past the paper stage until a company out of Brownsville built a pumping station not long before Yoakum's railroad arrived.

Away from the townsite at Mercedes, ARGL&I built a settling basin, a large canal with several branches and a pumping plant on the river. The company set restrictions for their town: commercial buildings must be brick, stone or concrete, and residences had to cost a minimum of $2,000. They then set about luring northern buyers to the tropical paradise with an extensive publicity campaign. Prospective buyers could visit the region by rail if they wanted a look around. Part of the advertisement plan was to send fruit and sugar cane to distant fairs, displaying what the Valley could do.

With their irrigated fields, ARG first promoted the area as perfect for grape growing then quickly added citrus fruit and vegetables. John McAllen was already growing 40 varieties of grapes on his nearby ranch. Success was swift. The first hotel popped up in Mercedes in 1907. A year later, the town had a population of 1,000 plus a school, feedstore, bank, and newspaper.

Benjamin Franklin Yoakum and Uriah Lott never realized the grandest of their railroad dreams. In 1913, the Frisco Line went into bankruptcy, and the Interstate Commerce Commission ordered the sale of Yoakum's other rail projects to pay the debts. The Gulf Coast Lines were acquired by the Missouri Pacific in 1925.

What Yoakum started in the Valley, however, could not be stopped. By 1920, the irrigation system his company created had three large canals, five pumping plants, reservoirs and settling basins, and extensive drainage works. Most importantly, other entrepreneurs, capitalizing on transportation and shipping provided by the Brownie, were rapidly following suit. Valley ranches were subdivided, and northerners were actively lured to southmost Texas for the next twenty years.

Texans know that one particular product came to be most associated with the Valley. In 1914, a Nebraska developer named John Shary bought 16,000 acres and planted white, seeded grapefruit. The first commercial yield, packed in onion boxes, was shipped north in 1920. It took another decade before a grower discovered a red grapefruit growing on a pink grapefruit tree. Redder bud mutations continued popping up, often named for the farmer who owned the trees. Any good Texan can tell you that Ruby Red Grapefruit from the Rio Grande Valley is the world's most delicious. It is also the state's most lucrative fruit crop. In 1993, the Texas Ruby Red was named the official Texas state fruit.

Chapter Twenty-Eight

Ignacio Zaragoza

The next time someone cries "cultural appropriation" on Cinco de Mayo, tell them that the hero of that celebrated battle in Mexican history was a native-born Texan.

Granted, Ignacio Zaragoza did not stay in Texas very long. Even before the Texians seeking separation from Mexico won their surprising victory at San Jacinto, Miguel Zaragoza Valdes and Maria Theresa de Jesus Martinez Seguin left their home in the village of La Bahia near the presidio in Goliad and resettled across the Rio Grande in Matamoras. Ignacio, the second child of what would eventually become a family of eight, was a mere five years old.

The Veracruz-born Miguel was an infantryman in the Mexican Army. He and Maria Theresa had met when his regiment was posted at San Antonio in 1825. Four years later, the unit was sent to Goliad. Maria was pregnant with Ignacio. The military family was used to relocating. There may have been a short stay in San Luis Potosi prior to Matamoras, but in 1844, they settled in Monterrey, Nuevo Leon. Ignacio entered a seminary there on the path to priesthood.

He was still in his teens when his nation was at war with the United Stated from 1846 to 1848, and his new hometown was the site of a major battle. It was enough for him to want to leave the seminary to follow in his father's military footsteps, but his pleas to enlist as a cadet were denied. Zaragoza was not accepted into the army of Nuevo Leon until 1853, initially serving as sergeant but soon becoming captain of his regiment.

Politics in 19th century Mexico was always a moving target, and no one was more slippery and resilient than Antonio Lopez de Santa Anna. He had famously switched from the liberal Federalists to the conservative Centralists, setting off revolutions in Texas, Zacatecas, and the Yucatan. Periodically, Santa Anna left the government in disgrace or defeat only to return. The 1854 Plan de Ayutla was a coup to overthrow him and reestablish a republic. Newly minted army officer Ignacio Zaragoza joined this liberal cause.

The successful fight became a catalyst for other Mexican rebellions and installed presidents who brought liberal reforms to curtail the power and government budget of the church. This War of the Reform was an ongoing conflict with conservative troops, and with Zaragoza taking part, it ended with liberal victory.

The conservatives in Mexico refused to accept their losses. In attempting to cling to some semblance of legitimacy, they borrowed heavily from the Europeans. Understandably, the newly elected president of the Mexican Republic, Benito Juarez, suspended payments of these dubious debts. To the French in particular, it was the excuse they had been seeking. The French enticed Spain and Britain to join them in a tripartite expedition, and their forces reached the port of Veracruz in 1862. The Europeans were gleefully aware that the United States was preoccupied with its Civil War and was rendered wholly incapable of enforcing the Monroe Doctrine to keep European powers out of the Americas.

Once it became undeniable that the French aims went far beyond debt renegotiation, the British and Spanish withdrew from the scene. It left France a clear field to turn Mexico into a satellite state. President Juarez quickly organized a military response and placed General Ignacio Zaragoza, by the Minister of the Army, in command.

The Mexican army outnumbered the French, but their equipment was far inferior, and their battle experience was almost non-existent. Mexican military might had been sapped by the Americans barely a decade earlier. Zaragoza led 4,000 men east to meet the French with hopes of giving his troops a taste of gunfire. The two small armies met at the Summit of Acultzingo. Surprisingly, it was the French who suffered almost 500 casualties to the Mexican's 50. When Zaragoza returned to this headquarters, he inspired his men by saying, "The French fight well, but our soldiers are better at killing."

Falling back to the stronghold of Puebla, east southeast of Mexico City, Zaragoza placed garrisons at two high-ground forts, Loreto and Guadalupe. He kept his last 3,500 men to confront the French directly.

Zaragoza's opponent across the battlefield, General Ferdinand La-trille, was certainly not lacking in overconfidence and vanity. He wrote: "We are so superior to the Mexicans in organization, discipline, race, morale and refinement of sensibilities, that from this moment, in command of our 6,000 brave soldiers, I am the master of Mexico".

At mid-morning on May 5, 1862, Zaragoza's Mexican soldiers and indigenous Zacapoaxtla forces beat back the initial French attack. The Mexicans positioned themselves in the dip between the two fortified hills while artillery from above pounded the interventionist army. A charge by French Zouaves reached far up Cerro de Guadalupe only to be beaten back by the rifle corps. Another attack from French marines was repulsed by Mexican bayonets. Finally, the Pachuca Guard charged on horseback and drove the French into retreat by late afternoon. Zaragoza wrote President Juarez that "the arms of the nation have been covered with glory."

General Ignacio Zaragoza (Library of Congress)

The victory at Puebla was a sweet one, but it was a case of winning a battle and losing a war. French Emperor Napoleon III was not easily deterred. His reinforcements eventually numbered 39,000, and though it took a year, the French and their allied Mexican ultra-conservatives took the City of Puebla and chased the people's government of Benito Juarez. The church, the army, and the wealthy were restored to power by 1863. The followers of Juarez and the duly elected republic fled north, moving the capital first to San Luis Potosi, then Monterrey, Chihuahua City, and finally El Paso de Norte, known today as the City of Juarez. Financial support and some volunteers from the United States bolstered the Juarez forces.

Death in the 19th century was ever looming, and it came for Mexico's newest hero on September 8th, a mere four months after his great battlefield victory. Ignacio Zaragoza died of typhoid fever at the achingly young age of 33. He did not live to see the right-wing monarchists ultimately defeated and their imported Emperor Maximillian put in front of a firing squad in 1867.

Zaragoza's success at Puebla survives him to this day, however. Cinco de Mayo was celebrated not only in Mexico but in Mexican communities in California and Texas in the 1860s. Border towns like Del Rio and Eagle Pass held Cinco de Mayo fiestas in the 1890s, drawing some of the Anglo neighbors to the party. Even after the significance of the day died away south of the Rio Grande, it clung to importance for Mexican Americans along the Texas border. When the influx of Mexican immigrants rose dramatically during their Revolution of the 1910s and 20s, mutualistas, aid societies which also happened to sell insurance policies, formed in the large cities of Southern Texas. In Houston, the annual Cinco de Mayo celebration given by the Sociedad de Benito Juarez on Navigation Boulevard was a noteworthy party.

The Zaragoza home is representationally preserved on the grounds of the Presidio la Bahia at Goliad. The three-room, adobe house, in typical South Texas style of the Tejanos, was a crumbling mess when Texas Parks and Wildlife took to reconstruct it in the 1970s. Colonel James Fannin had tried to destroy the military housing near the presidio prior to his attempted flight from General Urrea in March 1836.

The Texas celebration of Goliad's most famous son began long before the state turned his birthplace into a museum. The first General Zaragoza Society is believed to have been started at Los Olmos in Bee County in 1886. The one in Goliad dates to 1944 when they began what remains an annual Fiesta Zaragoza near May 5th.

Tejano scholar and writer Americo Paredes wrote in the 1950s of a ballad performed by a guitarrero named Onofre Cardenas at a Cinco de Mayo celebration in the Zapata County town of San Ygnacio in 1867, just five years after the battle itself. Paredes translated a lyric as: "God save thee, brave Zaragoza, unconquerable general of the border; I and all free men salute your flag that waved unceasingly in Puebla."

Chapter Twenty-Nine

Crystal City Internment Camp

B etween 1942 until 1948, more than two years after WWII ended, six thousand civilians from across both American continents were interned at a large camp roughly 120 miles southwest of San Antonio, not far from the Texas – Mexican border. The Crystal City camp held Japanese and Japanese Americans, Germans and German Americans, and a few Italians and Italian Americans, and each group developed its own camp culture. It was officially a secret, and Jan Jarboe Russell, who wrote the definitive book about the camp, called it "as close to a Siberia as we had in America."

Like other internment camps in the United States, Crystal City was far from the East and West Coasts where we had important military installations and port infrastructure. There was the added benefit that the place had been a migrant camp prior to Pearl Harbor. The government added 50 more acres to bring the total space up to 290 acres behind high fences, armed guard towers, and barbed wire.

The internees were called enemy aliens, and what differentiated Crystal City from the inmates at many other camps was that there were fathers. Unlike the 120,000 Japanese taken from the West Coast to War Relocation camps that were a total mixed bag, Crystal City held nothing but families. In thousands of cases around the United States and beyond, the German, Italian, or Japanese born men were simply arrested and hauled off, leaving their families lost and struggling. At Crystal City, families could be reunited if they volunteered to remain behind the wires and under the watch of armed guards at a place where the penalty for escape was death. No one at Crystal City ever tested that.

Thirty-six thousand men were arrested under the Enemy Alien Act early in WWII. Arrest did not require that a crime be committed, a person simply had to fall into one of three criteria. No charges were pressed, the target simply got a knock on the door one day or was roused from their sleep one night. Category A was the most easily understandable. Those were members of the American Nazi Party or an organization that swore loyalty to the Empire of Japan. To be labeled an enemy in Category B depended largely on one's occupation. Community leaders were taken so they could not rally other foreigners to the enemy cause, so Buddhist and Shinto ministers were immediate suspects. Engineers who could blow up a bridge and photographers who could surveil military installations were rounded up.

Category C should have been the most chilling to American sensibilities. Those were people interned solely based on the accusation of a neighbor who felt that the foreigner next door did not appear loyal. Once arrested, the term of confinement was indefinite. Lawyers or appeals did nothing. Enemy Alien fathers had very little choice about what to do. The only way that they could bring their families together was to voluntarily agree to be reunited at Crystal City.

In violation of the Geneva Convention, the Crystal City camp mixed nationalities. The German families came first, but when space was needed to house so many Japanese, another section of the camp was added. Those two sides did not generally mix. The dozen or so Italian families were scattered about. Since some internees were brought from Allied countries in South America, many people spoke Spanish instead of English, German, or Japanese.

Life for the internees at Crystal City was highly regimented. The day began with mandatory roll call, and everyone was required to tumble from the barracks and show their faces. An American flag was hauled up the pole every morning. All of the adult internees had a job. They worked on camp projects or maintenance; they made the food or grew the food. Some foodstuff was brought in from outside, so no one went hungry.

Shizuko Ina waits in line to be assigned a family number at a War Relocation Center in San Francisco in April 1942. Shizuko and her husband, Itaru Ina, were interned in Utah and Northern California before being separated in 1945. They were later reunited at the Crystal City Internment Camp in April 1946. (Library of Congress)

The children, almost all of whom were natural born American citizens, went to school. There were three choices – an American School
taught by certified Texas teachers, a German School taught by those
camp internees, and a Japanese School taught by Japanese internees. One
of the biggest issues in the camp became a chasm of disconnect between
the Americanized children and their fathers. The grown men were not
only bitter and angry about their imprisonment, but they were rendered
even more impotent by being forced to surrender much of the family
decision making to the U.S. government. The conflicts were especially
pronounced between the fathers and their older sons.

Since almost none of the internees were from South Texas, the concept
of summer heat that approached 125 degrees was difficult to grasp. Fat
rattlesnakes and angry scorpions were a new challenge. At the camp
hospital, sixty percent of cases were related to depression. There were
suicide attempts. The loss of liberty took a mental toll.

Stress was mitigated by physical activity. There was a swimming pool
built by German internees. Football teams were formed, and eventually the Germans played the Japanese, but the size difference favored
the German boys every time. The Japanese held judo and kendo contests, and the Germans became enamored with baseball. The adults on
each side busied themselves with their respective councils who served as
spokespersons to the top camp officer, Joseph O'Rourke, who was an
Irishman from Buffalo, New York. The Japanese elders' first big request
was for tofu. That meant nothing to the Americans in charge, but a hut
was provided for use as a tofu factory to be staffed by internees. Though
there were initial difficulties with obtaining the right type of sea-based
soy, it did turn out tofu for the Japanese. On the opposite side of the
camp, the Germans requested beer. The initial response from O'Rourke
was to allow an alcohol-free beer garden, but eventually, a still provided

real beer. Though there was a prescribed limit of once a week, that was largely broken.

The Japanese boys developed a nightly custom of strolling the perimeter of their camp section and serenading the guards who were stationed there. A favorite tune was the popular *Don't Fence Me In*.

The camp at Crystal City was sealed off from the outside world. Newspapers, radios, and magazines were not allowed. There was a movie night, but films on offer were mostly comedies from the 1930s. Outgoing letters were censored, and incoming literature, even comic books, were gone through with a razor blade to cut out newsworthy bits. The news blackout was so successful that at the end of the war, many of the German and Japanese fathers refused to believe that their countrymen had been defeated.

One of the saddest memories that author Jan Russell repeatedly heard when she interviewed Japanese children who grew up at Crystal City revolved around the end of the school year in 1944. The American School had a number of children who had completed a course of study and were ready to receive diplomas. O'Rourke decreed that to celebrate the occasion there would be a prom. The Japanese council's protest that good girls did not dance was overruled. This was an American school, and American customs would be observed. On the night of the prom, the Japanese men arrived and broke up the festivities. It remained a painful point for many even 50 years later.

Before the camp opened, Crystal City, Texas had a population of about 5,000, but the government installation raised it to 13,000. The town went from relying on only agriculture or the spinach canning plant to suddenly having jobs available. That was particularly true for the women who could work as translators, censors, and the omnipresent surveillance officers. Local women helped organize the camp's sewing, and all locals who worked there enjoyed more plentiful food than what they might get otherwise.

Perhaps the worst of all of it for the internee families came as the result of being a collateral part of the bigger war picture. Crystal City became the center of President Roosevelt's prisoner exchange policy. Many of the people who voluntarily agreed to be interned, also voluntarily agreed to repatriate if the government needed them. Thousands of them did. There were four large prisoner exchanges from Crystal City. In 1943 and '44, several thousand Japanese internees were traded into Japan for Americans there. Then came two enormous swaps for the Germans, one in '44 and one in 1945. The United States sent American born children into the world's worst war zones. They were just children who got caught up as a consequence of being in the internment camp with their parents. Despite the fact that their government had betrayed them, all of the relocated youngsters made it back to the United States and rebuilt their lives as Americans.

Chapter Thirty

Jovita Idar

I n 2023, Jovita Idar was celebrated when her portrait was placed on a United States quarter, but her name was little known to people outside of Laredo's Mexican-American community until this century.

She was born in Laredo in 1885, and from childhood, she was exposed to both the newspaper business and political activism. This was courtesy of her father who owned one of several Spanish-language newspapers in Laredo, *La Cronica*. In an overwhelmingly Catholic community, Jovita's parent bypassed the inadequate public school on offer and sent her to a Methodist institution called the Holding Institute. After graduating there, she earned a teaching certificate and took a job in the tiny Webb County town of Los Ojuelos. The poverty that she observed firsthand reinforced her desire to hasten positive changes in the Southwest Texas borderlands.

She felt that her best opportunity to contribute was back with the family newspaper. All of the Idars were of the same mind. Her start in the newspaper business coincided with extreme violence against Mexicans and Tejanos along the Rio Grande. *La Cronica* had already been taking on the racism, lynchings, and school segregation. They also took issue with the Catholic Church's poor treatment of women. Having just witnessed the uneven offerings of education, Jovita wrote that the children of Mexican descent should be learning not just about Washington and Lincoln but about Hidalgo and Juarez so they could proudly see the accomplishments of people who looked like them. She wanted bilingual education and better school opportunities for girls. She wrote: "Educate a woman, and you educate a family."

Unlike her father and brothers, Jovita initially wrote under the pen names of Ave Negra or Astrea. She surmised that might make her message be better received.

In 1911, the Idar family organized a cross-border conference that they called El Primer Congreso Mexicanista. The men and women who attended El Congreso for several days in Laredo were people who wanted to fight for the fair and equal treatment of Tejanos and improved economic opportunities. Energized by seeing women as active participants in the events, Jovita and others formed La Liga Femenil Mexicanista (the League of Mexican Women). She was chosen as their first president.

La Liga had both political and charitable goals. They worked for education in the Mexican border community, opening free bilingual schools and providing study sessions for women. She began a biweekly publication called *El Etudiante* that provided resources for bilingual teachers and carried a message against assimilationist Anglo-Americanized curriculums. Jovita wrote that "Woman must always seek to acquire useful and beneficial knowledge, for in modern times, she has broad horizons." Her writings and those of her family turned to the support of women's right to vote.

By the time the Mexicanist Congress met in Laredo, the revolution in Mexico was well underway, but by 1913, the killing had reached the border, including a bloody battle just across the river. Many Mexican American women were drawn to support the revolution in their ancestral land since the people were fighting for the same civic improvement and justice that they sought in South and West Texas. Leonor Villegas de Magnón, a close friend of Jovita Idar, founded a nursing organization called La Cruz Blanca, the White Cross, to serve the revolutionaries. Jovita crossed the border to help, traveling as far as Mexico City.

Jovita Idar during her journalistic career.

She returned to Texas and began writing for a paper named *El Progreso*, but one of the paper's articles landed them in very hot water. It was an editorial protesting President Woodrow Wilson's decision to send United States Army troops to the border. Wilson would soon develop a reputation for coming down oppressively hard on his critics, including with violence and arrest. In defense of his policies, the Army and the Texas Rangers took a close interest in *El Progreso's* printed attack.

Multiple Ranger battalions had been dispatched to the border to protect American interests against the Mexican Revolution, and, especially in the Rio Grande Valley to the south, they were also carrying on a bloody purge against people with brown skin whether they were Mexican or American.

With that violence as a backdrop, a band of Texas Rangers arrived with orders to destroy the newspaper *El Progreso*. They were met at the door to the small building by Jovita Idar who refused to let them pass to carry out their illegal mission. Though she talked them down that day, the following one saw the Rangers return. This time they smashed the printing press and the rest of the office to pieces, silencing their critic, at least for the moment.

Jovita Idar continued to write and advocate for her causes. After her father, Nicasio, died in 1914, Jovita and her brothers took over *La Crónica*. She also worked on other papers, including *El Eco del Golfo*, *La Luz*, *La Prensia*, and *Evolución,* a weekly newspaper she started herself in 1916 with a thousand-dollar printing press. At each stop, her activist passions continued to burn brightly. Her launch of *Evolucion* also placed Jovita Idar as the first woman newspaper publisher in Texas.

Jovita married Bartolo Juárez in 1917 and the couple moved to San Antonio a few years later. She turned over her paper *Evolucion* to her brother Eduardo. At age 35, her idealistic, muckraking journalistic career was over, but she continued to be involved in the fight. She helped establish a free kindergarten and taught hygiene and childcare classes to Latinas. Her writing was largely confined to a Methodist publication called *El Herald Christiano*. Jovita also worked as a translator at the county hospital and endeavored to get citizenship for Mexican immigrant workers. She and her husband founded a local Democratic Club and tried to positively impact life in San Antonio's Latino community.

Jovita's excellent writing was infused with striking optimism, and that is traced to her journalist father's egalitarian, can do views. That positivity reflects the way she and her siblings were raised. Take for example this short paragraph that she penned prior to WWI, half a dozen years before women even got the vote: "Women recognize their rights, proudly raise their chins, and face the struggle. The times of humiliation have passed, women are no longer men's servants but their equals, their partners." Would that were always true.

Gulf Coast

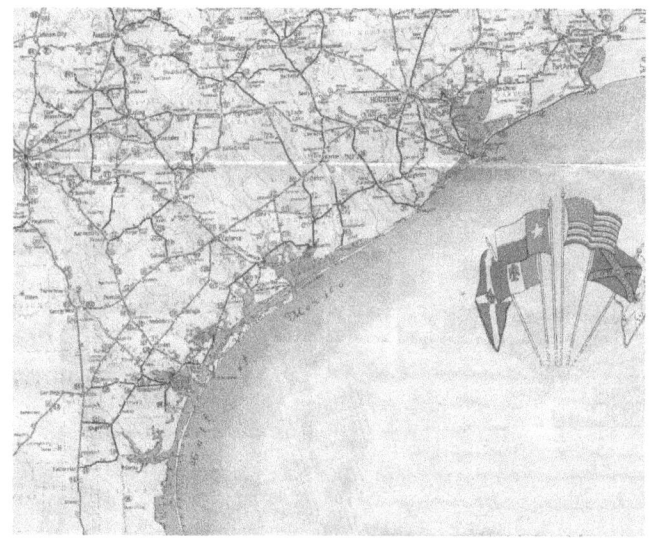

Chapter Thirty-One

Indianola

The first time in world history that mechanically refrigerated beef was ever shipped, it left from the port of Indianola. Steamship magnate Charles Morgan, the New Yorker who influenced Texas commerce as much as anyone in the last half of the 19th century, had commissioned a ship with a magical new hold. Double-walled and lined, 50 by 25 feet, it was cooled by a refrigerant that was "rapidly moved" by a steam-powered fan. The 30 beef carcasses that went aboard the *Agnes* in Indianola in July 1869 arrived in New Orleans perfectly cold. The *Picayune* reported that it was "pronounced by all who saw and tasted it to be the best beef ever brought into the market." It was a proverbial game changer. Safely transporting butchered beef meant carrying at least four times more peak product per shipload without having to dispose of live cattle waste.

Two years later, the same Charles Morgan had acquired controlling interest in a small railroad that connected Indianola to the Texas interior. It was an opportunity that presented itself after San Antonio businessmen vacillated over investments that would have greatly raised their city's profitability. Morgan secured a lease to bring his tracks right through the Indianola business district and ran it the length of his long wharf. It was one of several big steamship wharves that projected from the town's waterfront into Matagorda Bay.

The question, then, is how a city so prosperous could vanish from Texas maps.

The town of Indianola, initially called Indian Point, was founded by a Texas politician/ newspaper man, Samuel Addison White, and his friend on a stretch of beach on the west side of Matagorda Bay. White had acquired the property in 1842 and built a small house there. The land may have remained just another relaxing piece of bayside Texas if it had not been for immigration.

Two years before the town's official 1846 founding, Prince Karl of Solm Braunfels had declared that run of sand to be the official landing point for the thousands of immigrants that he intended to send from the German states to Central Texas. For a brief time, it was called Karlshafen.

Landowner White agreed to let the Prince's settlement venture, the Adelsverein, use a spot near his home as a staging ground, but no one was ready for the influx of several thousand Northern Europeans. If the immigrants were unprepared, the Prince was even more so. There was initially no housing for the new arrivals. A few of the foreigners saw opportunity right where they landed instead of following the somewhat bumbling prince to the settlement of New Braunfels. One arriving German started a lumber yard, and another quickly opened a bank in a tent.

Most of the task of capitalizing on the townsite fell to Anglo businessmen, and they had an early stroke of great luck. The United States declared war on Mexico, and they needed spots along the Texas Gulf Coast for rear supply of their armies. For over a year, heavy steam-powered vessels anchored off Indianola's beach and lightered men and materiel to shore. Unfortunately for the German immigrants wishing to head to the Comal, the Army also outbid for every haulage team and wagon in

Texas. One small group of young, newly arrived Germans made the best of it by joining the Army.

The military usage firmly established Indianola, still known as Indian Point and Brown's Addition, as an important port in the western Gulf of Mexico. The government gave an even larger boost when they constructed an Army depot to supply forts on the western frontier. A steamer began regularly scheduled stops for the Army, and they built their own wharf that extended 250 feet into the bay to a water depth of six and a half feet. The depot remained for 30 years.

By late 1847, there was a post office, and stagecoach service to the interior began a few months later. Within the next five years, there were hotels, stores of every kind, a newspaper, a city hospital, and soon, Indianola was the seat of the new Calhoun County. The bulk of the fresh development was three miles down the beach, closer to the mouth of the bay. By decade's end, the name Indianola was formally adopted, and the original settlement near Sam White's house became known as Old Town.

The growing city not only became a gateway to South Texas for Army troops, but more importantly, Indianola was earning a name as "The Mother of Western Texas." Since the railroads from Houston, Galveston, and the east did not reach Austin until 1871 and San Antonio until six years after that, the port at Indianola provided the shortest land route to where goods and people needed to be. It rather quickly became the second busiest port in the state, albeit a distant second. As more and more immigrants arrived, bound for the Texas interior, facilities to welcome them rose up, too. There were also warehouses and infrastructure to keep them supplied.

The United States Navy took an interest in Indianola during the Civil War. They blockaded the entire coast, but in October 1862, they came ashore and stayed for a month during which time they occupied the small rebel fort there and looted the town before leaving.

The first attempt at a railroad to Matagorda Bay fell victim to the war. As part of a scorched earth policy just after the first arrival of the Federal troops, Confederate General John Magruder ordered the burning of thousands of railroad ties at Indianola. The destruction may have slowed the logistics of moving inland, but Union forces returned at the end of the following year and occupied the town again. Though there were plans and movements to make an attack into Texas from the coast, the U.S. troops biggest accomplishment was holding the southerners' attention and causing general angst while they decisively won the war in the primary theaters to the east.

Indianola in September 1860

Indianola's demise lay in one simple fact: nothing lasts forever on the Texas Gulf Coast, particularly at sea level. Earlier small storms that delivered slight damage. After one such August blow, town officials even went so far as to congratulate themselves on the sanctity of the location they had chosen. They were very mistaken.

On September 15, 1875, the newly established Signal Service and weather observation post at Indianola, one of two on the Texas coast with Galveston being the other, got the first chance to record data from a Gulf hurricane. Once it passed Key West, the infant weather service could only guess at location and conditions until the Southwest Louisiana coast was brushed by wind and waves. Fully loaded ships leaving Indianola on the 13th and 14th sailed directly into the mouth of the storm.

When it made landfall, the town was especially full because out-of-towners crammed the hotels and boarding houses for a sensational murder trial. As the wind and water continued to increase, scared people jammed into the concrete-walled courthouse. Many looked to flee inland only to find the train at the depot rendered useless by saltwater that inundated the prairies behind the town for miles. Matagorda Bay came roaring through the Indianola streets, and when the water, which reached a height of 15 feet above normal at the bay shore, receded, only eight buildings were judged to be without damage.

Estimates of the dead ranged from 150 to 300. Bodies were strewn for 20 miles. In the first day after the storm, 60 of the bodies found could not be identified. Their faces had been obliterated by floating or flying debris. Some survived through the sheer luck of choosing the right structure in which to shelter.

Most of the residents lost the stomach for life at the beach no matter how lucrative it might be. The Morgan Line interests dithered about a rebuild but finally opted out. It and other economic engines would not return. The hardiest of townsfolk remained and rebuilt while others discussed relocating their homes and businesses to slightly higher ground on the north side of Powderhorn Lake. They never got the chance.

Another hurricane hit Indianola dead on just eleven years after the first one. Modern weather experts judge it as stronger than the Storm of 1875, but there was much less town to damage this time. What was there was wiped away by the wind and tidal surge, and for good measure, a fire brought about by crashing kerosene lamps. This time, even the weather Signal Station did not survive. By the following year, the site of the city had been abandoned and any remaining vestiges of structures were cannibalized for material.

Though the former residents of Indianola, at least those left alive, got the message that nature always triumphs, the same did not hold true everywhere. In late August, the *Galveston News* published a letter from someone calling themselves "Old Galvestonian." The writer smugly wrote, "It simply demonstrates that we are the safest place on the Texas coast…Galveston cannot be overflowed."

Chapter Thirty-Two

Roy Benavidez

Though some may equal it, no story of bravery could surpass that of El Campo's Roy Benavidez. He overcame obstacles from early childhood: poverty, bullying, and abuse because of his ethnicity and short stature. Like other Mexican Americans, Benavidez was refused service in some places and ate many meals from the back door of a café. He responded by developing toughness and an inner drive.

Orphaned by age eight, Roy found a family in the Army. Benavidez was of Mexican and Yaqui Indian descent. He was born near Cuero, but after first losing his father to tuberculosis and then his mother to the same disease, he was sent to live with his aunt and uncle in El Campo. He was separated from his half-sister but found himself living with eight cousins. The family were sharecroppers and migrant farm workers, and when Roy, formerly Raul, got to 7th grade, he had to quit school to work more hours in the fields and at the El Campo Firestone store. When he came of age, he joined the Texas Army National Guard, and then at 19, the regular Army.

Benavidez started his Army career with a tour in Korea, a country only two years removed from war. From there, he had stints at Fort Chafee, Arkansas, Augsburg, Germany, and then in a divided Berlin.

Along this route, he learned some valuable lessons about camaraderie and controlling his temper. Those flashes of pique had bought him a demotion from corporal to private first class and deferred his chance to go to Airborne School. Eventually, he made it.

After five years in the 82nd Airborne Division, Benavidez was sent to Vietnam in 1965. Roy credited an Australian warrant officer with teaching him important jungle survival skills, and he applied for Special Forces training. He never heard back.

His skills did not prevent him from stepping on a landmine a year later, still during his first tour. Severely injured, Benavidez was shipped back to Texas to Brooke Army Medical Center in San Antonio. Doctors told him that he would never walk again, but Roy proved the doctors wrong. He developed the habit of dropping out of his bed at night and crawling across the floor so he could repeatedly try to pull himself up against the wall. Ignoring doctor's orders, he first got his toes to wiggle, then his feet to flatten out, and eventually, he pulled himself upright. Six months later, largely through his sheer personal discipline, Roy and his wife walked into the doctor's office and demanded to return to active duty. Benavidez strolled out of the hospital and was reassigned to the 82nd in North Carolina.

Once again, Roy Benavidez applied for Special Forces, and this time the paperwork went through. The training was rigorous: parachute jumps, five mile runs with a 70-pound pack, light and heavy weapons drill, and a 12-day survival and navigation course. In January 1968, Benavidez went back to Vietnam for another tour. This time he was a Staff Sergeant and a member of the Special Operations Group. Much more training followed, most of it involving helicopters and exfiltration of soldiers under fire. The call sign given to him by his fellow SOG soldiers was Tango Mike Mike which stood for "That Mean Mexican."

On May 2, 1968, a twelve-man Green Beret team was dropped across the Cambodian border west of Loc Ninh, Vietnam. Their job was to gather intelligence in an area that was heavily and constantly patrolled by the North Vietnamese Army, but they ran into such heavy and over-whelming fire that they radioed back for an extraction. Three helicopters were sent but none could land due to the substantial onslaught from the enemy. As the choppers returned to base, SSgt. Benavidez, on his way back from mass, heard a radio distress call, grabbed an aid bag, and jumped aboard one of the aircraft, asking that they take him back to the combat zone. He was alone and largely unarmed.

Benavidez dropped from the helicopter, which was unable to land, and ran toward the men who were pinned down about 75 yards away. By the time he reached them, he had wounds to his face, head, and right leg. He repositioned the surviving men so that they could repel the enemy until a rescue chopper could land at the smoke canister Roy had thrown.

The next task was to secure the dead body of the team leader and the classified notes and operating instructions that man was carrying. American communications equipment also needed to be destroyed. On the way to accomplish that task, Benavidez took small arms fire to his abdomen and grenade fragments in his back. At the same moment, the hovering helicopter pilot was mortally wounded by ground fire and his aircraft crashed. Despite all of his injuries, Roy pulled the wounded off the downed helo and set them into a defensive perimeter while he called in tactical airstrikes to his position. Then he administered first aid as best he could. During that work, he received another bullet to the thigh.

When the next extraction aircraft returned, Benavidez safely shep-herded his wounded comrades aboard. Four of them were hit so badly that Benavidez carried them to the open helicopter door. On his second trip with a fallen brother in arms, he was clubbed in the back by an enemy soldier and forced to defend himself with hand-to-hand combat. By that time, Benavidez was holding in his own intestines as he continued his self-appointed mission.

He had accomplished these tasks using found rifles and his knife, and constantly exposing himself "to withering enemy fire," he saved the lives of "at least eight men." As a literal parting shot, Benavidez killed two enemy soldiers who were rushing the aircraft from the tail gunner's blind spot.

By the time Roy Benavidez himself was brought aboard the rescue helicopter, he had suffered four gunshots, a broken jaw, a deep bayonet wound, and 32 shrapnel hits. He could not see because of the heavy volume of blood flowing into his eyes. Back at the base, medics first zipped Roy Benavidez into a body bag. He was unable to move, speak, or even open his eyes, but mustering his last measure of strength, he spat in the doctor's face to notify the medical team that he was still alive.

Roy Benavidez was awarded four Purple Hearts, adding to the one he had received when he stepped on the land mine. He was presented with the Distinguished Service Cross, Meritorious Service Medal, and the Texas Legislative Medal of Honor. For several years, the nation's highest honor eluded him, however. The commanding officer of Benavidez' unit had only nominated him for the DSC believing that there were no eyewitnesses to his heroism. It was years later that the record of that firefight was brought to the attention of General Westmoreland, the officer who had pinned the DSC to the sergeant's chest. Westmoreland submitted Roy Benavidez for the Medal of Honor, and it was finally placed around his neck by President Ronald Reagan in 1981.

After that day in May 1968, Benavidez spent almost a year in hospital back in San Antonio before serving at Fort Riley, Kansas and Fort Sam

Houston. He retired from the U.S. Army in 1976 with the rank of Master Sergeant.

Life after the Army included a continuation of service in a different form. Benavidez traveled to schools and organizations speaking to and mentoring young people and encouraging them to find their own futures and embrace hard work. He was also an advocate for education and underprivileged children, and he successfully lobbied Congress to provide, increase, and protect benefits for disabled veterans.

Master Sergeant Roy Benavidez with his Congressional Medal of Honor (Veterans Affairs/US Army via Wikimedia Commons)

When the Defense Department finally began reviewing options for changing the names of military posts honoring Confederate generals who had been traitors to the United States, John Nova Lomax, a friend and collaborator of this author, was writing for *Texas Monthly*. Lomax wrote articles and letters trying to gain traction for renaming Fort Hood near Killeen to instead honor Roy Benavidez. As we all knew at the time, getting the military to name an installation, let alone the third largest military base in the world, after an enlisted man was a tall order. It was instead renamed for the deserving Richard E. Cavazos, the U.S. Army's first Hispanic four-star general and a native Texan, as well.

Master Sergeant Roy Benavidez received the Congressional Medal of Honor for valor that is Herculean even by the standards of that vaunted award. In his own words: "Faith and perseverance will win out over sheer ability every time."

Chapter Thirty-Three

Vietnamese Shrimpers vs. the Klan

K lansman and White supremacist Louis Beam amassed one of the worst reputations for terrorism in late 20th century Texas. In the 1970s, he was arrested for bombing the transmitter of Houston's Pacifica radio station and for a machine gun attack on the local Communist Party office. The charges were later dropped, not completely surprising since the Houston Police Department was still riddled with Ku Klux Klan members at the time. Later in the decade, Beam was arrested for attempting to assault the leader of the People's Republic of China during his visit to Houston. The following decade, he faced charges of kidnapping his toddler daughter and then seditious conspiracy to overthrow the United States government. In each case, Beam managed to skate away from prison time.

Over three decades with the Klan, Aryan Nation, and other violent racist organizations, Beam threatened, harassed, attacked, and targeted all manner of people. In his own words, he spoke of "the joys of killing your enemy" and repeatedly used the catchphrase "Where ballots fail, bullets will prevail." But there was one fight as the 1970s turned to the 1980s that Louis Beam decidedly lost.

At the end of the Vietnam War, an estimated 270,000 refugees moved from Indochina to the United States with the majority settling in California and Texas. The Houston area still has the second largest Vietnamese American population in the country. The new arrivals sought to do what they knew, and many of them who had been shrimpers and fishermen at home set themselves up with the same kind of work on the Texas Gulf Coast. They bought the smaller, older boats that the established Texas fishermen no longer wanted. One shrimp broker called the boats "junk," but that did not stop the American fisherman from suddenly raising the price of what had been a $3,000 boat to $10,000.

Still, the Vietnamese shrimpers made them pay off. They were so successful that the American shrimpers, who had cynically capitalized on the immigrants at first, began to cry foul.

A 12-year shrimping veteran at Kemah, Frank Jurecski, summed up the opinion of many of the Americans: "I just think it's unfair competition. They work as a family unit. They have a wife, kids, aunts and uncles working together. Our customs aren't like that."

On the other hand, the newcomers worked on rainy and windy days when the American fleet stayed in the Galveston Bay coffee houses and bars. They also worked longer hours. On some days, they brought in thousands of pounds more shrimp than the American boats.

"The American boats go out late and come in early so they can't expect to make good money," shrimper Chuong Tran told the *Houston Post*.

While the Americans may have been merely whining about their competitors outworking them, they had a very valid point about fears of too many boats disrupting the rhythm of the bay and depleting the long-term shrimp and fish population. Some of the Vietnamese were also regularly fined for not using the turtle excluders required by the federal authorities to help the endangered Kemp's Ridley Sea Turtle. The nets filled up faster without them.

Along with resentment, rumors began to spread among the Gulf Coast locals. False stories abounded that the refugees were getting free homes worth $50,000 or that the Vietnamese were receiving exorbitant government support. Figures in late 1979 showed that 82% of the refugees over 16 years old were working 40 hours a week or more and another 15% were working part time. Less than 5% of immigrant families were on any sort of assistance, and that averaged $36 a month. Pauline Van Tho, a former senator in South Vietnam who was working as a resettlement coordinator for Catholic Charities, said that many of the families had as many as seven wage earners.

None of those facts persuaded their American critics. Then criticism turned to violence. Billy Joe Aplin of Seadrift was killed by two Vietnamese brothers in what a jury determined was self-defense.

Governor Bill Clements set up a task force hoping to control the situation, and in April 1980, following the shooting death, a voluntary agreement was reached between all parties to hold the number of shrimp boats on the coast steady. At the time, there were about 1,300 licensed commercial fishing vessels in the state. The consensus was skeptically lauded at Palacios and Sabine Pass where the fear of overcrowding was great. On Galveston Bay alone there were 70 American shrimping boats and 55 owned by the Vietnamese refugees. American law did not permit a non-citizen to own and operate an ocean-going boat.

If state and federal authorities hoped that the freeze on new boats would end the violence, they were heartily disappointed. Small groups of American fisherman and shrimpers had begun to form on the Texas coast, and they requested Louis Beam and the Texas Ku Klux Klan to join the fray and help them. Beam gladly accepted. In his typical rabble-rousing oratory, he told the Anglo shrimpers that they would take back the country from immigrants "the way our founding fathers got it – with blood, blood, blood." In a show that his rhetoric was stronger than his grasp of history, Beam promised, "It's going to be a hell of a lot more violent than it was in Korea or Vietnam."

At the same rally, Beam set fire to an old skiff which had "USS Vietcong" painted on the hull. As he dropped the torch on the accelerant, he told the cheering group "This is the right way to burn a shrimp boat. This is an in service training." A few days later, two Vietnamese shrimp boats were the victims of arson, one in Seabrook and one in Kemah. Gasoline and diesel fuel had been splashed across the decks and poured into the hull then set alight. Fortunately for the victims, the arsonists failed to understand that closing the deck hatches also deprived the fires of oxygen. Still, the damages were severe.

Over the following days, crosses were burned on Vietnamese yards, threatening notes were mailed to the owner of a marina where Vietnamese boats docked, and other supporters received Klan cards in the mailboxes. On March 15, 1981, the entire simmering affair burst onto the national news after Beam and other heavily armed men in full Klan costume rode a shrimp boat around the Clear Lake waterfront firing blanks from a cannon and with a human effigy hanging from a yardarm.

Enter the Southern Poverty Law Center and its co-founder Morris Dees. They filed a series of injunctions asking that the Klan be ordered to stop all intimidation of the refugee shrimpers and their supporters. The SPLC also wanted the Klan to close five paramilitary camps it had set up around the area. Attendees were trained with grenades, explosives, machine guns, and hand-to-hand combat. The leader of the White fishermen stated that 50 or 60 followers had trained in Beam's camps.

Louis Beam and his fellow White supremacists turned their attention to Dees. Beam issued threats against the attorney and several of his co-counselors including Houston lawyer David Berg who had been brought onto the case. At a hearing, Beam sat across the conference table from Dees repeatedly mouthing "You die. You die." On another occasion, he pantomimed shooting several of the lawyers on the street.

The judge agreed that all of the injunctions were necessary, and they were granted. Though police protection and watchfulness continued for some time, the intimidation stopped, and the paramilitary camps were closed. By 1985, Houston newspapers were reporting that peace existed between the two shrimping communities.

Philip Zelikow, another Houston attorney on the case, called it "an extraordinary moment for the Vietnamese in which their new country intervened to protect them."

Morris Dees recalled later attending a blessing of the Vietnamese shrimpers fleet. In addition to sun glinting off the badges of United States Marshals, Dees said: "I could see the pride in the faces of these family members as they found a place at America's table."

Chapter Thirty-Four

Sam Houston's Twilight

I n the mid-1850s, Sam Houston left the Democratic Party of his mentor Andrew Jackson because he felt that the party had changed. He joined the American Party, a group more commonly known as the Know Nothings because, in their secretive early years, party members were instructed to respond to outside questions by saying "I know nothing." It was an anti-immigrant party, alarmed and angry with the out of control influx of Irish and German newcomers. They were anti-Catholics opposed to what they saw as the potentiality of an improperly educated and easily manipulated voting bloc who placed loyalty to the pope above fealty to the obligations of an American citizen.

Surprisingly for others, but not for Sam Houston, the party arguably had the most friendly policies toward the American Indian, backing a plan by Chippewa Chief George Copway to create an Indian state from the territories in the Northwest and give indigenous people citizenship, the vote, and elected representatives in Congress.

Houston embraced all of those premises, but the biggest reason for his defection may have been that the Democrats, with their whole-hearted backing of the Kansas-Nebraska Act, had doubled down as the party that supported the expansion of slavery, a stance that Sam felt would inevitably end with the dissolution of the United States. When Houston was one of only two southern senators to vote against the legislation, he was widely vilified back home in Texas. That term in the U.S. Senate was his last.

A mustachioed Senator Sam Houston during his last term in Washington (Library of Congress)

In 1857, Sam returned to Texas to run for governor as an Independent, and he suffered the only electoral defeat of his life at the hands of radical secessionist Hardin Runnels. Two years later, there was a rematch. Runnels had repeatedly threatened the federal government with ultimatums, saying that Texas would leave the Union unless he got his way. The Democratic Party of Texas wanted to reopen the Trans-Atlantic slave trade that had been ended by federal law in 1808.

Sam preached Unionism above all else, calling himself "an old fogy." He opposed everything Runnels stood for, and he especially harped on the sitting governor's failure to protect the Texas frontier from Comanches, Kiowa, and the cross-border raids of Juan Cortina. When the returns were counted, it was clear that Texans had forgiven Sam for his vote against the Kansas-Nebraska Act. The large German population overlooked his Know Nothing past, too. He won 57% of the vote. In some western frontier counties, Houston, the Independent, garnered more than 90%.

Fourteen months later, Sam Houston found himself out of a job.

His unemployment did not come about because of his own doing, though, perhaps the most questionable moments of his career took place early in his term. In the waning days of his Senate time, Sam Houston had proposed imposing an American protectorate on all of Mexico. As governor, he revived the plan. Houston made several moves, including conspiring with the Knights of the Golden Circle, to invade and capture Northern Mexico. Texans were upset with Cortina's raids, but Governor Sam also felt that once the Mexicans were taken from the sway of their priests and schooled in the ways of a true republic, they would become a more viable and "self-supporting" people. He badgered the U.S. Army for arms and support, but ultimately, in the face of great national opposition and fearing for his ambitions for the presidency of the United States, he backed off the scheme.

There were small groups pushing Sam for the biggest office in the land in 1860, just as some had done in 1856. The bulk of those with political power had turned against him, however. Even in Texas, the great founding hero Sam Houston was vilified as "shallow" or even a "low, spiteful, cunning, hipocritical (sic) man." The Constitutional Union Party, formed to save the Union at all costs, was his opportunity. Houston was only 11 votes behind former Tennessee Senator John Bell on the first ballot, but he was drubbed on the second. His brief thoughts of running for president as a "people's candidate" went nowhere.

The final campaign of Sam Houston's amazing life was not one for office. It was a fight to stop Texas from leaving the Union. With the election of Abraham Lincoln, wild conspiracy theories popped up everywhere in the South. Rumors of abolitionist fiends coming to Texas to set fires, poison wells, and steal the slaves spread as if they were real news. As the South disintegrated, and South Carolina, in December 1860, became the first state to secede, Governor Houston secretly summoned those Texas Rangers loyal to the nation to join him for a fight. Secessionist fire eater Edwin Ruffin of Virginia wrote in his diary that all Southern states would soon leave the Union and that the only fly in the ointment would be "that old scoundrel and traitor to the South, Houston." A senator from Georgia, Alfred Iverson, openly called for Sam's assassination.

Sam Houston spoke to belligerent crowds imploring them not to do as other southern states were doing. He pointed out that Texas alone had a hostile frontier and questioned whether this new alleged nation would protect it. When the secessionist convention voted to take Texas out of the Union, the heartbroken Houston seemed resigned to accept it. Still, in the three weeks between the convention and the vote of the people on whether to ratify their radical move, Sam Houston tried to rally the vote for the United States.

The new President Lincoln held Sam Houston up as a shining voice of Union in a South gone crazy. He sent a secret emissary to explore the idea of making a stand in Texas as opposed to Fort Sumter. Sam did not commit to the plan. Houston tried to steer separation sentiment into Texas again being an independent republic, but none of it worked.

He warned Texas citizens what was coming: "Your fathers and husbands, your sons and brothers will be herded at the point of a bayonet... You may, after the sacrifice of countless millions of treasure and hundreds of thousands of lives, as a bare possibility, win Southern independence, but I doubt it." When the secessionist convention, a body that Governor Houston repeatedly pointed out had no elected authority, ordered all state officials to swear an oath of allegiance to the Confederate States, Sam Houston refused to do so. The "quasi-government" declared the governorship vacant and appointed the lieutenant governor, Edward Clark. Houston was beaten, but he was not done talking.

"I am ready to be ostracized sooner than submit to usurpation," Houston said. "Office has no charm for me that it must be purchased at the sacrifice of my conscience and the loss of my self-respect. I shall calmly withdraw from the scene, leaving the Government in the hands of those who have usurped its authority; but still claiming that I am its Chief Executive."

There were last ditch efforts to send 50,000 United States troops to the port of Indianola to support Houston and Union, but the newly deposed governor did not have the heart for it. He moved out of Austin in March 1861 with all the family's belongings and went to his mother-in-law's home at Independence. The Houstons were broke.

On his way from the Governor's Mansion to exile, Sam was not yet too weary to stop in Brenham for an impromptu speech. Those who crowded to hear him were not on his side, but the greatest Texan stared them down and told them that "the vox Populi is not always the voice of God." In case anyone at all had doubts about where he stood, Houston added that "the hiss of the mob and the howls of their jackal leaders cannot deter me nor compel me to take the oath of allegiance to the so-called Confederate government."

Crowded out at Independence, the family settled for several months at Cedar Point, a cottage Sam had built on Trinity Bay in westernmost Chambers County in 1837. Margaret Lea Houston had lived there when she first married Sam. What the former leader of Texas liked most about the place was that he could easily sail down to Galveston. That was where his oldest boy, Sam Houston, Jr., was training with the Second Texas Volunteers. His father had wanted the boy to take a safe and cushy assignment at Galveston, telling junior that Texas needed him, but the young man joined the Confederate regiment under command of Sam's old friend and roommate, Ashbel Smith. Sam Houston, still tall but stooped, sat quietly and watched his boy march and drill.

When time came for the unit to shove off, the regiment's colonel, John C. Moore, invited the great man to review the 1,100 fresh troops. Sam donned his old suit and sword from San Jacinto and gave a few rousing words which included eliciting a cheer or two for himself.

The old warrior later gave a speech from the balcony of the Tremont Hotel in Galveston despite threats made against his life. One observer recalled "the deep basso tone, which shook and commanded the soul of the hearer." Houston spoke of one of his favorite subjects: Sam Houston. He told the crowd that he had made Texas, and that they knew it.

"You have always prospered most when you have listened to my counsel," he told his listeners. Once again, he criticized the hysteria for war and told the people, "I and you will sink in fire and rivers of blood."

It certainly proved true for Sam Houston, Jr.. In April 1862, the young man took a Minie ball to the groin at Shiloh. He was presumed dead on the battlefield until a Union soldier noticed him bubbling out small breaths of blood. Some on the United States side were still great admirers of the boy's father for his stand against the Kansas-Nebraska Act, and they saw to it that the old senator's son was nursed back to health. Biographers write of the August day when Margaret Houston was tending her vegetables and saw a man on crutches at her garden fence. He was "all skin and bones," but she eventually recognized him as her son.

Both parents, relocated once again, this time to Huntsville, were thrilled to have their son home safely, and did not relish the notion of him reenlisting. Sam, Sr. conspired to get junior signed on to a months-long trip to Mexico with close family friend Charles Power. It kept the boy from harm's way.

Occasionally, Houston journeyed over to the state prison and shot the breeze with Union officers being held there after capture on the Texas coast. He also corresponded with a few diehard believers about once again leading Texas. By June 1863, the once powerful Sam Houston was failing. He traveled to the hot springs at Sour Lake in a vain search for curative waters, but his eyesight was gone, and his old battle wounds were barking at him louder than ever. The "Raven," the great hero of San Jacinto, "the Big Drunk," died in his bed at home that July. His wife was so broke that it took quite some time before she could afford a tombstone for his grave.

Chapter Thirty-Five

Jack Johnson

N o Galveston native, or B.O.I. as the locals designate the honor, ever reached the international fame of boxer Jack Johnson. Though not much over six feet and 220 pounds, his nickname in the fighting world was "The Galveston Giant." He was once considered the greatest heavyweight boxer of all time, but his bigger impact on the planet was the racial upheaval his victories brought in the deepest days of Jim Crow.

Johnson's parents had been enslaved. By the time their son Jack came along, his father was a school janitor and his mother a laundress, and they owned a house at 808 Broadway in the integrated Twelfth Ward of the city's East End. He was a member of the mixed-race 11th Street and Avenue K gang. The fighter wrote of this blurring of segregation lines in his 1927 autobiography: "As I grew up, the white boys were my friends and my pals. I ate with them, played with them, and slept at their homes. Their mothers gave me cookies, and I ate at their tables. No one ever taught me that white men were superior to me."

The family's economic situation was not dire, but with nine children to feed, it required Jack to forego classes at Central High School, the first Black high school in Texas, and go to work. He got gigs at a barbershop and a gambling parlor and for a time in his teens roamed the country from job to job. A carriage shop owner in Dallas introduced the young man to boxing. Returning to Galveston, there was work as a stable-boy and longshoreman. While working as a janitor at a gym owned by German-born heavyweight Herman Bernau, Johnson scraped together enough money to buy a pair of boxing gloves. His first prize money, a dollar and a half, came from whipping another dockworker in a bout staged on the beach.

The same summer, when he was 17, a professional fighter named Bob Thompson breezed through town with an offer of $25 for anyone who could stay in the ring with him for four rounds. Johnson did it but called it the "hardest money of my life." Stating that there was "nothing more for me to do in Galveston," Jack went north to Chicago, and though he made some strides in the business, he did not find stardom. He did beat his first big time White opponent, and he experienced the first cancellation of a fight by a police chief citing the importance of racial separation.

By the start of 1901, Jack Johnson was back in Galveston where a group of White businessmen had arranged for him to fight pow-er-punching pro Joe Choynski at Harmony Hall, a Masonic building at 21st and Church Streets. There was only one possible hitch. Many states had legal prohibitions of prizefighting that dated back decades. Texas started in 1889 by requiring a $500 license but made fighting for money a felony two years later. In 1896, Judge Roy Bean evaded Texas Rangers, who had been sent to Langtry to shut down a heavyweight bout, by setting up a makeshift ring on a sandbar in the Rio Grande.

The Johnson – Choynski fight went off despite potential legal ob-stacles. The Rangers showed up just in time to see Choynski knock out Johnson in the third round. Since neither man could afford the $5,000 bail, they were thrown in a cell together for 23 days. With Choynski being Jewish, there were likely scant worries over offending anyone's sensibilities. Galveston Sheriff Henry Thomas was in no special hurry to let them out since he was admitting the public every afternoon to watch the two heavyweights spar. Choynski, who was extremely impressed with Johnson's "cat-like reflexes," told Johnson that "A man who can move like you should never have to take a punch." Johnson soaked up the lessons on defense in the ring. When the grand jury declined to indict either man, they both left town.

Johnson ended up in California and began moving up the sport's ladder. On February 3, 1903, Johnson beat Ed Martin in Los Angeles to gain the unofficial title of "Negro Heavyweight Champion." Gaining his next meaningful opponent took five years.

Interracial boxing matches happened all over the world. Johnson had won and lost several, including a takedown of a title holder's brother. The exception came in the most prestigious weight class. The unwritten rule was that top heavyweights were not to fight Black men. The world's ultimate boxing belt was to remain in White hands. The *Los Angeles Times* and the widely read *Police Gazette* were among major publications calling for heavyweight champ Jim Jeffries to take on Johnson. Instead, Jeffries retired in 1904 saying he had faced all "logical challengers."

It would take two more White champions and a mega-offer of $30,000 plus a major portion of the film rights to lure Tommy Burns into a title fight against Jack Johnson. It certainly did not hurt that Johnson himself had been stalking Burns' other fights, buying a ringside seat and throwing taunts and insults instead of punches. The bout took place in Sydney, Australia in December 1908. The beatdown that Johnson laid on Burns was vicious. In the 14th round, when Burns could no longer continue, local police stepped in to stop the match and the embarrassment. Though his official purse was only $5,000, Jack Johnson was the heavyweight champion of the world.

Two things happened with the rise of a Black man to the top spot in the sport. First were the efforts to stop circulation of the fight film. Boxing was a great fit for early motion picture cameras. Unlike baseball or other sports, the action was confined to a small ring, and easy to film. Eager sports fans gladly shelled out cash to see movie reels shown later in theatres. In pre-WWI America, the most popular sports were baseball, boxing, and horse racing, so there was money to be made. There was also purported trouble in letting the world see an African American best a White.

The other issue was in finding someone, anyone White, to wrest back the heavyweight crown. Leading the charge was a man with a national voice. Famed writer Jack London repeatedly called for a "great white hope" to step forward and take back the belt. Several tried, only to lose badly to Johnson who enjoyed flashing his gold-capped smile as he beat them into submission. London specifically kept up the pressure on Jim Jeffries to "emerge from his Alfalfa farm and remove that golden smile from Jack Johnson's face. The White Man must be rescued."

Finally, Jeffries consented. Billed as the Battle of the Century, though the century was but a decade old, a special arena was constructed in Reno, Nevada. There were 16,000 paying customers and well over 1,000 gatecrashers. There were also a record nine movie cameras to produce the epic film of Jeffries regaining White supremacy. The crowd cheered their champion who had undergone rigorous training to compensate for his four-year absence from the ring and to shed dozens of extra pounds. There were also threats of a sniper in the crowd.

Johnson and 110-degree heat took their toll on Jeffries, stopping him in the 15th round. Jack knocked Jeffries down three times that round before Jeffries' corner men jumped into the ring to stop the fight and save their man further beating. Afterward Jeffries manned up and declined to blame his conditioning. "On my best day," he told a newsman, "I couldn't have beaten Jack Johnson."

Hundreds of thousands of people around the globe had followed the fight action via telegram reports. In big cities everywhere, throngs gathered in the streets to hear the end-of-round results shouted through a megaphone. As the Black crowd began celebrating Johnson's victory, Whites attacked them. On Main Street in Houston, one man punched a Black woman in the face. Nineteen Blacks were killed in the U.S. on the fight night of July 4. As with the Burns fight, police around the country were instructed to break up screenings of the fight film. Bans also existed in other nations where the notion of White supremacy needed to be coddled. South Africa. India. The Philippines. After two years of White hand wringing, Congress banned the distribution of prize fight films altogether.

If he was not beatable in the ring, Johnson's detractors went after him in court. It was well known that the Black boxer liked the company of White women. He married some and had affairs with others. Not surprisingly, it amplified the hatred against him. In 1912, Johnson was on top of the world, but when he made a trip from Pittsburgh to Chicago with a White prostitute named Belle Schreiber, federal authorities were waiting. Johnson was arrested for violating the Mann Act, a previously unprosecuted law intended to rein in the sex industry. During the trial, the prosecutor was offered $100,000 toward his future defense if he would kill Johnson. With Schreiber as the primary witness, the all-white jury sentenced Jack to a year and a day in prison.

Jack Johnson and wife, Etta, in 1910 (Library of Congress)

Refusing to accept his conviction, Johnson fled the country. He spent the next years traveling the world and living in Europe, South America, and Mexico. His fights came on a sporadic schedule.

Champ Jack Johnson finally surrendered his title in Cuba in 1915. He was defeated by Jess Willard in the 26th round of a title fight that was scheduled for a brain-addling 45 rounds. Unlike the excuse makers for Jeffries, no one mentioned that Jack Johnson had lacked meaningful challengers for five years.

The World War severely limited Johnson's ability to both travel and earn prize money. In 1920, Johnson, then 42, finally surrendered himself to U.S. officials. He completed his sentence at Leavenworth Federal

Prison in Kansas. Reportedly prison officials staged five fights during his time there.

Chapter Thirty-Six

Sam & Rose Maceo

G alveston in the mid-20th century had a motto: The rules of the mainland don't apply. It was more than just a slogan. It was the ironclad truth, and the people behind the laissez-faire attitude were brothers Sam and Rosario Maceo.

The Maceos had arrived on the island in 1910, and soon wrangled jobs as barbers in two of the highest profile venues in town. Sam had a chair at the brand new Hotel Galvez, and Rose was in the shop at Murdoch's, the most famous of the stilted bathhouses that jutted out over the Gulf of Mexico. They were quickly supplementing their income with shady business.

They arrived in a city that already had a reputation for small to medium organized crime operations, but with the onset of Prohibition, the stakes were raised considerably. There were two syndicates in Galveston in the 1920s: one was known as the Beach Gang, run by Ollie Quinn and Dutch Voight, a German Texan from Brenham. Their rivals were George Musey and Johnny Jack Nounes of the Downtown Gang. Though the two generally co-existed, there were occasional fatalities between the outfits.

With its prime location on the coast, the island became a main port of entry for Texas' illegal booze. It was not uncommon to see a line of liquor-laden ships at anchor just on the far side of the U.S. territorial limit. The bobbing marketplace was known as Rum Row.

Nounes, who started life with the surname Nonus but altered it slightly out of respect to his Portuguese immigrant family, was a flamboyant figure. He was friends with Frank Nitti, the enforcer for Al Capone. Nounes and his lieutenant, a one-armed, first generation Syrian American named George Musey, had dreams of an empire unconstrained by the causeway. Sadly for Nounes, his high profile caught the eye of federal authorities. In 1924, he drew two years in Leavenworth Penitentiary for bootlegging. Caught again unloading a shipment at Seabrook, he drew another two-year stretch. This time, Musey went with him. By the time Nounes returned to Galveston, the island's crime was no longer his.

The Maceo Brothers had gone to work for the Beach Gang not long after they arrived in Galveston. Ollie Quinn became the Maceos' mentor. In the 1910s, the gang was making a large share of their money from organized big-time poker games. With Prohibition, the Maceos expanded into bootlegging. They and Quinn opened the upscale Hollywood Dinner Club in 1926 at 61st and Stewart. Needless to say, it offered alcohol and gambling.

Thanks to a smooth and even personality, Sam Maceo became the face of their operations. He had a special ability to hobnob with politicians, including on the state level, and the brothers' clubs became popular with Hollywood celebrities, as well. By the time the U.S. Treasury department investigations cost the brothers the Hollywood Dinner Club, they had several other businesses to take its place. Their headquarters were located at the Turf Athletic Club and Turf Grill located at 23rd and Market.

Gambling in the Studio Lounge was accessible by private elevator on the 2nd floor of the 3-story building.

The Maceos also owned the Sui Jen on the seawall at 21st. At the end of its extremely long pier was the Grotto which had gambling. That operation was enlarged and turned into the Balinese Room, the longest lasting of the Maceo properties and one that would be made famous in song.

Their clubs, particularly the Balinese, featured top flight entertainment – Phil Harris, Frank Sinatra, Sophie Tucker, Glenn Miller, Duke Ellington, Joe E. Lewis, Tommy Dorsey, and Guy Lombardo appeared multiple times. With the brothers' efforts, Galveston on the cusp of WWII was a version of what Las Vegas would eventually become. People vacationed in Galveston from all over, and on any given night, the town was particularly swarming with Houstonians.

Any competition that arose was squelched. George Musey, who had unsuccessfully fled to Canada to avoid arrest, returned to the island from prison in 1935 and opened a nightclub of his own. One night, he was called outside to speak to a visitor. The man turned out to be Windy Goss, a Maceo associate, and he shot and killed Musey on the sidewalk. At the subsequent trial, Goss was acquitted on grounds of self-defense.

In addition to the high-profile nightclubs, the Maceos owned dozens of bordellos along Post Office Street. They also had slot machines in virtually every bar and half the food stores in Galveston County and all the way to Dallas. In 1937, the Feds charged Sam Maceo with running a nationwide narcotics ring. He fought extradition and was eventually acquitted of the charges in 1942. The general word on the island was that Sam had been framed by rivals.

The Maceos were exceptionally popular citizens because most Galvestonians knew that their employment was boosted by what they saw as a victimless crime operation. In fact, locals credited them with keeping real crime off the island. Tourism brought in money, and the Maceos sponsored big events like Splash Day, a Christmas party, and various beach concerts. They sent orphans to college. They paid workers to put a new roof on a needy Black church. When a car dealership was in danger of bankruptcy, they suddenly got a big order to supply a brand new car for every priest in Galveston. The Maceos footed the bill. In 1947, when the worst industrial accident in American history hit Texas City, it was Sam and Rose Maceo who led the relief effort with a huge bash starring Frank Sinatra and Jack Benny.

The brothers sometimes partnered with the richest family on the island, the Moodys. During WWII, it was the Maceos and W.L. Moody, Jr. who built the Pleasure Pier following a hurricane that had damaged many of the city's entertainment venues. The two were simply continuing the Free State of Galveston.

In 1947, a 30-year old car and insurance salesman named Herbie Cartwright was elected mayor on a platform of keeping Galveston a regulated open town. He got along with the Maceos famously, and also made needed improvements to his city. That included adding more lanes to Broadway to let traffic flow in and out of town more smoothly. The move was not popular with Mr. Moody whose front yard was affected.

Cartwright's election coincided with the steep decline of political corruption in Texas. At least the above-board kind. Two years after the election, Texas Attorney General Price Daniel authorized raids to shut down the Maceos. They were not successful. The defenses that the organization marshaled started with advance warning from the mainland. As soon as the law came through Kemah or Dickinson, two towns filled with their own Maceo gambling houses, the folks in Galveston knew about it. In some cases, with enough notice, many of the 1000 some odd slot machines were hurriedly moved to warehouses. At the Balinese, the gambling apparatus in the last room of the over-long pier was craftily hidden. Craps tables were turned into pool tables, and roulette wheels folded up into wall panels.

Though they dodged those proverbial bullets, Sam and Rose Maceo began working on a move. The State of Nevada had legalized all gambling in 1931, and by the end of the 1940s, things in Las Vegas were starting to hum. The Maceos became the largest owners of the new Desert Inn. Their old pal Jakie Freedman, who ran a swanky gambling club in Houston called the Domain Privee, bought into the Sands. The Texas boys were moving west. Unfortunately, life intervened. Sam Maceo was diagnosed with cancer and died at Baltimore's Johns Hopkins Hospital in 1950, shortly after the opening of their swanky Desert Inn. His death was national news.

The Maceos had sold their Galveston operations to several associates. Vic and Anthony Fertitta were the most prominent, and they had continued things as usual at the Balinese. The fun must always come to an eventual end, though, and new Attorney General Will Wilson was especially intent on ending Galveston's. Under his orders, the Texas Rangers, holding a boozy stakeout at the Jack Tar Hotel across Seawall Boulevard, raided the famous club for 64 straight nights. Every time they tried to race through the mile long winding pathway to the room where they knew gambling was in progress, the band would bust out into "The Eyes of Texas," and every patron would jump to their feet and sing along, further blocking the angry Rangers.

The State of Texas eventually won, and the Free State of Galveston closed about 1957, but not before two of the greatest moments in the history of Texas Senate hearings. When a committeeman, seeking scapegoats, asked Galveston County Sheriff Frank Biaggne why he had never raided the Balinese Room in 20 years on the job, the sheriff replied. "I can't get in. I'm not a member."

Mayor Herbie topped his sheriff. A senator asked Cartwright if he knew that there was gambling and prostitution in Galveston.

"Of course, I did. I'm the mayor," he answered.

"Then why didn't you stop it?"

The mayor looked at the senator and replied, "God knew what was happening in Galveston. If he didn't want to shut it down, why should I try?"

Houston

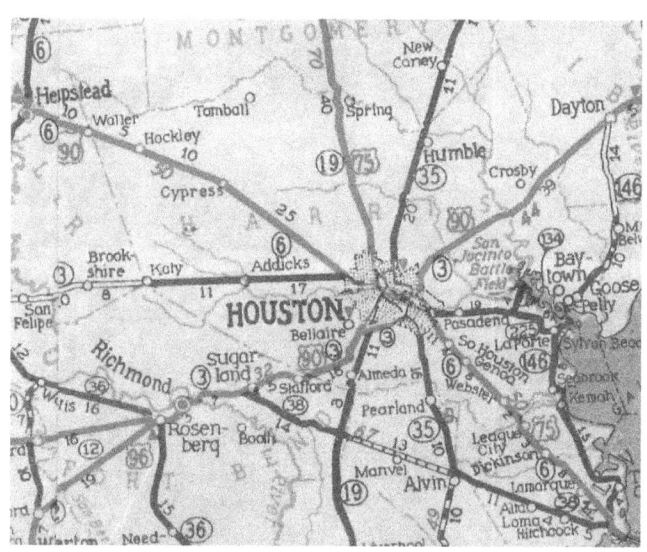

Chapter Thirty-Seven

Sugar Land 95

Texas in 1867 was largely broke. It had not suffered remotely as much as the other states of the defeated Confederacy. Texas saw far less fighting on its soil that any of its traitorous brethren. On the other hand, because of that relative lack of interference, there had been some great individual fortunes amassed in Texas from running contraband cotton through the Federal blockade or wagon training bales overland to Matamoros where it could be shipped to Britain. The state coffers were much less robust.

One of the plans for income was to contract the entire state prison system out to a private entity. Under this arrangement, the parties who took it over leased out the state's inmates and pocketed the proceeds. Such systems operated throughout the South, and evidence suggests several were worse than the one in Texas. Georgia's is often noted as being particularly brutal, but penal servitude in Texas should never be remembered as easy.

The first two times the state awarded contracts to operate its prisons, the contractors cut expenses on feeding, housing, and caring for the prisoners to the point where Texas officials were forced to nullify the deals. Inspections in the last years of the 1860s and early 1870s were infrequent, but when they took place the results were startling. The men from Austin found a large number of the leased convicts who were malnourished and wearing tattered clothing that barely covered them after weeks without being changed. The imprisoned men regularly endured beatings, and with threatening guards looming, the inmates were extremely hesitant to speak up about any abuse.

In 1875, Texas signed a private prison deal for the third time, and it proved to be, if not a charm, at least economically profitable for the men in charge. They were two Fort Bend County planters named Ed Cunningham and Littleberry Ellis. Cunningham lived in San Antonio most of the time, and Ellis had a primary home in Austin, but their money came from their adjacent farming and milling operations along the Southern Pacific owned railroad tracks that ran southwest from Houston.

Not only were they making good money with their leasing program, but unlike their predecessors, Ellis and Cunningham also satisfied the state inspectors, though those G-men were almost certainly not getting a true and full picture. The partners invested in the prison infrastructure and leased the convicts out to private farms, railroads, and industries. The biggest customers for prison labor were Ellis and Cunningham's own plantations. The two were so successful that in 1883 the state saw the possibilities and took back the prison leasing system in order to pocket more money for themselves. Ellis and Cunningham still remained the biggest users of convict labor. Depending on the ebb and flow of their yearly needs, each of those two plantations might employee 300 convicts or more at a given moment.

L.A. Ellis owned 2,200 acres and leased more than twice that much. His plantation was called Sartartia, and it grew cotton and corn. The biggest crop, however, was sugar, a labor-intensive undertaking that at certain times of the growing season required workers in the field almost around the clock. Ed Cunningham's operation was similar in makeup, but markedly larger. Both men owned sugar mills including Ellis' Imperial mill. They also had multiple cotton gins on their land along with general stores and warehouses. Cunningham built a short railroad, and Ellis had a system of movable track to bring the cane to the mill and refinery. By the 1890s, both Ellis' Sartartia and Cunningham's Sugar Land warranted post offices. Each was its own small town.

Throughout the life of the leasing system, the demand for inexpensive convict labor sometimes outpaced the supply. Large landowners and businessmen could no longer simply buy workers as they had under slavery. Just as in ante-bellum times, enslaved workers labored in many areas besides field work. Leased convicts worked in industry, unloaded ships at the docks, and built several Texas railroads.

After the Civil War, many Texas counties regularly doled out harsh sentences for misdemeanor offenses, and a disproportionate percentage of the recipients of these punishments were African American males. A perusal of convictions and sentencing makes the disparity clear. Though Blacks made up roughly a third of the overall population of Texas, they always topped 50%, and sometimes 60%, of the state's prisoners.

Their sentences for the same crime were also more harsh. Stealing a pocket watch or being a vagrant sometimes earned a Black man in Texas a two to three year term at hard labor. They were also much more likely to be leased out under the late-19th century system. Official state policy set the cost of leasing a Black convict higher than a White because the lessor and lessee both knew that those men would be worked harder. The sugar plantations of Ellis and Cunningham used African Americans exclusively. It was spelled out in their written contracts. White convicts were more likely to be leased out for building railroads or working in a factory.

The population of Texas prisons around the start of the 20th century was between three and four thousand inmates. Ninety-five percent were male, and roughly half of those were leased out as convicts. The death rate among those men was about three to four percent. In 2019, the death rate across state prisons in the U.S. was 0.33%. That puts the likelihood of death for a convict in Texas during leasing days about ten times that of inmates now.

Another major downside of the leasing system for the inmates was that the end of their sentence did not necessarily equate with their release. Those convicts who were unfortunate enough to have their time expire in the middle of harvest season usually found themselves working for several more weeks or even months before they were sent on their way.

There had been rumblings against convict leasing for years, but the Progressive Era, which very often failed to live up to its name, proved to be the undoing of the system in Texas. The state legislature outlawed convict leasing in 1910, and the law took full effect two years later. The state's owned-and-operated prison farms likely did not feel any different for the prisoners at all. The crops they grew were used to feed guards and prisoners with excess sold in the market and profits accrued to the State of Texas. There was simply no further hiring out to private businesses.

At Sugar Land and Sartartia specifically, Cunningham and the Ellis heirs were in heavy debt by 1906. Cunningham's business was in receivership. Littleberry Ellis' two oldest sons had been murdered. Over the next few years, the holdings of both families were sold off. Sugar Land was purchased by Issac Kempner of Galveston and W.T. Eldridge of Eagle Lake. Eldridge was in favor of continuing the use of the convicts, but Kempner, the money man, insisted on free labor, and the company town for Imperial Sugar was born.

Convicts with a cane car and the moveable track at Sartartia plantation about 1900 (Sugar Land Heritage Foundation)

The eastern portion of Sartartia got rolled into what became Sugar Land, but most of the Ellis land was sold to the State of Texas and became the Imperial Prison Farm. It was renamed as the Central Unit in the 1930s. Central housed prisoners who worked in the fields for many more decades, and other units were spun off nearby. Prison farms on the Sartartia land after 1912 were segregated into White, Black, and Latino populations. By the 1990s, the old Sartartia land underneath the Central Unit was becoming very valuable. A good portion of the property was ceded to the Texas Department of Transportation for Highway 99, the Grand Parkway. A few years later, the City of Sugar Land wanted the remainder for expansion. The last of Central closed in 2009.

Today, along Interstate 69 or US Highway 90A, East Fort Bend County is a never-ending sea of upscale suburbia dotted here and there with private country clubs. The Fort Bend Independent School District, which had only a single high school in the late 1970s, now has twelve.

There are also 15 middle schools and 51 elementaries, and it keeps grow-ing. In early 2018, during construction of a new education center in the district, a cemetery was unearthed. Some believed that it was used to bury Black convicts during the leasing system. Other prison cemeteries existed in the area, including one at the old Imperial Prison Farm that was designated as an Historic Texas Cemetery in 2007. Over the next months, a total of 95 unidentified graves were discovered at the new site.

Reginald Moore, an activist born in Houston, had been a consistent but lone voice urging the City of Sugar Land to do the right thing. Moore was a hulking man who had played football at Yates High School in the 1970s and spent many years as a longshoreman, but he also worked for a time as a guard at the Jester Unit near Sugar Land. That is where his interest in the convict leasing history started. It was his belief that those inmates deserved some sort of recognition for laboring in what he and many others considered a rigged and unjust system. The city honored Ellis, Cunningham, Kempner, and Eldridge, the latter being a man who himself murdered two people and was twice acquitted, but nowhere was there a mention of the slaves or convicts who did the physical work of creating the town.

For a few years, city officials tried their best to ignore Moore when he regularly railed at city council meetings or harangued in city offices. Some officials believed that Moore's requests to be hired as a contractor to create a memorial was a kind of veiled extortion. They occasionally listened to Moore, but few could say they did so politely. Then came the unearthing of 95 graves.

By law, the Texas Historical Commission oversaw the archaeology and exhumation. Many more clues pointed to the 94 men and one woman primarily being former convicts from the days of leasing. For some time, there were recriminations and finger pointing over the right course of action, but the school district finally gave in, though Reginald Moore did not live to see it. The exhumed remains were reburied at the site where they were found in November 2019, this time with community members present to offer respects. As of 2024, the school district was still fundraising to create a memorial space for study and reflection. DNA research to identify the 95 individuals continues.

Chapter Thirty-Eight

John J. Herrera

The son of a law enforcement officer, John J. Herrera graduated from Sam Houston High School in 1934 where he was inspired by his speech teacher, Lyndon Baines Johnson. Herrera had grown up in a large family, the third of ten or eleven children. Though the Herreras were descended from the Canary Islanders who were pioneers of San Antonio, John J. was born in the hamlet of Cravens, Louisiana, a town not far from what was then called Fort Polk. The senior Herrera, Juan Jose, had left his job as a San Antonio policeman to temporarily become a sheriff there.

John J. Herrera no doubt grew up knowing of his distinguished ancestry. His 3xgreat grandfather was Jose Francsico Ruiz, one of the most important men in colonial Bexar and a signer of the Texas Declaration of Independence. His 2xgreat grandfather was Blas Maria Herrera, a famous scout during the Texas Revolution. His own father had fought with Teddy Roosevelt in Cuba. Whether or not this served as an impetus for young John J., he was described as driven and hard working. He later told family members that "He knew what he wanted to be as a young boy," and he worked hard to get there.

Herrera sold papers on the streets of downtown Houston and shined shoes as a boy. Due to various hardships, he was 23 when he got his high school diploma. He spent three years as a janitor for the city. While he was enrolled at Houston's South Texas Law School, he drove a taxi and worked common labor jobs in rice or cotton fields. He got his degree in 1940 and passed the bar three years later. By that time, he and his wife were raising the first of their six children. Throughout those years, Herrera held on to his dream of making an impact in Texas politics.

He became an activist for Mexican Americans in Houston even before he completed his law degree. His efforts in those years brought fair hiring, first for Hispanics in city government in the 1930s and then in WWII-related industries through the President's Employment Practice Commission. It was his efforts that also brought about the naming of wartime Liberty Ships for Mexican American war heroes. Though unsuccessful, Herrera was the first Latino political candidate in Harris County history. There were four losing campaigns for the state legislature between 1947 and 1958. The losses did not dissuade him from his work in the slightest.

Herrera, like fellow Houstonian Felix Tijerina before him, served as national president of the League of United Latin American Citizens. Herrera had been the one to revive LULAC Council 60 in Houston back in 1939. That council became arguably the most active in the nation. Serving in various LULAC offices, Herrera spread the group's message and mission by organizing 53 new councils in Texas, New Mexico, and Arizona. After his term as national president, he served as LULAC's national legal advisor for more than a decade.

His most noteworthy impacts, though, came from civil rights cases. Herrera was involved with *Delgado v. Bastrop ISD*, a 1948 case that declared segregation of Latino students to be illegal. He was part of a team headed up by a San Antonio lawyer named Gustavo C. Garcia, one of the more colorful civil rights lawyers Texas ever produced. Garcia was five years younger than Herrera but had more experience as an attorney. He went to the University of Texas on a scholarship then stayed on for law school. Garcia served as a prosecutor and an Army lawyer in postwar Japan, and he had already successfully sued to close a "Mexican school" in Cuero and in Westminster, California. The Delgado case was filed to end the practice in Texas, and in addition to Herrera, the team included future Congressman Robert Eckhardt and had the backing of the G.I. Forum, LULAC, and the Los Angeles Civil Liberties Union. The Texas attorney general had even agreed with Garcia, but Bastrop was one of many districts stubbornly maintaining their segregated schools for Latino children. The court victory forced integrated campuses but still allowed separate classes based on a student's level of English language skills.

Six years later, Herrera was again on a Gus Garcia-led team of lawyers. This was for the appeal of a case pitting Pete Hernandez against the State of Texas. Hernandez was a farm worker indicted for murder in the town of Edna, one county north of Victoria. His trial lawyers argued that justice could not be dispensed by an exclusively White jury system, but the court ruled that Mexican Americans were White and therefore merited no special consideration. They stated that it was not a problem that no Latino had served on a Jackson County jury for 25 years. Garcia, Herrera, and a San Antonio attorney named Carlos Cadena took the appeal. The Texas Criminal Court of Appeals sided with Jackson County saying there were only two racial classes – Black and White.

In Washington, Garcia and Herrera, both admitted to practice before the United States Supreme Court, successfully argued against the systematic exclusion of Mexican Americans from Texas juries. It was the first Hispanic civil rights case to reach the U.S. Supreme Court. The court found that Mexican Americans did indeed constitute a distinct class of citizens given the quarter century of no jury service and the fact that the Jackson County Courthouse had separate bathrooms – one marked "white," and one labeled "colored men and hombres aqui." Chief Justice Earl Warren wrote the unanimous opinion in favor of Hernandez. It was the first time the Fourteenth Amendment had been applied to Latinos.

One of the biggest moments in Mexican American civil rights in Houston came on November 21, 1963. President John F. Kennedy, Vice President Lyndon Johnson, and their spouses stopped in to offer a quick hello to a state LULAC meeting being held in one of the ballrooms. JFK's entourage was in town to honor Congressman Albert Thomas as part of a four city swing through Texas hoping to shore up support for the following year's election. Greeted by raucous shouts of Viva Kennedy!, the presidential party stayed much longer than planned. Each man said a few words, and Jackie Kennedy thanked the crowd in prep school Spanish. The next day around noon, Kennedy was shot dead in Dallas.

John J. Herrera had greeted the party the previous evening and introduced them to the crowd. He had also no doubt reflected that he had shined shoes in the Rice Hotel as a boy. Herrera mourned JFK's loss greatly. The following year, he served as cochairman of Houston's Viva Johnson Club.

In later life, John J. Herrera stayed focused on community issues. He also worked as a union organizer, establishing an even dozen worker's organizations. He served on draft boards during Vietnam. He was the dean of Houston's Mexican American Bar Association, a legal advisor for Imagen de Texas, and a founder of SER Jobs for Progress. In a nod to his illustrious and cherished heritage, Herrera was a member of the Sons of the Republic of Texas.

Mostly, he continued his law practice. His was a small firm in the Scanlan Building with only two other lawyers most of the time. One was his friend Jose Rojo, who went to back before the JFK and LBJ event at the Rice Hotel. Most of the firm's cases were criminal defense.

His niece, Sarita Page, worked in the office as a teenager and recalls that her uncle still "wanted to give a voice to Mexican Americans and to make sure that they had proper legal representation." She remembers a generous man and an office "full of characters." In the courtroom, even in his 70s, Herrera remained animated, sometimes dropping in poetry, Shakespeare, or even a song into his defense.

Page also recalls John J.'s words: "You can't think about what your client has done, you have to concentrate on defending him to the best of your ability. Remember that they are human and make mistakes just like the rest of us." Herrera handled more than 1,000 murder and capital cases in Texas courts.

The honors for John J. Herrera are several, both before and after his death in 1986. He was a lifetime honorary member of both LULAC and the American G.I. Forum. There were several honors bestowed by Hispanic organizations, and an elementary school on Houston's near Northside bears his name.

Chapter Thirty-Nine

L.L. "Shorty" Walker

With apologies to residents of the City of South Houston, the area does not appear remarkable. It was, however, the site of the first airplane flight in Texas history on February 18, 1910. The event was sponsored by the Western Land Company and the *Houston Post* with the goal to lure potential land buyers to the grassy prairie at Spencer Road and Galveston Highway. Spectators were also required to pay a dollar each to witness the spectacle of Texas' first powered flight.

The sponsors were paying French aviation pioneer Louis Paulhan a cool $20,000 for his show. Paulhan, his wife, and two assistants arrived in Houston by train on the previous Tuesday and brought the pieces of two planes to the would-be flying field for assembly. There were two – a Bleriot monoplane and a Farman biplane. Windy, muddy, and overcast conditions dictated that the Farman be used. Men carried the craft, basically a large box kite with a motor, into position, turned the rear propeller, and Paulhan took to the skies. He circled the field and landed to the great satisfaction of the crowd.

With a lull in airplane development in the United States after the initial euphoria of the Wright Brothers first powered flight in December 1903, the Europeans, particularly the French, took the lead. Paulhan had received the first pilot's license ever issued by France only one year prior. In South Houston, he was nearing the end of his four-month U. S. tour after setting successive altitude records in New York, Los Angeles, Salt Lake City, and Denver.

Three of the paying customers in South Houston proved to be more taken with the event than others. Lesley Lewis Walker, Louis F. Smith, and Gus Hahn were Houston machinists according to the city directory, but that did not begin to tell their story. The men were into motorcycles and engines and things that went fast, and they became so interested in the airplane that they decided to build one themselves. Plans were common in various scientific enthusiast magazines, and for good measure, Smith had marked up his cane so he could surreptitiously measure Paulhan's plane.

The year 1910 became a busy one for heavier than air flight in Texas. Only two weeks after the Paulhan exhibition, Army lieutenant Benjamin Foulois flew at Fort Sam Houston in San Antonio. He had barely more than three hours previous flight time in the one-year old biplane the Wrights sold to the U. S. Army Signal Corps for $30,000. It was the only airplane the Army owned, and it had been sent from Virginia and Maryland down to Texas to find better flying weather. Foulois' superiors gave him the order to "teach yourself to fly." On a Fort Sam parade ground, he had his first solo flight and his first crash. He altered the biplane's elevators after consulting with Orville Wright by mail.

Meanwhile, L.L. Walker, known to most by the nickname "Shorty," spent much of his free time that year building a knockoff version of the French monoplane designed by Louis Bleriot. Armed with plans and photographs, Walker worked in a garage. He started the year with a job as a mechanic at the Bayou City Car Company but broke his wrist in two places that July while cranking a car engine. When he recovered, he moved on to the Auto and Marine Company at their new digs on Capitol Street at Milam. That is where the airplane was completed.

Walker, son of a Midwest lumberman and a Swedish mother, had started working in automobile shops in Orange at the age of 15. He soon moved to Houston and found work in several of the city's first auto sales and repair businesses. After an abortive attempt at college in Stillwater, Oklahoma, he signed on as a drill press machinist in the new Panama Canal Zone for several months. As the saying goes, lubricating oil ran in his veins.

The Bleriot monoplane had carried its original builder on the first flight across the English Channel in 1909. The design was an easy one for Walker to copy from a set of plans he bought out of a British magazine for $100. It was a partially covered box-girder construction made of spruce and magnolia wood and taut wire. The Bleriot specs called for a French 3-cylinder Anzani motorcycle engine, but that was out of both Walker's reach and price range, so he used a 35 horsepower Kemp Gray Eagle motor that he ordered from Muncie, Indiana. It weighed more and produced less horsepower, but it was available. Longtime *Houston Post* writer and amateur historian George Fuermann said that Walker's creation flew at a top speed of 30 mph and an altitude of 300 feet.

By August 1910, Walker's airplane was complete, and he towed the craft to a field near Bellaire. He had one last obstacle to overcome. He did not know how to fly, so he spent several days hopping around, barely above the ground, before trusting himself to truly go aloft. It was the school of trial and error. When he was satisfied, and with a few friends on hand, L.L. "Shorty" Walker became the first Houstonian to fly an airplane. According to Houston aviation historian Michael Bludworth, "No one had the presence of mind to write down the exact date." The best guess is September of 1910. A rival claim by another early Houston aviation man, Harold Hahl, seems to have no merit.

L.F. Smith and Gus Hahn spent over $13,000 building their airplane in a garage in South Houston. Smith, who spent his life as a genius tinkerer and inventor, was often seen in oil-stained clothing. That earned him the moniker of "Greasy." Smith & Hahn were so happy with their design they kept building them at their small factory located within a literal stone's throw of the place where Paulhan had flown.

Shorty Walker taking off in late 1910 for an attempted flight from Houston to Galveston. He got as far as La Marque. (University of Houston Special Collections. Houston & Texas History)

In January 1911, a two-week aviation meet was held on the prairie east of Bellaire, and five Houston aviators took part including Walker, Smith, and Hahn. The highlight of that show was provided by the flying troupe of John Moisant, a Frenchman who had learned to fly from Louis Bleriot himself. The biggest flying stars of the day soared in and out of the fluffy clouds above Houston, reaching altitudes of 5,000 feet, but Moisant himself was not there. He died the previous December during a crash at New Orleans, and that city named their first airfield in his honor.

With his success, Shorty Walker spent some time barnstorming around Texas and his birth state of Missouri charging admission to small town folk curious to see a man fly, but it did not pay as much as he earned working on cars. He remained a staple in the growing airplane world of South Texas which, along with Southern California, was attracting dozens of daredevil men, and a few women, who sought to touch the clouds. Fred Dekor, a Norwegian engineer who changed his name to avoid criticism from his parents, bought a Shorty Walker-made airplane dubbed the "Green Dragon" and hopped with it all the way from Houston to the West Coast.

Dekor also flew a Smith & Hahn produced biplane on the barnstorming circuit, though that plane failed him when he tried to become the first person to fly at Brenham in 1912. The Brenham feat was accomplished a year later by J. Hector Worden, the world's first Native Indian aviator, and, after missions for the Mexican Federalistas, the first pilot to take part in armed combat. Also in 1913, the U.S. Army Signal Corps, the outfit connected with Benjamin Foulois, made Texas City the home of American military aviation. After the pilots complained of strong coastal winds and mosquitoes bigger than their airplanes, the 1st Aero Squadron moved to San Diego.

By the outbreak of the first World War, there were a few hundred flyers in the United States, but the Army was invested in utilizing many more in combat over France. Shorty Walker was among the experienced pilots brought in as civilian instructors. He went to San Antonio to teach would-be military aviators first at Stinson Field then at the Army's own Kelly Field. From there he had instructor stints at Newport News, Virginia, and in New York, Illinois, Wichita Falls, and Lake Charles. In February, back in Houston, Walker was severely injured when his car overturned giving him a broken leg, arm, several ribs, and feared internal injuries. On Armistice Day, he was teaching night classes in auto mechanics at Houston's Central High School.

Shorty Walker kept tinkering with airplanes and engines for the next 50 years, but his vehicle of choice changed. By the start of the 1920s, his name frequently appeared in the local papers as the builder of racing cars. Specifically, he loved Fronty Fords. The name was short for Frontenac, a company owned by the Chevrolet Brothers. They had lost control of the car company that bore their name, so they began making parts for other cars. Their most popular product was a cylinder head that could double the stock Model T's horsepower. Fronty Fords won the Indianapolis 500 in 1920 and 1921, and they were the bailiwick of Shorty Walker and many of the diehard racers at Gulf Coast Speedway which sat near the modern intersection of Bellaire Boulevard and Stella Link, the same parcel of land that hosted the Houston aviation meet of 1911 and Walker's first airplane flight.

By the late 1930s, Walker was more into boats than cars or planes. He operated a marine and aircraft propeller business on 80th Street in Harrisburg. Occasionally, he got together with people like "Greasy" Smith to do some "hangar flying." In July 1960, the features insert of the *Houston Chronicle* ran an article on Shorty who was then living in the Garden Villas neighborhood. The 72-year old Walker regaled the writer with some exploits and admitted that he had flown as recently as the previous year. "But I can't say just how recently," Walker added with a chuckle. "Or I'd be in trouble at home." He died of heart failure just three weeks later.

Chapter Forty

Francis Moore, Jr.

Houston was filled with interesting people in its earliest years, but perhaps none were as accomplished as Francis Moore, Jr., and few were more disliked. Moore was prickly, pushy, superior, self-aggrandizing, and seemingly never let an opinion go unexpressed. Skinny, six-foot tall Francis Moore was described by Texas historian Stephen L. Hardin as a "bluenose."

He came by his New England qualities honestly. He was born in Salem, Massachusetts in 1808, the son of a Harvard-trained doctor. Moore lost an arm in a childhood accident, but he refused to let that deter him. At age 20, his family moved to Livingston County in western New York, just south of Rochester, and Francis studied medicine like his father. Six years later, he moved a bit farther south to the town of Bath near the Finger Lakes District. There he studied law and taught school. A girl named Elizabeth Mofat Wood caught his eye, and life might have been perfect in the idyllic town except that in 1836 Francis Moore, Jr., like thousands of other young men around the United States, caught the fever for Texas.

He left New York with two friends, brothers Jacob and James Cruger. They arrived in June, almost exactly two months after the rather unex-

pected victory at San Jacinto and a subsequent disastrous retreat that
sent the Mexican Army packing south of the Rio Grande. In spite of
not really having anyone to fight, Moore and the Crugers signed on with
the Buckeye Rangers, an Ohio unit of maybe 100 men. Moore was the
company's assistant surgeon. The group served as a personal guard for
Texas official David G. Burnet and remained in service until the threat
of a Mexican reinvasion was deemed to have passed.

Moore liked what he saw of Texas enough to stay and invest. He
bought interest in the *Telegraph and Texas Register* from Thomas Borden in March 1837. That made Moore partners with Thomas Borden's
older brother, Gail. Just a few weeks after the purchase, Moore and
Borden moved the newspaper operation from the town of Columbia
to the new community of Houston to follow the capital of the Texas
Republic. Within the month, Gail Borden sold his share to Moore's pal
Jacob Cruger.

A melancholic Francis Moore, Jr.

Though they were partners, Francis Moore, Jr. was the *Telegraph*'s editor, and he never hesitated to opine about how the city of Houston and the Republic of Texas should be run. His view was that the people of the United States were looking to see Texas fail, and he denounced all activities that might give the Americans reason to denigrate his adopted home.

Moore railed about elected officials who carried a criminal record back in the United States, his disliked "red-nosed" drunkards, idlers, gamblers, and mountebanks - the exact types of men who overflowed Houston. Moore editorialized against the practice of carrying weapons and vilified both dueling among gentlemen and knifings among the lower sort, who were called rowdy loafers.

Little of this earned him friends. Sam Houston, with whom Moore generally disagreed, said that Moore's one arm could "write more malicious falsehoods than any man with two arms." Houstonian Edward Stiff called out the "slabsided, knock-kneed" Moore for wearing the same clothes every day – "the same Kentucky jeans pants, the same pair of stitchdowns, the same long and flowing blue green robe, and the same redoubtable ancient drab beaver hat."

In addition to the editorial comment, Cruger and Moore's paper published official documents of the Republic, ran excerpts of popular fiction, and did job printing on their press to bring in extra cash. Francis Moore, Jr. had a passion for science and mapping. Putting those to work he turned a series of articles on the natural resources of Texas into two books in the early 1840s. They carried the repetitive titles of *Map and Description of Texas* and *Description of Texas*.

Ultimately, Moore was not content to shape Houston solely through opinion. In 1838, he was elected as the city's second mayor, and one could argue, the first municipal leader of note. Being hizzoner did not mean that Moore gave up being the town's main newspaper editor. He did both, and the editor, under the penname Citizen, often praised the mayor's decisions.

On the occasions when gentlemen and rowdy loafers intersected, Moore was there to demand justice. During his first term in office, he oversaw the hangings of two men after amazingly short trials. One was an escapee from the Goliad Massacre, David James Jones, who drunkenly murdered a well-to-do man from New York. Another episode which caused Moore to preach in print was the fatal shootout precipitated by Jackson Smith, a member of one of Houston's best families, at a crowded racetrack. Francis Moore derided the events but stopped short of naming Jackson Smith or his cohorts by name.

His protective attitude toward Texas, a place it sometimes seemed he viewed with thin contempt, came through loud and clear in one editorial: "Her enemies abroad (and they are not few) have enumerated with malignant satisfaction, crimes committed with impunity...It is time for Texas to speak – to annihilate their hopes and rebuke their craven spirits, by exacting judicious compliance with the law, and enforcing its entire execution."

Under Moore's mayoral administration, the city built a market house and passed a city charter. The first police officers were hired, and Houston bought a town lot and a fire engine for the first volunteer fire company. Moore resigned his office in early 1839 and returned to western New York long enough to lure Elizabeth Mofat Wood back to Houston. They were married in 1840.

In November 1839, Francis Moore, Jr. shifted his attention to a bigger stage and started the first of three consecutive terms as the Republic's senator representing Harris, Galveston, and Liberty Counties. In his role as chairman of the Education Committee, Moore oversaw the chartering of the first ever college in Texas, a school at Rutersville in Fayette County. The Congress rejected the school's first application because they did not like the espousal of Methodism. The non-denominational charter was approved in 1840.

Moore left the legislature and returned to his job as mayor of Houston in 1843. He left after that term but later returned for two more, serving cumulatively for seven years. He focused on improving roads and built the first city bridge over Buffalo Bayou. Moore even designed the city seal which is still in use.

On the private side of things, Moore got involved in a variety of business ventures including being a backer and officer of more than one railroad company. The Houston & Texas Central was the first of those which saw success and completion. The Houston Plank Road Company, created to build a 50-foot-wide route from the city to the Town of Washington, was another business which Moore helped organize.

There were few limits to his energy. His family attended the Episcopal Christ Church, and he spent three years being the church's representative at diocesan conventions. When Texas finally got another chance at annexation to the United States, Moore jumped at the opportunity to represent Harris County at the convention.

Moore's interest in mapping and geology was a lifelong one. When setting up Rutersville College, he had insisted on geology being added to the curriculum. In 1845, the *Telegraph* sold copies of Augustus Mitchell's map of Texas, Oregon, and California, a cartographic work that inspired thousands of people to emigrate westward. Moore was not only among the first in the nation to sell the map, but he added his own annotations. Among those who used the maps for their relocation were Brigham Young and the Mormons.

Jacob Cruger sold his interest in the *Telegraph* to Moore in 1851, but just four years later, the newspaper business had run its course. Francis Moore, Jr. sold out to a New Hampshire man named Edward H. Cushing. He and Elizabeth and their many children, there would eventually be nine, moved to New York. Francis studied geology and paleontology at the New York Geological Survey in Albany. With his newfound knowledge, Moore landed a job for the Philadelphia Academy of Natural Sciences. He returned to Texas gathering shells and fossils for the Society. In the late 1850s, he began angling for the position to head the Texas State Geological Survey but lost out to another. He settled for practicing law in Texas until Sam Houston, once a nemesis and now a friend, took over as governor in 1860 and appointed Francis Moore to be his geology man.

In the winter of 1860 into 1861, Moore traveled the state making observations. In March 1861, he went to the Trans-Pecos region and gathered ore samples. He returned to Austin that June excited about the rich mineral resources of the area. Instead of a happy reception, Moore found that Texas had joined the Confederacy, Sam Houston was kicked out of office, and the job doing geological surveys had been abolished.

Unlike many other Yankees turned Texans, including E.H. Cushing who had bought the *Telegraph*, Francis Moore, Jr. believed in Union forever. He left Texas for the last time and moved to Brooklyn.

In the midst of the Civil War, Moore journeyed to Minnesota to explore the Lake Superior area and assess its potential for copper mining. He died there, likely from a burst appendix, in the early fall of 1864. Francis Moore, Jr., a man who did so much to put Houston on a good pathway forward, is buried in Brooklyn. He lies in the same cemetery as Augustus Allen, the last of the city's two founding brothers.

Chapter Forty-One

Glenn McCarthy

H ouston was overrun with oil wildcatters in the first half of the 20th century, and many of them sported outsized personalities. Only one of them, however, was the inspiration for a James Dean movie character, graced the cover of *Time Magazine*, and loved boozing so much that he created his own brand of bourbon in a crockery bottle with a derrick stopper.

McCarthy may have been born in Beaumont, but he was pure Houston. His father worked in the oil fields, and he got his son a job as a waterboy at the derricks at the age of eight. Glenn's wages were a half dollar a day. After living for a while in Port Arthur, the family returned to the Bayou City where young Glenn was a star athlete at San Jacinto High. He then signed to play football at Tulane. After an injury, he transferred to Texas A&M where he soon got expelled for hazing. His third college team was at Rice Institute, and it was a good one. His Rice team finished 8 and 4 overall. For good measure, McCarthy was also a heavyweight A.A.U. boxer for the Owls.

Ultimately, college was not where Glenn McCarthy wanted to be. At about the same time, he dropped out of school and married Faustina Lee, the daughter of successful Houston oil man, T.P. Lee. McCarthy later claimed that he had a dollar and two quarters to his name at the time. Whether that story holds any truth or not, Glenn convinced his father and brother to work with him drilling a well in Hardin County. It was a dry hole. Two years later, however, he had cobbled together more funding and worked a lease he managed to acquire near Anahuac. This one proved to be a gusher. It could have produced as much as 3,000 barrels a day, but the East Texas Field had brought a glut of crude onto the market. Texas regulators held him to just 20 barrels daily. Still, it showed that Glenn McCarthy had the touch.

In oil crazy Houston, once his first strike became known, reporters found the football player turned oilman noteworthy, even if the news was less than spellbinding. Two years after that first hit, his Number 2 Preston test well made the *Chronicle* in March 1934 for "running about 250 feet higher than in the No. 1 test, a mile west of the present well, drilled last year." His Preston No. 2 was "about four miles west of La Porte and about 500 feet north of Spencer Highway." Truth was that, in the early and middle 1930s, McCarthy's young wife and daughter made the papers more often than he did for such big stories as a motor trip through Oklahoma or "presiding over the punch bowl" at a San Jacinto High School tea.

In 1936, the stories about McCarthy's wells became more numerous. His success at Cotton Lake near Baytown was one big reason. A year later, he found more oil at Amelia in West Beaumont, then drilled a dry hole at the new Friendswood Field, but overall, his news was routinely good. McCarthy struck oil 38 times in his first decade in the business. Halfway through that period, he announced to the Houston press his plans for a $200,000 mansion on "the southwest fringe of Braeswood." As of the decade's end, only two of Houston's ubiquitous oil million-aires had outspent him in that regard.

Industry people noticed McCarthy's successes. He had found 11 new oil fields according to most metrics and extended the range of several others. His hits at the Chocolate Bayou Field north of Alvin were one of those good fortunes. Just after WWII, Glenn McCarthy hit on the highest-pressure gas well ever drilled at that point. That Brazoria County well had the potential for 300,000 cubic feet of gas a day. As time went on, his every move was imitated.

McCarthy's knack for buying good oil leases extended to his real estate investments, even if by accident. He paid $154 an acre for the land that would later hold the Astrodome and NRG Park. Some 4,800 acres of his property later became the Sharpstown development. He floated grand ideas for his home town including a 22-story high rise apartment building as part of a planned development on land he owned at Main Street and Bellaire Boulevard, a lonesome stretch of prairie in 1945.

A proposed new Houston airport in Bellaire was another McCarthy cause. He and the ultimate Houston influencer, Jesse Jones, pushed hard for the project. They claimed that the then-Municipal Airport site, called Hobby today, had "outlived its usefulness." They brought in America's greatest WWI flying ace, Eddie Rickenbacker, to hype the new airfield. Rickenbacker also used the occasion to bad mouth "lowdown, despicable" communists and criticize the City of Houston who had recently upbraided Eastern Airlines for the non-payment of landing fees. Rickenbacker was the president and general manager of Eastern at the time, and his friendship with McCarthy was genuine. He brought the Texan on as a director, and later chairman of the airlines.

In 1945, McCarthy and several other Houston sportsmen were involved in a bid to create the Transamerica Football League, planned with eight teams including in the new-to-the-big-leagues markets of Houston and Denver. Later, he unsuccessfully tried to lure the Cleveland Browns to Houston and touted a 110,000 seat covered stadium to house them. In 1948, McCarthy was pushing for the gridiron behemoth to be built on 100 acres he was prepared to donate near Playland Park out South Main, the site later used for the Astrodome. Before the plan evaporated, another location at Waugh and Memorial Drives was also proposed.

Glenn McCarthy relished his Irish ancestry and spoke of it often. His views on the subject became widely known. When an Irish sea captain visited Houston, he told the *Chronicle*, "I have read much about Glenn McCarthy. He seems to symbolize Texas – its vigor, its creative imagination, its tremendous reach."

McCarthy at his peak was known across America, in large part because he welcomed the publicity. In addition to his various oil companies, he owned a local radio station, KXYZ, several small-town newspapers, the Shell Building, a movie company, and two banks. He invited reporters aboard his "Flying Office," a DC-3 kitted out with a lounge, a desk area, and a well-stocked bar. He bought a souped-up P-38 fighter plane and raced it against other rich men, making heavy side bets.

The attention-seeking Glenn McCarthy's biggest splash came in 1949 at a time when his net worth was estimated at $200 million. On his Main and Bellaire property, he opened the enormous Shamrock Hotel at a reported cost of $21 million, a tenth of his holdings. The hotel had been more than three years in the making. Movie star Pat O'Brien was there for the groundbreaking. The Shamrock was lavishly appointed in 63 shades of green and boasted a swimming pool large enough to host water skiing exhibitions. For the grand opening, on St. Patrick's Day, of course, McCarthy threw a million-dollar party replete with wealthy oilmen and Hollywood stars. He could afford it. "The King of the Wildcatters" had over 400 producing wells at the time.

*The Shamrock Hotel nearing comple-
tion, probably in late 1948. (University of Houston Special Collections. Conrad
Hilton College of Hotel and Restaurant
Management)*

McCarthy made darn certain that the whole country would hear about his exquisite new hotel. He arranged to have over 40 press correspondents on hand and set up Dorothy Lamour's radio program to broadcast from the Shamrock's Emerald Room. That was the largest of the hotel's nine dining options, able to accommodate a thousand diners. He premiered his first movie production at the grand opening, a film called "The Green Promise" starring Walter Brennan and 10-year old child actress Natalie Wood. To get all of his Hollywood guests to Houston, McCarthy arranged the Shamrock Special, a 16-car Super Chief with Pullman berths for more than 100 people and two lounge cars supplied with enough hooch to float the train to Texas if needed.

"Diamond Glenn" was the inspiration for Edna Ferber's Jett Rink
in the book *Giant* which was ultimately made into a Texas epic with
Rock Hudson, Elizabeth Taylor, and James Dean playing, at the end of
the film, a drunk and surly McCarthyesque character. Those scenes fit
with the bedlam that played out at the real Shamrock's opening that was
both overcrowded and overserved. Movie Columnist Erskine Johnson
described the gala as "like trying to eat dinner in the Notre Dame backfield." In the long run, not many people cared. They got their celebrity
autographs, tittered at real shamrocks flown in from Ireland, and stole
the "world's largest bath towels."

Only a few years later, in stark contrast to the glamour of the Shamrock and high times with his movie star friends, Glenn McCarthy was
bankrupt. The federal government stepped in to loan him $52 million to
pay off his debts. He recovered his footing, and he sold the world-famous
Shamrock to Hilton Hotels in 1955, just six years after his million-dollar
party.

McCarthy was not ready to leave the limelight just yet. He reopened
his beloved Cork Club in 1957 at the Central Bank Building on Main
Street, recreating what he had at the Shamrock, perhaps even complete
with the fist fights he was known to get into.

Ultimately, Glenn McCarthy settled into a life lived in an unobtrusive
two-story house in La Porte, away from the spotlight which had shone
on him so brightly.

Chapter Forty-Two

NAACP Convention of 1941

N ew Deal programs spent $41.7 billion to help a nation decimated by the Great Depression, but to African Americans, it could also be called the raw deal. Though enough benefits trickled through the framework of discrimination to bring about a wholesale shift among Black voters from the Republican to Democratic party, most of the New Deal benefits remained off limits. The Federal Housing Authority did not loan to Blacks wanting to buy in "White neighborhoods," the Civilian Conservation Corps operated segregated camps with fewer spots for people of color, and the National Recovery Administration offered Whites the first and best jobs. The New Deal agriculture policies paid landowners more to leave fields fallow than to hire on sharecroppers, and that brought horrific times for the 40% of American Blacks who earned their livings that way. Even Social Security did not apply to multiple job categories in agriculture and domestic house help that were disproportionately Black.

At the Start of WWII in Europe, when American defense industries ramped up with Lend-Lease for the British and then with a belated flurry of war preparedness needs for the U.S., once again it was Whites who got the jobs. Millions of newly created positions were not open to African Americans. A mass protest had been successful in opening a few spots on the construction crew of an Army base near Kansas City, but only after the workers joined a segregated union. Nothing at aircraft factories or shipyards was available. In those cases, both bosses and unions remained strictly segregated.

Journalist Roy Wilkins, who was second-in-command at the National Association for the Advancement of Colored People, wrote: "According to my information every airplane factory in the nation is lily white, with not even a Negro janitor to sweep their floor... The way the unions are handling the situation, it works out that the only practical difference is the bosses hit the Negros with clubs while the unions use a thinly-padded blackjack."

The top civil rights groups in the country demanded a better deal. The NAACP wanted the 1935 Wagner Act, the watershed law for organized labor, amended to refuse certification to unions who discriminated. For over a year, they requested a meeting with President Roosevelt while at the same time lobbying Congress for an investigation.

That was the scenario in early 1941 as the NAACP readied to hold their annual convention in Houston that summer. Posters had begun to appear in the Bayou City with the tagline "Fight Now for Action."

More radical than the NAACP brass was A. Philip Randolph, the socialist head of the Brotherhood of Sleeping Car Porters. If any powerful man in America was willing to push the boundaries to gain fair access for Black jobseekers, it was him. Randolph issued a press release on January 15 threatening a mass march on Washington. He announced that they were prepared to bring "ten, twenty, fifty thousand Negroes on the White House lawn" if their demands were not met. To other audiences he used the number of 100,000 Blacks descending on the nation's capital, maybe more. Though they were not in at the start, the NAACP got involved over the following months, working more closely with Randolph than any time before or after.

Randolph set the march date for June 30, the day after the NAACP convention in Houston ended. His counterpart with the organization was Walter White, a light-skinned, blue-eyed Black man who had been leading the NAACP for a decade. White was the country's most widely recognized spokesman for African Americans, and he made sure that the NAACP was represented at all the march organizing meetings and encouraged the members and local branches to take part.

Walter Francis White, longtime NAACP President (Library of Congress)

At the start of June, with the meeting in Houston just three weeks away, Randolph sent letters to FDR, his wife Eleanor, and the secretaries of War and the Navy to address the crowd when they gathered for the march. The administration began to fear that Randolph and the NAACP might actually pull this March on Washington idea off.

On June 13, White and Randolph met with Eleanor Roosevelt and Aubrey Williams, head of the National Youth Administration, in the office of New York Mayor Fiorello LaGuardia. The NYA, thanks to the efforts of Mary McLeod Bethune who sat on their advisory committee, was one of the only government agencies trusted to give Blacks a fair shake. The First Lady, who, unlike her husband, cared about civil rights, nonetheless asked the two men to call off the planned rally. Some more moderate Black leaders bailed from the coalition. White and Randolph held firm. They demanded an executive order in exchange for canceling the march.

Four days later, Aubrey Williams called to say that the President, the War and Navy Secretaries, and the heads of the Office of Production Management would meet with them the next day at the White House. FDR set the tone by asking for patience, but the two Black men were inflexible. Walter White told the President that they had "been getting the runaround everywhere" and that "the Negroes as a mass must do something." There were more inconclusive meetings the following day that included LaGuardia, then White left for Houston and the convention with a positive feeling.

The NAACP meeting was booked from June 24-29 at the Good Hope Baptist Church at Saulnier and Wilson Streets in Fourth Ward, which is called Freedmen's Town today. The group's goals were stated at the outset. They wanted equal pay for Black teachers, the elimination of the poll tax and all-White primary elections, and "admission for Negroes to all departments of military service." Still, it was the planned march, which had been pushed back one day until July 1, that had everyone abuzz. At the same time as the NAACP confab, 5,000 Black Baptist Sunday School leaders were also meeting in Houston, and though it caused "fireworks," they passed a resolution in support of the March on Washington.

Herbert Agar, the White editor of the *Louisville Courier-Journal* and an opponent of segregation, gave opening remarks. Walter White read a congratulatory telegram from President Roosevelt. The keynote came from Roscoe Dungee, publisher of the *Oklahoma Black Dispatch*. His stirring oratory included this: "National unity cannot be effected through bigotry and intolerance. The very essence of democracy rests in the precincts of freedom."

As the Houston conference attendees heard speeches and choirs, A. Philip Randolph was on the East Coast still working on draft language for an executive order. Once it was deemed acceptable, White gave approval from Texas by telephone. That was opening day of the NAACP's 32nd annual convention.

Randolph flew to Houston the next day to address the conference at the evening session, and he "dropped a bombshell... when he announced the executive order" and told attendees that the march had been postponed. Randolph talked of "mobilizing their bargaining power" and told the assembly to "engage in the constructive movement to wipe out discrimination in national defense industries and every department of the federal government in which it is evident." He told those in Houston that FDR's order was a victory, "But our efforts must not and will not stop here. We want jobs."

Many in the youth divisions of the March on Washington committees were angry that Randolph had "sold out to Roosevelt" and that they were not even consulted about it. Ironically, that came on "Youth Night" at the conference in Houston. Also that evening, the NAACP gave a special award to Richard Wright for his book and play *Native Son*.

Walter White spoke up to defend Randolph and noted that the march's executive committee unanimously agreed that the mass event should wait "until such time as it was necessary." That time came in 1963 at the march made famous by Martin Luther King and heavily promoted by A. Philip Randolph.

The end result of White and Randolph's push with the President was Executive Order 8802 which banned racial discrimination in defense industries on June 25, 1941, in the middle of the Houston NAACP conference. It was the first presidential directive on race since Reconstruction. The first two points in the order decreed that all defense contractors and vocational training programs for defense production could "not discriminate against any worker because of race, creed, color, or national origin." To handle "complaints of discrimination in violation of the provisions of this order," 8802 set up the Fair Employment Practices Committee.

It looked good on paper, but when many Blacks actually applied for defense jobs, the industry overall refused to cooperate. It took more pressure, but FDR strengthened the FEPC in 1943 by increasing its budget and establishing a full-time staff located around the country. By the end of the war two years later, eight percent of defense jobs were held by Black workers, though most were relatively low-paying, unskilled positions. Blacks in government jobs had tripled since the start of the war.

Two bills were put forward to make the FEPC permanent after the war's end, but both were defeated by Southerners in Congress. Those same committee heads cut off funding for the agency, and in 1946 it was formally dissolved.

Roughly a year after the demise of the FEPC, President Truman issued Executive Order 9981 which ended segregation in the military. That was by far the biggest step yet in the fight for civil rights. Truman was also the first president to address an NAACP convention when he did so in 1947.

Deep East Texas

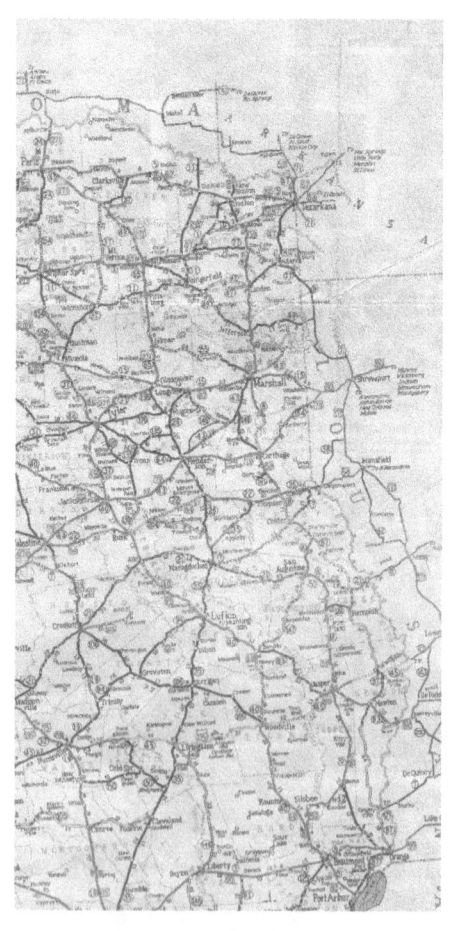

Chapter Forty-Three

Wiley College

Historically Black Colleges and Universities have produced an American Vice President and a renowned Supreme Court Justice. There have been athletes and actors, filmmakers and poets. World-shaping civic icons Booker T. Washington and W.E.B. DuBois, who were often at odds over the best course to pursue for the betterment of their race, were HBCU graduates. So too was Nobel Prize winner Martin Luther King, Jr.. These venerable institutions offered hope to people who had largely been deprived of it in the United States.

By the time Texas got its first institutions of higher education for African Americans, there were well over a dozen such schools in the East. The Freedmen's Aid Society of the Methodist Episcopal Church established Wiley College just south of Marshall in 1873. They started with two small wood-frame buildings on four acres, but within a decade, the school moved to a 70-acre tract in Marshall's downtown. The coed student body numbered 160 that year with a faculty of seven.

Like many of the first higher ed schools for freed people, Wiley offered high school level and industrial education courses along with the college curriculum. Many involved in education believed that American Blacks were best served by an education that prepared them for limited opportunities. Add to that the simple fact that only ten years before the college was founded, there had been no advanced schools for the state's Blacks at all. The first college graduate at Wiley, Henry B. Pemberton, received his B.A. in 1888. That same year, three students received teaching certificates from the Normal Department.

Wiley College was also far from alone in the fact that the school president and all of the faculty were White missionaries. That remained the case for the first 20 years of the college's existence. After losing their first Black president to a writing and publishing job, Wiley hired Matthew Dogan, a man who stayed in the position for 45 years.

The State of Texas certified Wiley as a college in 1882, but the school had no admission requirements. Dr. Dogan's biography reported that "all who came were admitted and assigned to such work as they were able to pursue with profit." The first college course of study included English, History, Mathematics, Bible study, and a small amount of public speaking.

The education system for Texas African Americans kept growing. The first high school for Blacks in the state opened in 1885, and 11 years later, when Dogan took office, every major city in Texas had one. Some of those pupils continued into colleges like Wiley, and by that time, Prairie View A&M, Houston Negro College, Paul Quinn, Huston, and Tillotson. When Dogan took the reins, Wiley College had grown to almost 300 students. Though only eight were taking college courses that year, 37 were in the college preparatory department.

Ironically, it was a devastating fire in 1906 that made the school take the next step. Five of the eleven campus buildings were destroyed, and as long as they were being rebuilt, a president's home was added. Dr. Dogan also applied to Andrew Carnegie for $15,000 to build a library including requesting an exception from raising the normal matching funds. Pulling a string or two for the request was Booker T. Washington, whose secretary, Emmett Scott, was a graduate of Wiley. The school's Carnegie Library, along with some of the other new buildings, were constructed by students.

The City of Marshall had a private library for Whites starting in 1902, but Blacks in the area used Wiley's Carnegie Library until the city opened its first integrated library in 1974. It was the last decent sized town in Texas to add that needed amenity. The longtime librarian at Wiley's Carnegie facility was Gertrude Mason, the first Black admitted as a member of the Texas Library Association.

In 1929, Wiley finally shed the high school and industrial courses on its books. A few years later, the Southern Association of Colleges and Secondary Schools made Wiley the first Black college in the state to receive an "A" rating. The association made it crystal clear, however, that Wiley College was still not eligible to become a member institution.

Throughout its first half century, Wiley College shared experiences and growing pains with other Black colleges in Texas and across the South. They often struggled by on shoestring budgets. They faced racist backlash from many in their communities. Their students were almost always prohibited from using the best of local facilities.

It was an event in Wiley's 51st year that charted a unique path for the school. A newly hired English teacher named Melvin B. Tolson decided to start a debate team in October 1924. It quickly became his passion project. The debate team met at Tolson's home on Tuesdays and Thursdays and basically picked each other apart. The constant goal was to challenge one another's logic and thought processes. They concentrated on elocution and delivery. Stumbles, ums, and aahs were hammered from speech patterns. Hand gestures were honed down to only what was needed to make a point.

Tolson taught his debaters to make a case for whichever side of an argument they were given. They analyzed the pros and cons of issues regardless of their own personal beliefs. They were pushed from their comfort zones and taught to defend positions with which they totally disagreed. Their teacher assigned extensive reading lists to the members of his new Wiley Forensic Society. He wanted them to know history, economics, government, and sociology inside and out.

For the first several years, Wiley competed against other Black colleges. In beat up old cars, they traveled the South pitting their skills against the likes of Fisk, Morehouse, Howard, and Wilberforce. They stayed in hotels and guest houses that advertised "for the Negro trade." Because they were not allowed to join the national debate society Pi Kappa Delta, Tolson formed Alpha Phi Omega to serve historically Black colleges in the same capacity. Wiley developed a reputation for being the best debate team in its pool.

Race and Jim Crow in the world of college debate was not as absolute as some other arenas of society by 1930. Though the notion stirred controversy, some White universities agreed to face the Black debaters from Marshall, Texas. Since Wiley was not part of Pi Kappa Delta, the contests were unofficial. Technically, no winner was decided.

Their first matchup took place in early 1930 at the Seventh Street Theater in Chicago. It was a Black-owned venue. The White-owned halls did not allow mixed race crowds. Their opponents were law students from the University of Michigan. Soon after, they faced the team from Oklahoma City University in the first interracial debate in the South. Melvin Tolson thought the Black and White meetings did more good than harm.

"In the South," he said, "I have seen ex-slaves shaking hands with the grandsons of the masters after the debate."

The White newspapers almost never covered events at Black colleges, but word still got out. Before Jesse Owens and his gold medals. Before Joe Louis was champ or Jackie Robinson took his first major league swing, Black Americans were often short on victories.

After Wiley completed another undefeated debate season in 1934-35, Tolson arranged an "Interracial Goodwill Tour." The debate topics that year included some still unresolved questions such as "Should the incomes of presidents of corporations be limited?" and "Should health care be available to all at public expense?"

In the early spring, Texas Christian University made history by inviting the Wiley College debaters onto its campus to face the Forensic Frogs. Wiley was the consensus victor, and afterward, Tolson complimented the Horned Frogs debaters and added "we were never received more agreeably anywhere."

Hobart Jarrett, Henry Heights, and James Leonard Farmer, Jr. (Wiley College Yearbook 1936. Wiley College Library)

Wiley went up against the University of New Mexico in the auditorium of El Paso's Negro High School. Next was San Francisco State Teachers College, the final stop on the way to face the reigning Pi Kappa Delta national champions, the University of Southern California. Wiley debaters Hobart Jarrett and Henry Heights went up against the Trojan duo in front of a crowd of 2,200. It was another no-decision event, but later interviews affirmed that Wiley carried the evening.

Melvin Tolson's forensic society students did not just talk a good game. Some of them made a case for what was right. James Farmer Jr., who joined the team at age 14, became a major civil rights leader, co-founding and leading the Congress of Racial Equality.

At Wiley College, new students held a large sit-in in March and April of 1960. James Farmer himself joined busloads of CORE Freedom Riders in Alabama and Mississippi a year later, meeting violence and getting arrested for his protests.

The Wiley team got its national recognition in 2007 when Denzel Washington directed a movie called "The Great Debaters." Oprah Winfrey, a product of HBCU Tennessee State, was the producer, and Washington starred as Melvin Tolson. After the film was released, Washington personally donated a million dollars to the college. Combined with other donations that poured in, the debate program was restarted.

In the 2013-14 debate season, Wiley College finally achieved the official national championship they had been denied in 1935. They were the first HBCU to win it. The Wiley team even faced USC again. Their head debate coach, Christopher Medina noted, "Back in 1935, it was interesting because we left the building as equals. And this time, we're entering the building as equals." One can only imagine that if Melvin Tolson were around, he would smile to see that Wiley drew the affirmative side of this topic: "Civil Disobedience is Necessary in Order to Achieve Legitimacy."

Chapter Forty-Four

Martin Dies, Jr.

I f Martin Dies, Jr. had a posthumous press agent, they might be wondering why history so vividly remembers Wisconsin Senator Joe McCarthy and ignores the first man to have his name inextricably linked to "Un-American" activities. If Dies was perhaps not quite as feared as a ruiner of lives and careers, it was a sign of his times and no reflection on his diligence in seeking the limelight.

He was the son of a United States Congressman and father of a Texas State Senator, all with the same name. Late in life, this middle Martin Dies was referred to as senior, but he was Martin Dies Junior during his most influential years. The eldest Dies was a successful lawyer in Woodville in Tyler County, moving up to marshal, county judge, and then the district attorney serving that and several other Southeast Texas counties. At the end of that job, Dies tried the landscape in West Texas long enough that his son Martin was born there in 1900. After that, it was back to Beaumont and a job as counsel for the fledgling Gulf Oil Company. Then came five quiet terms in Congress. If Martin Dies, Jr. needed a lesson in ambition, he had a role model close at hand.

Junior left the University of Texas for law school at National University in D.C., then returned home to practice law first in Marshall and then in Orange. It is no coincidence that those towns were at opposite ends of the congressional district that was so connected with his family. The Texas 2nd District followed the Sabine from Harrison County all the way down to the Gulf, running from one to three counties west from the river all the way. Martin Dies, Jr., leaving a job as district judge, began serving as its representative in 1931.

Fortune smiled on the young man from the start. John Nance Garner was the House Minority Leader poised to become Speaker. He was an extremely powerful fellow Texan in the halls of the Capitol, and he made sure that the protégé who had been sent to him by the voters of the 2nd District was appointed to the influential House Rules Committee. When the election of 1932 swept in Franklin Roosevelt and his New Deal, Dies' Democrats in the House jumped from a 14-vote majority to an advantage of almost 200. At first Martin Dies, Jr. went along with the crowd and supported Roosevelt's initiatives, many of which provided needed relief for rural areas and farmers steamrolled by the Great Depression.

All that changed soon enough. In his heart, Martin Dies, Jr. was far from a New Deal progressive. Early in the Depression years, he had written that the "large alien population is the basic cause of unemployment." It was not a unique viewpoint. Many inveterate segregationists were blaming the Depression on either foreigners or African Americans. Senator Theodore Bilbo of Mississippi wanted to deport 12 million American-born Blacks to Liberia. Though racial integration was never on the table for Franklin Roosevelt and the New Deal Congress, by 1936, Dies felt that they had gone too far. His mentor, Vice President Garner, largely agreed, though it took Garner a few more years to break with FDR.

One particular area of policy that Dies detested was the administration and Congress' support of labor unions. He soon found a vehicle to not only attack labor, "Harvard men," and go after New Deal programs in general. It was the perfect way to self-promote on a national scale.

In 1937, Martin Dies, Jr. and Congressman Samuel Dickstein of New York City began moving toward the formation of a new committee. Dickstein was a Lithuanian immigrant. The son of a rabbi, the family had come to Manhattan's Lower East Side when Dickstein was only two years of age. Arriving in Congress in 1923, he followed his interest and became chairman of the Immigration and Naturalization Committee. Dickstein and Dies joined forces in 1932 to outlaw Communist Party membership. Two years later, with the rise of the Nazis in Germany, Dickstein joined John McCormack, a Bostonian who later became House Speaker, in going after Nazis in the United States. Their committee introduced the phrase Un-American Activities, but by 1938, Dickstein had lost the leadership role to Martin Dies. Forty years after his death, claims surfaced that Dickstein was both corrupt and a Soviet operative.

The official charge of the Special Committee to Investigate Un-American Activities under Chairman Dies was to scrutinize both right and left wing organizations that were seeking to undermine American life and government. Expectations were that Nazis and sympathetic fascist organizations would be the Dies Committee's primary targets, but that did not prove to be the case at all. The German American Bund and the Ku Klux Klan were both under heavy influence from Germany where Nazi Party leadership expected America's right wing organizations to keep the United States out of the war in Europe. When the committee looked into the Klan specifically, their lead counsel, Ernest Adamson, proclaimed that: "The committee has decided that it lacks sufficient data on which to base a probe." John Rankin, a Mississippi Congressman and a longtime member of the Un-American Activities Committee, said on the record: "After all, the KKK is an old American institution."

Congressman Martin Dies, Jr. and his ever-present cigar. (Library of Congress)

Instead, Dies increasingly led his committee into attacks on communists and communist sympathizers, even in the World War II years when the Soviet Union was America's close ally. During those war years, Dies failed to target Nazi spies in the United States. He fixated on labor unions and quickly began to use his committee to make accusations against New Deal officials and even Roosevelt cabinet members.

From the beginning, the Dies Committee had its critics, the FDR administration among them. In 1938, just a year after the committee's start, Secretary of the Interior Harold Ickes ridiculed Dies to the press by saying: "They have found dangerous radicals there led by little Shirley

Temple." Temple, then 10 years old, had indeed been included on a committee list of celebrities who had sent messages to a leftist French newspaper called *Ce Soir*.

The committee's criticisms of the Hollywood stars came from J.B. Matthews, the Kentucky son of fundamentalist Methodists who became first a Progressive then a socialist and finally an organizer for the American Communist Party. In the late 1930s, Matthews experienced an abrupt about face. He became one of the very first anti-communist informers to testify before the Dies Committee. Matthews went on to create a profession for himself as an anti-communist researcher, first for Dies, then for the Hearst News organization, and later for Senator Joe McCarthy's committee. Matthews developed the habit of tarring with a broad brush and including many hundreds of non-communists in his accusations. Shirley Temple was lumped in with Clark Gable, Robert Taylor, and James Cagney for "lending their names for ...propaganda purposes," though he specified that these people were not themselves communists.

Labor Secretary Frances Perkins, the first-ever female cabinet secretary, called such accusations of the likes of Shirley Temple "preposterous revelations." In turn, the committee went after Perkins and the Labor Department. Dies was adamantly against the Fair Labor Standards Act because it provided a minimum wage. His statement was that "what is prescribed for one race must be prescribed for the others, and you cannot prescribe the same wages for the black man as for the white man." Dies Committee member J. Parnell Thomas, a New Jersey Republican and another longtime anti-communist crusader, sponsored a bill in 1939 to impeach Secretary Perkins.

Several of the committee's accusations made an impact. Frank Murphy, former Detroit mayor and sitting governor of Michigan, had worked with Frances Perkins to negotiate an end to the General Motors sit-down strike in 1937 that led to the rise of the United Auto Workers. Testimony before the committee, however, branded Murphy as either "a Communist or a Communist dupe." He lost his 1938 bid for reelection. President Roosevelt subsequently appointed Murphy to the Supreme Court.

In 1940, Martin Dies published a book about his exploits to save America. It was titled *The Trojan Horse of America*, and it concentrated entirely on ferreting out supposed communists. Dies and his committee found such people everywhere. One particular committee target was the WPA's Federal Theatre Project and Writers Project. Congressman Thomas labeled "practically every play presented" by the Theatre Project as "sheer propaganda for communism or the New Deal."

In 1941, Dies filed for the Texas seat in the Senate that had been opened by the death of Morris Sheppard. He finished a distant fourth and returned to his previous agenda in the House. His next large target was Vice President Henry Wallace. Specifically Dies claimed that 35 members of the veep's Board of Economic Warfare had been members of communist groups. He specifically targeted Maurice Parmelee who was not only a commie but a nudist.

It was the next organization in the Dies crosshairs that cost him. The Congress of Industrial Organizations, one of the two major labor groups in the country, was accused of having 280 Soviet-funded organizers in its ranks. The CIO countered by organizing a voter drive in the 2nd District of Texas and fielding a candidate to oppose Dies in the primary. The Congressman decided not to seek reelection.

The Committee, rebranded as HUAC, continued without Martin Dies. In 1953, he returned to Congress for a few more terms. He badly lost another race for Senate in 1957, as well. In 1959, after holding no important positions during his second Congressional stint, Martin Dies, jr. retired to Texas to practice law.

Chapter Forty-Five

Father Antonio Margil

The sparkling historical gems in San Antonio are certainly the stars of the show, but Texas once had Spanish missions scattered far beyond those. The famous complex in Goliad that is so educational to visit today is a reconstruction that started in the 1930s courtesy of the New Deal. There are three amazing old mission churches in the El Paso area, but that was not part of Spanish Texas. The rest of the Texas missions are known today from archaeology or a few scattered ruins, but the intersection of indigenous Texans with the first Europeans can still be seen and touched in a few unlikely places.

The Spanish saw no real need for Texas until they were afraid they might lose it to the French. The placement of their initial missions in the state reflects that. They were in East Texas, and date back as early as the late 1680s. The building boom continued for the first two decades of the next century, and that included Mission Nuestra Señora de los Dolores de los Ais that was built in 1717 near Ayish Bayou, not far from today's town of San Augustine.

Mission Dolores was founded by Antonio Margil de Jesus, a Franciscan priest who had left his home in Valencia, Spain to serve at the College of Santa Cruz de Queretaro in south central Mexico. Father Margil had already served at missions in modern day Guatemala, Yucatan, Costa Rica, and Nicaragua before he came to East Texas as part of an expedition led by Domingo Ramon.

The two men came from different backgrounds. His later admirers report that Father Margil believed in penance and self-discipline. He eschewed sandals in favor of walking barefoot, even across the rocky and thorny Texas landscape. He fasted often, always denied himself fish or meat, and is said to have spent most of his nights in prayer rather than sleep.

Father Antonio Margil depicted in sandals (San Jacinto Museum of History)

Domingo Ramon was a second-generation Spanish military officer. He was awarded leadership of the East Texas entrada in Mexico City in September 1715, and his second in command was a most unlikely fellow. Louis St. Denis, a French cavalier, had been captured on the Rio Grande and sent to the capital city as an enemy and illegal trader. His explanations pleased the Spanish colonial authorities enough to not only spare him, but to employ him. They assigned St. Denis to guide Captain Ramon and act as the commissary officer.

The group went by ship to the Rio Grande then struck out over land on April 27, 1716. Among the 75 travelers were 12 priests, counting Father Margil. They were needed since Ramon's charge was to establish four missions along with one presidio to keep the French safely at bay across the border in Louisiana. The rest of the expedition was a mix of soldados and civilians. Seven of the soldiers brought their wives and families, and these were the first Spanish women in Texas. There were also livestock, horses, and other equipment and supplies.

The first mission they set up was a replacement for Nuestro Padre San Francisco de los Tejas. Ramon's version was built on the opposite bank of the Neches River from the 1690 original, moving it from Houston County to Cherokee County on a current Texas map. Two of the priests were left behind to run the operation. Unlike the well-known limestone missions in South and West Texas, the East Texas missions were smaller complexes built of wood and other local materials.

Three more missions were founded before the year was done. In July, it was Nuestra Senora de la Purisma Concepcion for the Hasanai Caddos on the east bank of the Angelina River. Nuestra Senora Guadelupe came next, sharing a name attached to a mission near El Paso de Norte. San Jose de los Nazonis was established in what is now Nacogdoches County for the Indians of that name. At each stop, priests left the expedition to do their order's work with the indigenous locals.

Louis St. Denis made a trip to Mobile over the winter, but dutifully returned to help Ramon found two more missions in early 1717. The first, where they left Father Margil, was Nuestra Senora de los Dolores, and finally came San Miguel de Linares de los Adaes. The latter one is just across the Louisiana border, 20 miles west of the French fort at Natchitoches.

In addition to the defensive benefit that the mission presence established in East Texas, the Franciscans were also accomplishing their goal of creating new subjects of both the Spanish Crown and the Catholic Church. The various Texas Indians who were being missionized received education in language and liturgy and learned a trade.

Domingo Ramon stayed in East Texas until 1719 when all of the Spanish there fled back to the safety of San Antonio. If not for disrupting the lives of their new Indian converts and putting a dent in Spanish trade, the episode, dubbed the Chicken War, was a comical overreaction. Upon hearing that the Spanish and French had become enemies in a European war, the zealous French commander at Natchitoches, Lt. Phillippe Blondel, led an attack on the mission at Los Adaes. Blondel and his command of seven men found only a lay brother and a single soldado with a few Indians on site. He took his two prisoners, stole the sacred vestments, then raided the mission henhouse. As he tried to mount his horse with flapping chickens tied to his saddle pommel, Blondel's horse unceremoniously dumped its owner in the dirt. The lay brother took advantage of the resulting confusion to escape.

The brother raced to Mission Dolores and informed Father Margil of the intelligence that Lt. Blondel had given him. The French had captured Pensacola and were marching with an army to capture the East Texas

Spanish missions. Margil and the others fled to the next mission south, and Captain Ramon ultimately led his panicked people and their livestock all the way back to San Antonio. Aside from the brave Lt. Blondel and his stolen fowl, there were no more French incursions into Texas. In fact, the French were ordered by their government to pursue more trade with the Spanish.

Following the fiasco of the Chicken War, as Spanish officials planned what to do about the shuttered East Texas missions, Father Margil and others continued their work in San Antonio. Margil, the omnipresent priest, received permission from the Marquis de San Miguel de Aguayo, the new governor of Coahuila y Texas, to establish a new mission in the city. The nearby missions, including San Antonio de Valero, were crowded with the refugees from East Texas. Margil's new mission was dubbed San Jose y San Miguel de Aguayo and is now considered the Queen of Texas missions.

Domingo Ramon also had more mission founding left in him. The Marquis de Aguayo sent him to the site of La Salle's old fortification on Matagorda Bay in 1721, where Ramon established the first of the La Bahia missions that eventually migrated inland to Goliad. Sadly for Ramon, he was killed by a Karankawa only two years later.

Also in 1721, the Spanish, led by Marquis de Aguayo himself, once again journeyed to East Texas and reestablished their earlier missions. This time, they remained for fifty years, finally abandoning their missionizing in the region in 1773. By that time, the Spanish had ruled over Louisiana for a decade, and the threat from the French had passed.

Three of the East Texas mission locations have been precisely confirmed by 20th century archaeology. Mission Dolores is among them. The City of San Augustine built a museum, campground, and archaeology lab at the site in 2000, and the Texas Historical Commission took it over in 2016. The hidden history nugget is the only East Texas mission site that can be visited by the public.

Nearby is a site that is equally rare. It is called Lobanillo Swales, and it is the largest remaining vestige of the Spanish highways in the United States. The swales lie at a somewhat tough-to-find pull in along State Highway 21 near the town of Geneva. They are privately owned by the El Camino Real de los Tejas National Historic Trails Association. From a small gravel parking lot, visitors can walk down a short section of rutted roadway that was carved out by thousands of animals, native Indians, and Spaniards over a few hundred years. Through similar quiet pine forests, travelers from Natchitoches made their way along this very ground headed as far south as Mexico City. The Lobanillo Swales are the best place to follow in the exact footsteps of the earliest Texans.

Chapter Forty-Six

Homer Rainey

T hose who impinge on academic freedom today have nothing on the group that went after Homer Price Rainey as part of an effort to purge liberals from the state during the early 1940s. Rainey, who became a national cause celebre over the crisis seemed, on the face of things, to be an unlikely target for his detractors.

Homer Rainey was born in Clarksville, barely west of Texarkana, but spent most of his childhood at Eliasville in Young County near Graham. He was an ordained Baptist minister by age 19 and youth director at his church. He was a star baseball player at Austin College who was good enough to pitch professionally, but who chose to stay in Sherman to teach and coach. He eventually headed off to get his master's and doctorate degrees from the prestigious University of Chicago. Rainey taught at the University of Oregon and served as president of Franklin College in Indiana and then Pennsylvania's Bucknell University.

In 1939, after an almost two year quest to find the perfect successor to President Yandall Benedict, the University of Texas brought Rainey home to be its leader. They chose him because of his sterling academic credentials and his honorable reputation. The honeymoon was a brief one.

UT Austin was the largest university in the South, but that hardly meant that it could not use some improvement. Rainey raised the size of the faculty, strengthened the graduate school, opened a Latin American Institute, greatly increased the library holdings, and upgraded a building construction program for the College of Fine Arts.

On the political front, however, there was soon trouble. Lee "Pappy" O'Daniel had been reelected governor in 1940 on a platform that included a statewide sales tax, but he was getting a great deal of stubborn pushback in the legislature. In the midst of this, Clarence Ayers, a highly respected economics professor, gave a routine talk to an Austin Rotary Club. Afterwards, he was asked about the governor's sales tax. Ayers explained his opposition, and things hit the proverbial fan. O'Daniel rallied a private group of top state business leaders to go after radical ideas and blamed the University for being the seat of it all.

Homer Rainey, his wife, and daughters as a happy family in January 1939. (Library of Congress)

He removed certain members of the UT Board of Regents including Major J.C. Parten who was Rainey's biggest supporter. They were replaced with right-leaning cronies of O'Daniel. His new appointees included Orville Bullington, a Wichita Falls attorney, Houston oilman Dan Harrison, and Fred Branson, a Galveston banker. The makeover continued unchanged when Pappy left for the United States Senate and Coke Stevenson became governor. Stevenson added Dallas judge John Bickett, and W. Scott Schreiner, a Kerrville rancher and capitalist. It was another new member, attorney and lobbyist D. Frank Strickland of Mission, who fired the first shot.

At his very first meeting, he handed an index card directly to Rainey. It contained the names of four tenured economics professors. Clarence Ayers was at the top. The cigar-chomping Strickland told the president "we" want those men fired because "we don't like what they're teaching." The specific offense was that these full professors backed the New Deal.

Rainey countered the request by explaining the way tenure worked, but not satisfactorily. Strickland did not see the value of having professors trained at Harvard or Princeton or Michigan. He was fine if they changed university policy, lost their accreditation and said adios to all those out of state teachers. The new Regents were prepared to get rid of tenure altogether. They felt Texas would be better off. Rainey sought an opinion from state Attorney General Gerald Mann. The AG backed the faculty and the president. After being shot down there, the Regents began what Rainey termed a "campaign of harassment."

As the Regents' anger and frustrations mounted, three young instructors named Peach, Gordon, and Foster, went to Dallas to counteract a manufacturers-backed movement against the forty-hour workweek. They ultimately spoke out in favor of organized labor and minimum wage laws in a letter to the *Dallas Morning News* after they were kept off a meeting docket by Karl Hoblitzell, the chairman of Interstate Theatres in Texas. After that incident, the Regents went over the heads of the faculty committee and fired the three young, untenured professors.

The next battle the Regents chose was about banning a book. At a specially called meeting, Orville Bullington brought the "vile" book *U. S.A.* by John dos Passos and read passages containing obscenities. He and other critics said the book was "anti-industrialist," and they demanded that the person who placed it on the optional sophomore reading list for English be terminated immediately. Faculty members present explained that the book was not required, and that it had been on the list for years, selected by a committee, not an individual. The meeting lasted almost all day as the Regents tried to find one culprit to fire. When that did not happen, the board themselves voted to ban the book. Longtime Regent Lutcher Stark, who knew this would make the book incredibly popular across Texas, sent someone down to the Drag to buy every copy at the University bookstore. He then proceeded to autograph those copies for everyone in attendance.

In the summer of 1943, the board gutted the proposed budget of almost all of the research projects in social sciences saying they did not want that sort of thing. The hard sciences projects remained intact.

Almost everyone in Texas could see where things were headed, but the final straw that caused Rainey to go outside normal channels came after the board attempted a gag rule on their university president in September 1944 by telling him to stop making public speeches.

Rainey took his fight to a very public level. He gave a speech in mid-October to the entire faculty over 16 points, all what he considered egregious transgressions from academic norms. The items were taken directly from the Board of Regents own agendas. Newspapers ran Rainey's points and asked the Regents to counter with their rationale. None was forthcoming. Instead, the Regents voted to fire Rainey on November

1st. No reasons for his dismissal were given. Marguerite Fairchild, only the second woman to ever serve on the UT Board of Regents, cast the lone vote to keep President Rainey.

The Longhorns student body went on strike over the firing, and more than 8,000 of them marched in protest from the Tower to the Capitol and then the Governor's Mansion. The outcry against Rainey's dismissal was so great that six board members almost immediately offered their resignations, and three were accepted by the governor. Harrison, Bickett, and Hilmar Weinert were gone. Strickland, Bullington, and Schreiner resigned but were pressured to remain. Rainey laughingly said that Governor Stevenson's new replacements did not improve anything. "They were the same type as the ones who went off, and in some cases worse."

Meanwhile the Southern Association of Colleges and Secondary Schools, the American Association of University Professors, and Phi Beta Kappa reprimanded the university or placed it on probation. The AAUP censorship lasted multiple years, until the organization was convinced that there were sufficient changes "in the attitudes and procedures of the Board of Regents."

Homer Rainey briefly hosted a radio show after his firing. He spoke of politics and called for academic freedom. The show was financed by a wealthy member at Rainey's University Baptist Church.

In 1945, the Young Democrats organizations around the state began to build a campaign for Rainey to run for governor the following year. The field in the Democratic primary, then the de facto election in Texas, was crowded with 13 candidates. Coke Stevenson declined to run for reelection.

Though he was clearly a lifelong devout Baptist, the rest of the field ganged up to attack him as a dangerous radical. Rainey was denigrated over academic freedom and labor union rights. Though he did not speak out about it, he was accused of harboring sentiments in favor of racial integration. Rainey finished a solid, but distant second to Beauford Jester, a WWI veteran and Corsicana lawyer who was then serving on the Railroad Commission. In the runoff, Jester defeated Rainey by a 2-to-1 margin. Jester then garnered over 91% of the vote against the Republican nominee in the general election.

The coalition of labor, minorities, and progressives who had backed Rainey got a few of their policy concerns addressed. Jester instituted prison reform, created a board for state schools and special education, and supported an anti-lynching law. In his second term, Jester implemented the Gilmer-Aikin Laws, the first solid school funding and teacher salary plan in state history. On the other hand, he enacted stringent anti-union labor laws.

In 1947, Homer Rainey left Texas to become president at Stephens College in Missouri. Nine years after that he became part of the education faculty at the University of Colorado. He wrote a book in his retirement called *The Tower and the Dome* about his time as president of the University of Texas. He died in Boulder in 1985 at the age of 89. Austin College, his alma mater, annually awards the Homer P. Rainey award in honor of his legacy. Most poetically, the Music Building on UT's South Mall, opposite Bendict Hall, was renamed for Homer Rainey in 1995.

Chapter Forty-Seven

Cherokee Treaty

The fact that the Cherokee share language roots with the Iroquois of New York and the Northeast suggests that they had relocated before. As the American Anglos moved into their ancestral lands from Virginia south to Alabama, they felt pressure to move again. Decades prior to Andrew Jackson and his forced locations that stole away the tribe's centuries old homelands, some bands saw the writing on the wall. They wanted to preserve their culture and lifestyle, and they felt that westward migration was the answer. As early as the 1790s, Cherokees from the Southeastern United States voluntarily settled in what would become Missouri and Arkansas.

By 1807, the first bands slid southward from their new Arkansas land and began to establish homes in modern Texas. They were not alone. Portions of several allied tribes came with them. That summer, a delegation of Cherokees, Pascagoulas, Chickasaws, and Shawnees visited Spanish officials in the settlement of Nacogdoches and asked permission to stay in the Spanish colony. Their request coincided with the desires of higher up Spanish authorities to have a buffer against American expansion. The Indians were welcomed with open arms, and over the next decade, a small number of family groups came and went from Northeast

Texas. As Americans pushed the frontier into the far corner of Arkansas Territory, more Cherokee moved south.

The Cherokee were farming people. They had horses and cattle. They built log cabins. Though they found wonderfully rich soil for farming, they also adapted to include big game hunting in their routine for the first time. Buffalo were slowly incorporated into their lives. That also brought the first conflict with their nomadic neighbors to the west, the Comanche and Kiowa.

When Duwali, also known as Chief Bowl, led 60 families into Texas in 1820, they first settled at the site of Dallas before being forced east by the Comanche. Duwali's people landed instead in modern day Rusk County, north of Nacogdoches. Their friends the Caddos had occupied the land, but with Caddo numbers in decline, they welcomed the Cherokee. Within two years, the new communities had a population topping 300.

Though the Spanish had signed on to granting the Cherokee their land, by 1821, the Spanish were no longer in charge. Just as the Texas Cherokee were settling into their new home, the years-long revolution against the Spanish Crown had yielded a Mexican government, and when the tribal leaders went to legally and permanently affirm their land grant with the new representatives, they were denied. One of the Cherokee's chief diplomats, Richard Fields, tried multiple times to achieve written title, but was met only with delays.

The 1820s also brought more and more Americans across the Red and Sabine Rivers into Texas. Those who chose to stay just to the south and east of the Cherokee lands were distrustful of their new neighbors, and the tribe largely reciprocated those feelings. Each found the other peoples to be a threat.

By the end of the decade, the Mexican government began to view the burgeoning American population as a threat, too. The Law of April

6, 1830 sought to shut off the flow of new Anglos into Texas, and once again a government in Mexico City warmed to the notion that the Cherokee could provide a buffer to the hordes of Norteamericanos. Unfortunately for the tribe, they lacked the lawyers and money to navigate the Mexican court system. The long-sought land title became a gleaming carrot just out of the Cherokee's reach.

By 1830, the Cherokee population topped the 400 mark, and the people had established three or more towns along Texas tributaries to the Sabine. Diplomat Fields was again sent out by Duwali, this time to forge alliances with other immigrant tribes. He visited the Shawnees, Delawares, Kickapoos, Alabamas, and Coushattas. The tribes which had recently come to Texas from the southeastern U.S. shared similar lifestyles and culture. It was crucial that they get protection and increase their power, not as much against the Whites but against the Comanche who were raiding them with greater frequency. The Comanche were not only formidable fighters; they outnumbered the immigrant tribes by 2 to 1.

As the first rumble of trouble between the White Americans and the Mexican Centralists flared in Anahuac in 1832, the Cherokee stayed loyal to Mexico. They were driven by hopes of the almighty land title. When tempers flared further, the Cherokee declared their official neutrality. The Provisional Government of Texas, however, recognized that if the Cherokee and other immigrant tribes chose to side with the Mexicans, they could constitute an entire second front in a potential revolution, an armed group of people at the rear. The would-be Texas government sent a team of commissioners to negotiate a treaty offering whatever was necessary to guarantee that the tribes would not be marching on the Texians as they were trying to fight Santa Anna's Centralist soldiers.

Sam Houston, newly appointed as the commander of all the Texian armies, was joined by John Forbes and John Cameron to get the job done. Though this pulled their top officer away from the Texian siege at Bexar, Houston was the natural choice. He had lived among the Cherokee in Arkansas after the breakup of his first marriage. He was an official member of the tribe. He had taken a Cherokee wife, and he spoke the language.

The terms that were reached gave the tribes less land than they hoped, but it would finally be the guarantee that they sought. If the Texans lost, the Cherokee could always revisit the claims that had been pending with the Mexicans for a decade and a half.

The agreement was signed in February 1836, and it included not just the Cherokee, but East Texas bands of the Delaware, Shawnee, Kickapoo, Biloxies, Quapaws, Choctaws, Alabama, Coushatta, Iawani, Unataquous, Tahoocattakes, and Caddo of the Neches. The treaty reserved the land between the Angelina, Neches, and Sabine rivers and the Old San Antonio Road for Indian use. In easier terms it was all of today's Smith and Cherokee Counties plus portions of Rusk, Gregg, and Van Zandt, as well. Texas promised not to tax Indian trade, though they could regulate it, and there would be an Indian agent placed in the Cherokee villages "whose duty it shall be to see, that no injustice is done to them, or other members of the community of Indians."

Sam Houston affixed his prominent signature a la John Hancock, and the other Texian commissioners and aides followed suit along with eight Cherokee leaders including Duwali, Big Mush, Corn Tassel, Samuel Benge, The Egg, and interpreter Fox Fields.

Political and military events began to conspire against the treaty within weeks. The worst scenario, that the Texians might win their unlikely revolution so quickly that the tribes never got a chance to help, is pre-

cisely what played out. The lone exception was that the Coushatta tribe
provided great aid to some of the thousands who were fleeing east in the
Runaway Scrape.

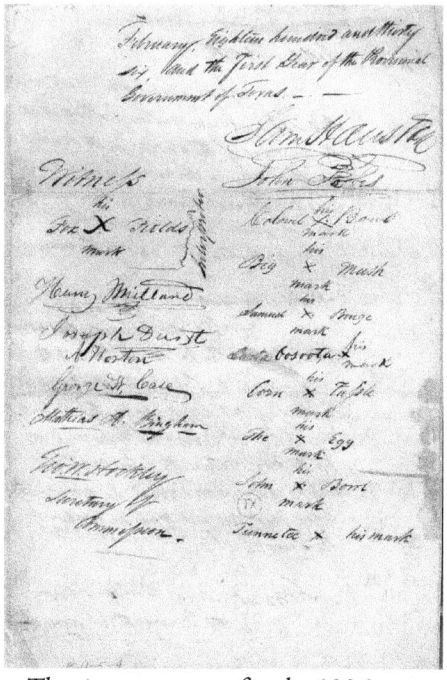

The signature page for the 1836 treaty.
(Texas State Library and Archives)

The history of the United States is littered with broken treaties between Anglos and Indians. Across America, there were plenty of transgressions committed by both sides after the accords were signed. Often, there were White men who cried foul when the treaties were later
disregarded, but one would be hard pressed to find any historical figure
who took the trashing of the articles he helped craft any harder or more

personally than the President of Texas, Sam Houston. To him, it was his sacred honor on the line.

With victory declared after San Jacinto and governing reality facing them, the new Senate of the Republic met about the signed treaty. Some members said that Houston, Forbes, and Cameron had extravagantly exceeded their charge. Virtually none of the senators saw any need for an alliance with the immigrant Indian tribes any longer.

The newest arriving settlers in Texas, those who began to pour across the border as soon as Santa Anna was vanquished, saw only good, cheap land occupied by Indians. Back in the United States, the tribal purges of Andrew Jackson were in full swing. The Trail of Tears was happening to the sisters and brothers of these same tribes, and the land-hungry Anglos saw zero reason why the Indians in Texas should be treated any differently. The Texas Senate shared these feelings, and they refused to ratify the Cherokee Treaty.

Duwali and the other chiefs associated with this treaty viewed this development as a true dishonor and betrayal. A threat of war between Indians and Texans hovered over the Republic for much of 1836.

As a man who thought a great deal of himself and his word of honor, Sam Houston was crushed. He reminded all who would listen that his tribe, the Cherokee, had agreed to let Texas pursue its dreams of separation from Mexico and stood quietly by during the Texians' darkest hour. Houston feared that his reputation among the tribe who had provided him a home would be forever ruined. There is no doubt that Houston's feelings were genuine and his pain and regret real. Evidence lies in words he wrote to Duwali, Chief Bowl, on April 13, 1836, a mere eight days before the battle at San Jacinto that would make the Texas Republic legitimate:

"I am busy and will only say how da do to you. You will get your land as it was promised in our treaty, and you, and all my red brothers, may rest satisfied that I will always hold you by the hand, and look to you as brothers and treat you as such!"

Within his powers as president, once he took office, Houston did everything he could to salvage something and assuage the tribes. He wrote to all of the chiefs promising to save what he could of the treaty. He established a boundary line separating their land, but that only served to anger the Whites even more. He coaxed the Cherokee to establish a group of rangers to scout the frontier to their west, and he even enlisted Duwali as the Republic's emissary to the Comanche. When Houston's term ended and the Constitution did not allow him to run again, he was replaced by Mirabeau Lamar, a man who openly spoke of "extermination" of the Texas Indians. For the Cherokee, the fatal die was cast.

Chapter Forty-Eight

Dad Joiner

There are as many rollicking tales of Texas oilmen as there are derelict well sites scattered across the state. A heartache for every broken drill bit, and few soaring successes. Few of those stories can match either the unlikely and unseemly path to success or the giant "what if" finish as that of Columbus Marion Joiner.

He was born in North Alabama just prior to the Civil War. His father died in battle, and his mother followed in death four years later. Joiner was raised by his sister who taught him to read and write using the Bible, the only book the siblings owned. He admitted to only seven weeks of formal schooling. After a few years away in his teens, Columbus Joiner returned home, married, and started a dry goods business in Muscle Shoals. It failed to hold his interest, and he moved north into Tennessee where he became a lawyer. He was successful enough around the age of 30 to be elected to a term in the Tennessee Legislature.

In 1897, Joiner moved again, this time to Ardmore in Indian Territory. He began acquiring cheap farmland through purchase or lease. Ten years into his venture, Joiner controlled well over 10,000 acres, but the financial panic of 1907 wiped him out. Once again, he was at a crossroads. He found his way forward, at age 47, in an oil business that was just taking off in Southern Oklahoma.

To be precise, Columbus Joiner was not an oilman. He was an oil promoter. He proved particularly adept at charming people into signing leases or investing in his drilling operations, and no type proved more vulnerable to Joiner's pitches than the recently widowed. Those bereaved women became the backbone of his funding.

At the same time, Columbus Joiner met up with a man going by the name of A.D. Lloyd. The fellow's real name was Joseph Idelbert Durham, and to say his past was sketchy would be a bit of an understatement. Lloyd had left a job as a drug store clerk and part-time medical student in Cincinnati to try his luck in the Idaho gold rush. He became a self-taught mining engineer and followed the profession to the Yukon and Mexico. For several years he toured the country as the title character in "Dr. Alonzo Durham's Great Medicine Show" selling his own petroleum-based elixirs. By the time he met Columbus Joiner, he had not only changed from Durham to Lloyd, he was also billing himself as a geologist.

With Lloyd providing scientific backup, the two men traveled in search of oil and investors. Joiner got into the habit of trading small portions of oil leases for necessities such as dinner, hotel rooms, and haircuts. Still, in spite of his lack of training, "Doc" Lloyd showed flashes of knowing what he was doing. Twice the pair fell just shy of discovering a major oil field. At Oklahoma's Seminole and Cement fields, Joiner and Lloyd were the first to drill in the right spot but lacked the money and decent equipment to go deep enough. They stopped drilling about 200 feet too soon.

In 1921, Joiner and Lloyd began to do business in East Texas, and eventually, the pair moved to Dallas. By this time, their operating procedure had been perfected. Not only were small pieces of their leases providing their living expenses, but such trades also furnished firewood to operate their ancient, steam powered drilling equipment. They even used the paper to pay for manual labor. Best of all, Joiner had figured out that he could sell off as many shares in an oil lease as he wanted – just as long as he didn't actually strike oil. Their business was the plot of a Mel Brooks comedy.

The location in East Texas was also tailor-made for the oil schemers. It was one of the poorest parts of the state, so the locals, having heard about rich oil finds in other areas, were mostly up for anything that provided the whiff of a chance. To top it all off, the major oil outfits had explored every inch of that part of Texas and announced to the world that it was barren of gas and crude.

"Doc" Lloyd handled that hurdle by putting on his geologist hat and producing a 1927 work of art entitled "Geological, Topographical and Petroliferous Survey, Portion of Rusk County, Texas, Made for C. M. Joiner by A. D. Lloyd, Geologist And Petroleum Engineer." In quasi-scientific terms it outlined the formations that indicated rich oil deposits were lurking underground. It stated that several major firms were buying up leases in the area. It flatly said that Joiner and Lloyd expected to find this oil at a depth of 3,500 feet. None of it was true, though. The big players had looked and passed. Only Humble still had leases in the area, and they hung on to them simply because they were so cheap.

One of Joiner's widow women was Daisy Miller Bradford who owned a 975-acre farm just west of Henderson in Rusk County. Joiner and Lloyd drilled their first well on her property in 1927, and they concentrated their funding efforts in the piney woods and fertile imaginations of the area. The pair were using a flimsy pine derrick, rusted third-hand equipment, and other people's money. With Tom M. Jones doing the drilling, they worked for six months before losing the well to stuck pipe. A year later, with a different driller, another second well was started 100 feet northwest of the first. At just over 2,500 feet, after 11 months of on-again, off-again work, the drill pipe twisted off and blocked the hole.

In May 1929, with Ed Laster, their third driller in as many years, Joiner and Lloyd started Daisy Bradford Number 3 about 375 yards from the second well attempt. At 1,200 feet, the well showed oil. Still facing intermittent money-based stoppages, and with a months-long pause while Laster and a rig hand recovered from an exploding boiler accident, drilling was paused at 1,530 feet in January 1930 to wait for better weather. It resumed in March, the month C.M. Joiner turned 70 years old.

A drill stem test in early September 1930 brought oil and gas, and by the time the well was completed at the start of October, the entire area was in a frenzy. Joiner and Lloyd's well was producing 300 barrels a day at first, but every major and independent producer in the area scrambled to buy up leases. Local farmers were only too happy to oblige by subdividing their mineral rights into small pieces. Within a year, rigs sprouted even in the yards of residential homes.

"Doc" Lloyd, after scouting the entire area, had wanted to drill a bit further west, but Joiner could not afford to move their dilapidated rig. The first independent to hit was the Deep Rock Oil Company, and in December, they hit a gusher one mile west of Daisy Bradford #3 that was soon flowing 3,000 b.p.d..

By Spring 1931, enough independent drillers had hit to determine that the East Texas Oil Field was enormous. When everything was mapped, the field covered 140,000 acres and ran 45 miles north and south and five miles across. It was the largest field ever discovered up to that time. Fortunes would be made, but unfortunately for Joiner, who was now being called "Dad" as the father of the discovery, it was someone else who would capitalize on his ground floor location.

Haroldson L. Hunt was a gambler living in El Dorado, Arkansas and dabbling in oil field properties. One of his biggest strengths was knowing when to capitalize on someone else's difficult situation, and while he was poking around in Rusk County, he learned that no one was as uncomfortable as Dad Joiner in the fall of 1930. The last thing Joiner had wanted was real success to spoil his moderate success, but that was exactly what had happened.

Even before the Daisy Bradford #3 well blew in, some investors were already asking that Joiner's leases be turned over to a receiver who could sort out the tangle of overextension. The first time things came before a judge, it was a wholly sympathetic one in Henderson. The Honorable R.T. Brown concluded the hearing with this bon mot: "I believe that when it takes a man three and a half years to find a baby, he ought to be able to rock it for a while. This hearing is postponed indefinitely." Unfortunately for Dad Joiner, another case was opened in Dallas.

H.L. Hunt had no more clue than anyone else whether or not the Joiner strike was for real, but he did have cunning and a few connections. He arranged for a relay team of scouts to make sure that he was the first person to receive news of the Deep Rock well just west of Daisy Bradford. If the Deep Rock well was a winner, too, then Hunt would know he was on to something since that site was almost surrounded by Dad Joiner's leases.

H.L. Hunt had no money of his own, so he enlisted a Henderson lawyer named J.B. McIntire and a Dallas haberdasher buddy named Pete Lake. The clothier supplied the capital in return for 20% of the deal, and those three men set out to isolate Dad Joiner from the rest of the world until potential good news from Deep Rock's site was known. At the Baker Hotel at Commerce and Akard in Downtown Dallas, Hunt, Lake, and McIntire kept Joiner liquored up and entertained by women. They were looking to con the con man by exploiting his weaknesses.

Stained glass at the East Texas Oil Museum at Kilgore College honors Joiner, Lloyd, and Hunt who brought great wealth to the area. (Library of Congress)

When the positive phone call arrived, Hunt made his offer to Joiner. He sympathized with the horrible legal trouble that Joiner faced and tut-tutted about the usual uncertainties of the oil bidness. In a few hours, Joiner was convinced, and he parted with 5,580 acres worth of leases in what would soon become the famous East Texas Field, a find so big that it destabilized the U.S. oil market and worsened the Great Depression. He accepted $30,000 cash plus a series of four notes totaling another $45,000 over the next nine months. The big cherry on top was $1,260,000 paid out of profits on the leases, but only if they produced. Hunt accomplished this deal without losing a dime out of his own pocket. He called it "the greatest business coup" of his career.

Dad Joiner's estate was valued at near $3 million as late as 1938, but when he died in Dallas less than a decade later, it was described as having just a "nominal value." As for A.D. Lloyd, he disappeared after a small slew of women who had seen his picture in the newspapers showed up wanting to talk about their children.

Acknowledgements & More

C reating books takes many hands, especially a work of history when the writer must locate then scour hundreds of reliable sources. That is if the writer is doing their job right.

Between my own personal library of a few thousand books and the growing number of primary source materials that are available digitally, I traveled untold numbers of history rabbit trails. I also had the chance to pull down books that I had not visited in years. That pleasure reinforced my policy to never get rid of a non-fiction book. I found old file folder of material when I was doing a regional history TV show, and I even plucked out a few paragraphs from an as-yet unpublished manuscript on Harris County school history. I love researching, so all of that was a joy.

That material, though, was compiled with help. The people at places like the Texas State Library and Archives and the Houston History Research Center have always been ready to aid researchers. A few of the stories got an assist from various site staff members of the Texas Historical Commission, another wonderful government agency in our fine state.

My pal Stephen L. Hardin is owed thanks for long talks about various Texas Revolution topics. Michael Bludworth, Houston's top aviation historian, pointed me in several great directions with Shorty Walker. All of the books that I consulted have authors who deserve thanks. That includes people like Gregg Cantrell and Jan Jarboe Russell, both of whom I met while working on previous projects. Attorney David Berg was someone I interviewed in the TV days, and the notes of that great visit helped with the Vietnamese shrimpers story. Those are just example names. There are many dozens of books and authors.

The good people at Rice University's Glasscock School of Continuing Studies let me do a remote synchronous course version of this material, and that really helped me flesh out the structure. As with several previous books, my good buddy and fellow writer Chris White helped with feedback and general camaraderie throughout the process. My wife, Anne, found time to fit proofreading into her already too full work schedule.

As mentioned in the foreword, I hope to write three more Undertold Texas books in coming years, but I also have other history non-fiction books and a growing number of historical fiction titles, too. All of that information can be found on my website at www.mikevancewriter.com While you're at the site, please sign up for my newsletter which can be done using the form at the bottom of any page.

www.ingramcontent.com/pod-product-compliance
Lightning Source LLC
Chambersburg PA
CBHW071142130626
46553CB00004B/1485